THE
"TOTAL WELLNESS"
ADVANTAGE

Yes, there is a path to total wellness, to a life of *no more suffering*. The author in fact found this path by spending 10 years studying what "rehab" centers in the U.S. did to successfully treat those suffering from acute stress, anxiety and depression. It is well-known that Hollywood celebrities often turn to such centers for help, hence the name of his new book, *The Hollywood Cure™ for Stress, Anxiety and Depression*.

Take a moment and think what a life free of emotional pain and suffering would be like for you. Imagine how you would *feel* on a daily basis if you could eliminate fear, anger, guilt, greed, hurt, lust, envy, resentment and remorse from your life. Miraculously, once these emotions have been dealt with, new understandings and insights will begin to impact your consciousness, as will their associated emotions that include peace, love, hope, harmony, joy, understanding, tolerance and compassion. This, then, should be your goal in life. And this is what this book offers.

"You cannot see the light
until you begin to walk the path."

An Excerpt from PART 5:

"I offer this final observation, and emphasize that this is very important to understand. There is another possibility in this 'romantic love' scenario and I suggest it is the ideal situation. Consider this: If you are able to bring *transcendent love*, which is not a purely unconscious act as is romantic love, into the relationship as well, then you have something quite remarkable, indeed very, very unique. In this instance, you have nothing less than pure, enthralling, ever-enchanting … *bliss!* And bliss has magical powers attached to it as it allows miracles to show up – not just once or twice, but on a regular basis. And a life sprinkled with miracles here and there is surely one that is worth living."

Some of the groups particularly vulnerable to depression and despair:

medical professionals

combat soldiers

high school and college students

law enforcement

Native Americans

dancers

actors and entertainers

prison inmates

business people

addicts

Source: *Brisbane Times* for "soldiers" photo; others from www.shutterstock.com

Also by Walter Doyle Staples

The Greatest Motivational Concept in the World

Think Like A Winner™

Power to Win

In Search of Your True Self

Everyone A CEO, Everyone A Leader

PRAISE ... from several world-renowned authorities who have commented on the many books by Walter Doyle Staples.

"If you're reading this *(In Search of Your True Self)*, consider yourself lucky — you've stumbled across one of the best books ever written. Walter Staples has put so much wisdom and so many practical strategies for success into his book that it could have been three books. What a treasure chest for anyone serious about greater success and more happiness in every area of their life."

Jack Canfield
Co-Creator, the *Chicken Soup for the Soul* book series

"Leaders are those who have a vision of excellence and have acquired the necessary skills to help themselves and others reach their full potential. By applying the principles in this book *(Think Like A Winner™)*, you are taking a major step in this direction."

Dr. Kenneth Blanchard
Co-Author, *The One Minute Manager*

"Helping people discover their richest possibilities and reach their greatest heights is an extraordinary gift, and one that Dr. Staples shares." *(Think Like A Winner™)*

Anthony Robbins
Author, *Unlimited Power* and *Awaken the Giant Within*

"This *(Think Like A Winner™)* is a scholarly motivational book. It convincingly presents workable formulae for releasing potential."

Dr. Norman Vincent Peale
Author, *The Power of Positive Thinking*

"Dr. Staples has written a complete manual *(Think Like A Winner™)* for personal and professional development. It will surely help many reach the pinnacle of success."

Art Linkletter
Author, Lecturer and Television Personality

"If you want to maximize your life's potential and at the same time enhance the lives of others, *Think Like A Winner™* is vital reading."

Dr. Robert H. Schuller
Senior Pastor, The Crystal Cathedral

"This book *(In Search of Your True Self)* has an important message – how to master the process of personal empowerment to help ourselves and others live fuller, more productive lives."

Dr. Denis Waitley

Author, *The Psychology of Winning* and *Seeds of Greatness*

"He's done it again! Dr. Staples has hit the major issues in personal performance head on. This book *(In Search of Your True Self)* opens your eyes to the critical determinant of happiness and success in life, and shows you how to develop everything you do."

Brian Tracy

Author, *Maximum Achievement*

"Nearly everyone knows that they have more talent and knowledge than they're using, but they're not sure what to do about it. Here is a book *(Think Like A Winner*™*)* that provides both understanding and action steps that will make a difference!"

James W. Newman

Author, *Release Your Brakes!*

"Dr. Staples has pulled all the magic together from a myriad of sources and blended it in his own special style into a fascinating journey into our minds, hearts and spirits. We'll all be blessed and inspired by this book *(In Search of Your True Self)*, as well we all face the challenges described within and possess the unlimited power to overcome."

Les Brown

Author, *Live Your Dreams*

"If you're looking for the key to success, look no further. Dr. Staples' new book *(In Search of Your True Self)* will tell you how to unlock the power within."

Peter McWilliams

Co-Author, *Life 101* and *Wealth 101*

"Throughout the history of man, all the great thinkers and philosophers agree that successful living is rooted in successful thinking. In a clear, easy-to-follow format, this book *(In Search of Your True Self)* provides a road map to transform the person you are into the person you want to be."

Michael LeBoeuf, Ph.D.

Author, *The Millionaire In You*

"A wise and practical book *(GMC: The Greatest Motivational Concept in the World)* interestingly presented."

Dr. Laurence J. Peter

Co-Author, *The Peter Principle*

DRUG-FREE AND CLINICALLY-PROVEN
WAYS TO MANAGE AND CONTROL YOUR
THOUGHTS, MOOD AND FEELINGS

The book all of Hollywood is talking about!

THE
HOLLYWOOD
CURE™

FOR
STRESS, ANXIETY
AND DEPRESSION

MEDICAL PROFESSIONALS

COMBAT SOLDIERS

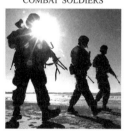

COLLEGE STUDENTS

SOME OF THE GROUPS PARTICULARLY VULNERABLE TO DEPRESSION AND DESPAIR

WALTER DOYLE STAPLES, Ph.D.
Author, *Think Like A Winner*™ and *In Search of Your True Self*

Staples Learning Inc.
Five Barclay Square, 223 Rebecca Street
Oakville, Ontario, Canada L6K 3Y2

STAPLES, WALTER DOYLE

THE HOLLYWOOD CURE™ FOR STRESS, ANXIETY AND DEPRESSION/
WALTER DOYLE STAPLES

1. SPIRITUAL GROWTH 2. PRACTICAL / POSITIVE PSYCHOLOGY
3. SELF-HEALING / MENTAL WELL-BEING

ISBN 978-0-9616385-1-1

About "The Hollywood Cure"™

To begin, let's consider for a moment the plight of Hollywood stars and other celebrities who regularly experience a wide variety of emotional and mental afflictions that include stress, anxiety, substance abuse, depression and despair, any one of which can bring on feelings of self-doubt and low self-esteem, even thoughts about death or suicide.

Some of these people have risen to unimaginable heights of fame and fortune in their career, only to fall back to earth with a loud and resounding *thud!* I liken this to being tossed out of a Boeing 787 at 33,000 feet, which seems to be an accepted occupational hazard of their roller-coaster industry and fast-paced lifestyle.

Their choice? Simple. It is to either pick up the pieces and begin anew, or succumb to their new "reality" and give up. We know a fortunate few will make the transition, some will struggle indefinitely, while many others will fail miserably. Interestingly, many of the successful ones will have sought out one-on-one counseling or entered "rehab" (e.g. a rehabilitation center), and the treatment they received as a result is very similar to what is presented in this text.

You might think that those who succeed in such situations must take some powerful and often mind-numbing drug over a long period of time to get well again. However, this is generally not the case. In a very real sense, it is their mind-set, personal perspective and ingrained habit patterns of thought that have to be transformed. This, then, is what is meant by the word "cure" in this book: *Your ability to recover from stress, anxiety, fear, phobias, depression and despair in ways that have proven in clinical trials to be just as effective as taking well-known anti-depressant drugs.*

Hopefully, if you are experiencing a particular mental or emotional challenge in your own life, you didn't have to fall nearly as far to get to where you are today. In other words, falling off a ladder or the roof of a house is not nearly as traumatic as being tossed out of a high-flying airplane!

Hence this important message to you. If the approach to ***total wellness*** described in this book – what is called *The Hollywood Cure*™ – can bring movie stars and other celebrities back from a state of utter desperation and despair to one of incredible hope and happiness, *it can do the same for you.* You need only learn and apply the same principles and techniques.

TO NOTE: Please see the 3-piece package titled **The "Total Wellness" Kit** described in detail on page 224. It includes (a) this book; (b) The Wellness Workbook (Annex 1–21); and (c) two (4 hours) DVDs.

"It is often tragic to see how blatantly a man bungles his own life and the lives of others yet remains totally incapable of seeing how much the whole tragedy originates in himself, and how he continually feeds it and keeps it going."

Carl Jung
(1875 – 1961)
Swiss Psychologist

Table of Contents

The Purpose of this Book. xix

The Hollywood Connection to the "Cure". xxi

Preface xxv

Foreword xxvii

PART 1
Cognitive Behavioral Therapy and Critical Thinking 1

PART 2
Practical Spirituality and Self-Image Psychology 21

PART 3
Mindfulness Meditation and Suggested Exercises 141

PART 4
Timeless Quotations that Inform and Inspire 163

PART 5
Frequently Asked Questions 195

Afterword. 217

The "Total Wellness" Kit 224

Life Coach & Mentoring 225

Keynotes & Seminars. 226

Bibliography. 227

About the Author 230

Permissions

Grateful acknowledgment is made to the following publishers for permission to reprint these works:

Broadway Books, The Crown Publishing Group, a division of Random House, Inc., 1745 Broadway, New York, NY 10019 for permission to quote from *Awakening the Buddha Within* (1997) by Lama Surya Das.

HarperCollins Publishers, Inc., 10 East 53rd Street, New York, NY 10022 for permission to quote from *The Tibetan Book of Living and Dying* (1992) by Sogyal Rinpoche; from *A Return to Love* (1992) by Marianne Williamson; and from *The Invitation* (1999) by Oriah Mountain Dreamer. (www.harpercollins.com)

Professor Swapan Majumdar, Viova-Bharati, 6 Acharya Jagadish Bose Road, Calcutta 700 170, India for permission to quote from *One Hundred Poems of Kabir* (1961), translated by Rabindranath Tagore.

Random House, Inc., New York, NY, for permission to quote from *Inner Peace, Inner Power* (1985) by Dr. Nelson Boswell; from *Memories, Dreams, Reflections* (1961) by Jung, C.G. and Aniela Jaffè; and from *The Way of Zen* (1957) by Alan Watts.

Walker & Company, 435 Hudson Street, New York, NY 10014 for permission to quote from *The Path: A One-Mile Walk through the Universe* (2003) by Chet Raymo. (www.walkerbooks.com)

Wilshire Book Company, 9731 Variel Avenue, Chatsworth, CA 91311-4315 for permission to quote two passages from *The Magic in Your Mind* (1961) by U.S. Andersen. (www.mpowers.com)

Shutterstock, 60 Broad Street, NY, NY 10004 for permission to use the photos on the front cover and page v.

Brisbane Times, Brisbane, Australia, for the photo of the three soldiers: "War games in Rockhampton, Freshwater Beach, 16 July, 2009."

DIVERSITY DECLARATION

Every effort has been made to provide information in this book that is acceptable to the widest and most diverse group of readers as possible regardless of race, color, creed, culture, ethnicity or gender, as well as any particular religious or spiritual following. Any errors or omissions in this regard, whether large or small, are unintentional and remain the sole responsibility of the author. Your suggestions about how to better accommodate these and other aspects of our modern, diverse society in the text are most welcome.

The Purpose of this Book

"**V**eni, vidi, vici" are the famous words spoken by Julius Caesar in 47 B.C.E. They translate in English to mean, "I came, I saw, I conquered."

Interestingly, Caesar's words can be applied to each of us in our own lives today. We are all born (veni), see what the world is like around us (vidi), then attempt to "conquer" a variety of challenges we encounter (vici) while trying to satisfy our personal needs, wants and desires. In this regard, some of us end up being more successful than others. It all depends on how you define "success," of course.

For reasons that escape me, I have had feelings of low self-esteem most of my life, something that I discovered is surprisingly common. On certain occasions as an adult, I have also suffered from many of the same maladies already mentioned, including stress, anxiety, fear, phobias, depression and despair. As a result, I have been actively (and often desperately) looking for a "cure" for these and related ailments. Now, after several years of in-depth research and study, I have found it. Specifically, I have found a drug-free and clinically-proven approach, one that has worked for me and countless thousands of others in similar circumstances in all walks of life and in all parts of the world.

I didn't "invent" this cure. It has existed for many years, in various disguises, and much of it has remained relatively unknown to the average person. I have had to undertake a diligent search to find it myself, an "exercise in elation," as it turned out. Interestingly, I found one part of the puzzle over here in this direction – **the West**; another part over there in that direction **the East**; and yet a third part in here and in no particular direction, namely **the inner confines of the mind**. I address and explain each of these parts in detail in the pages that follow.

You may recall Sally Field saying in the movie *Forest Gump,* "Life is like a box of chocolates. You never know what you're going to get." A wise statement to be sure, but it is incorrect in this sense: As you will discover later in the book, you *do* know what you are going to get in your life, namely a lot of pain and suffering, but even more importantly, that there are specific ways to avoid such a fate.

So my purpose in this undertaking is clear. It is, first, to help you overcome any mental or emotional challenges you may currently be experiencing in your own life; and second, to show you specific ways to move beyond such challenges and reach another much more exciting, much more meaningful level, one that is full of joy and bliss, of passion and purpose. It is a place I call *total wellness*. I look forward to seeing you there!

The Hollywood Connection to the "Cure"

*"Few are those who walk on water; most of us are simply
fortunate enough to find stones that someone else has placed
in life's pond and tread on them when the need arises."*

Ronald Cole
(1942 – 2009)
Canadian Writer, Businessman and Philosopher

Hollywood. Its iconic status as the entertainment capital of the world is
indisputable. With its reputation, however, comes other less endearing
descriptive terms including "gaudiness," "glitz" and "glamour," as well as
"superficial," "artificial" and "tinsel town."

Hollywood is also synonymous with "bigness" including big egos, big
dreams, big homes, big parties, big ups, big downs … and fragile lives. It
seems that here, in this town at least, a lot of people live on the edge.

So what does this have to do with the so-called Hollywood cure? In
other words, what is the malady that requires a cure and why is the word
"Hollywood" used to describe it?"

First, the malady is *depression* (and its many root causes that can include
low self-esteem, stress and anxiety) and its *tragic effects* which may include
drug or alcohol abuse, irrational acts of various kinds and thoughts of death,
including suicide. Second, the word "Hollywood" is used because <u>scores
and scores of celebrities enter "rehab" every year and receive treatment of
a kind that is described here</u>, in considerable detail, in this book.

Of course, many people in this city *do* suffer from depression but this
doesn't mean that Hollywood has exclusive rights concerning this problem.
In Hollywood, however, it does get more publicity and often a lot more.
We witness almost daily stars and starlets self-destruct on our TV screens
and in sensational tabloid headlines. Young or old, male or female, black or
white, it doesn't seem to matter. People's personal lives are put on display
for the whole world to see. And, for a variety of reasons, this has proven to
get our attention.

The trend towards more openness and frank discussion about depression can be very helpful, of course. As observers, we come to realize that anyone can be affected by this "dis-ease," that neither fame nor fortune by itself can buy health or happiness. When those suffering from depression are open and candid about their condition, it often leads to more public discussion and sharing generally of various treatment options and approaches. Depression is no longer seen as a failure from which people need to hide; it is accepted simply as another illness that needs to be understood and properly treated. People with this affliction just want to get help, get better, and get on with their lives.

The *National Examiner* featured an article on 3 March, 2008, with the names and photos of several Hollywood celebrities who have come forth concerning their own fight with depression. It included Cher, Delta Burke, Jean-Claude Van Damme, Patty Duke, Britney Spears, Connie Francis, Ned Beatty, Shelly Long and Bobby Brown. To read in detail about the pain and suffering of these people is truly heart-wrenching, just as it is for anyone in the general population dealing with this affliction.

Other famous actors have stepped up and commented on their own personal struggle with depression. In August, 2010, *Women's Day* magazine chronicled the following.

Olivia Newton-John: "When I was at my worst I took anti-depressants. If you are in a dark place, you may need to ask for help."

Jim Carrey: "You can smile at the office. You know? But it's a low level of despair," he told U.S. current affairs program *60 Minutes*.

Brooke Shields: "I really didn't want to live anymore," she says of her darkest days. "I wanted to leap out of my life."

Hugh Laurie: "Depression is a disease. It is the last great taboo—something people still don't want to talk about."

Mental disorders of various kinds have become a world-wide phenomenon, a virtual pandemic with no borders. The World Health Organization (WHO) currently states on its website that anxiety is "the most prevalent mental health problem across the globe." Indeed, the world seems to be under attack from the "S-A-D factor," a phrase I coined that refers to "stress, anxiety and depression." Interestingly, WHO also noted that "only 2 in every 5 people experiencing a mood, anxiety or substance use disorder seek assistance in the year of the onset of the disorder." This implies that the number of people who actually suffer from such ailments is likely greatly underestimated by those in the mental health community.

OK, enough of the background and on to the cure!

Of note is this comment by Aaron T. Beck, M.D., co-author of *Cognitive Therapy of Depression* (1979) that he made some years ago: "We now have a large body of research data and clinical experience which suggests that people can learn to control painful mood swings and self-defeating behavior through the application of a few relatively simple principles and techniques."

In the pages that follow, I describe **the three components** of the cure for low self-esteem, stress, anxiety and depression that I have found. Indeed, **the first** is Dr. Beck's area of specialization, Cognitive Behavioral Therapy (CBT), with the critical thinking it involves (an example of Western, left-brain analytical thinking); **the second** is practical spirituality (an example of Eastern, right-brain mystical thinking), and its self-image psychology component; and **the third** is mindfulness meditation (an inner body, contemplative approach designed to minimize and manage our internal thought processes in order to calm the mind), and how it connects us to the serenity and solace of our Source.

The following describes the primary thrust of this book:

CBT *by itself* has proven to reduce stress and anxiety, increase self-esteem and overcome moderate to severe depression as effectively as anti-depressant drugs in numerous clinical studies conducted over the past 40 years. (See PART 2 of the text for details on one recently conducted at the University of Pennsylvania.) As well, practical spirituality and mindfulness meditation *on their own* have proven effective in helping people deal with these very same as well as many other related afflictions. Each of these approaches has an important role to play in helping sufferers move from resignation to revelation, from superficiality to substance.

A NOTE OF CAUTION: In all cases, it is strongly recommended that those suffering from stress, anxiety, substance abuse, depression and despair, to whatever degree, promptly seek out professional medical advice. Indeed, there may be instances when drug therapy is the preferred course of action, at least initially. In such cases, the self-management approaches described in this book may well prove to be helpful adjuncts to such treatment, ideally leading to a faster recovery and less likelihood of a serious relapse.

When explaining to people what is described in this text in both formal and informal settings, I am often asked, "So, where exactly is the 'cure' in all of this?" I respond by saying, "Begin by exploring the menu that is in front of you. Pick from the three items that are offered, then diligently and methodically absorb and apply each one in a way that best suits your own particular needs, preferences and personality. The cure that you find may not be the same cure that another person finds. This shouldn't be any great surprise. We know some people like vanilla ice cream while others prefer chocolate!"

Preface

Some time ago, Nisargadatta Maharaj (1897 – 1981), the respected Indian teacher of Advaita Vedanta, shared with us the following affirmation:

"In my world, _nothing_ ever goes wrong."

This statement stops many people dead in their tracks when they first come across it. NOTHING! Is that really possible? Just think … what kind of life would you be living if you thought this way? As you go through this book, I suggest you come back periodically and reconsider this statement, and you will see that in fact it *is* possible. You *can* live in a calm, understanding, forgiving, non-conforming and non-judgmental way, knowing that everything happens for a reason and a purpose, and in each and every case, it serves you.

Armed with this new awareness, this new insight into the ways of the world, you have to ask yourself, "What could possibly hold me back from being the person I really want to be, from living the life I really want to live, from achieving the things I really want to achieve?" *As you will discover over and over again in this book, the correct answer is,* **"Only you!"** The old adage, "You are your own worst enemy" is 100 percent true. So one of the biggest challenges you face in life can be stated quite simply: "How can you *stop* being your own worst enemy?" You will find the answer to this question expressed in many different ways and on many different occasions as you read on.

If you apply the principles described in the text, your life will be very different indeed In particular, consider the suggestion that you listen to your ego, recognize it for what it is, then shut it down by ignoring what it is telling you. If you apply this one principle and this one principle only, you will have discovered one of the greatest secrets to personal well-being and life-long happiness.

Like you, I have had my share of pain and suffering in my life. And like you, I have diligently searched for a way to move beyond suffering and into peace. As all the ancient spiritual masters have discovered and shared with us, there is a way and it is this:

When you let go of the ego, you will be free of your pain.

Once you have a deeper understanding of what this statement actually means and begin to apply it (no matter how haltingly) in your own life, something quite remarkable happens: You will begin to *think* differently, *feel* differently and hence *behave* differently, and exactly in this order. To use a baseball analogy, this sounds pretty much like a home run to me!

Foreword

We all need to better understand the process we use to "think." The reason is quite simple:

The very first step in everything we do – or don't do – in life begins with the thoughts we choose and give the most importance to.

Of course, we can have exciting thoughts and feel excited, then act on them; or we can have depressing thoughts and feel depressed, and do nothing. So which of these two scenarios appeals the most to you? I think I know your answer. We all want to manifest a life-time of accomplishment and fulfillment, to do the things that make a difference in our lives and in the lives of others. Now you have this incredible opportunity – to live in a state of sustained happiness and well-being for the rest of your life!

The Hollywood Cure™ for Stress, Anxiety and Depression presents a definitive, broad-based approach to managing your everyday thoughts, and in turn your mood and feelings. It is a fascinating look at how you can live more fully and positively, and learn more about yourself and your rightful place in the world.

The text Dr. Staples presents draws on several primary disciplines – behavioral psychology, philosophy, theology, sociology, anthropology, science and others – to make its main point, namely that each of us is a "spiritual" being living in a "physical" world, yet many of us either don't know this or don't fully accept it.

As a consequence, many of us are not genuinely happy. We lack meaning, purpose and direction, and any real sense of passion in our lives. We feel unfulfilled, unworthy and unappreciated. We are *not* content; we are *not* at ease; we are *not* ourselves. We often suffer from a host of debilitating ailments that may include stress, anxiety, guilt, depression and despair, along with the many serious physical illnesses that these mental afflictions can bring on, including high blood pressure, heart disease, diabetes and cancer.

This necessarily limits our ability to live and function as we should, including our relationships with family and friends, our jobs and career, our finances, our personal goals and aspirations ... our ability to live abundantly and productively as vibrant, creative and joyous human beings. In other words, when both our mental and physical health are at risk, nothing else in our life can work very well.

Dr. Staples does us all a great service in this book. To support one of his main points – that each of us *can* think and feel good again – he convincingly and adeptly uses timeless insights, proven psychological principles, historical anecdotes, personal experiences, clinical research findings, humorous quips and insightful quotations from dozens and dozens of learned people in all walks of life – some very common folk while others are quite uncommon.

He explains that the underlying intent of all the great spiritual masters, from Lao-tzu and Buddha to Jesus and Mohammed, is remarkably similar: To encourage people to direct their hearts and minds *inward* towards the divine ("God" by whatever name) rather than primarily *outward* towards the world of form ("stuff" by whatever name). His effort is a remarkable work of love, understanding, dedication and caring.

A final point. Dr. Staples introduces us in his book to his central concept of hope and happiness in life which has nothing to do with the material world of fame and fortune. He states that "authentic happiness" follows naturally and spontaneously from simply *understanding who we really are*, our one and only true Self, and then deeply and passionately loving that Self. This he calls *unconditional self-acceptance*. He suggests this should be our primary goal.

In turn, this results in something quite remarkable: By acting in accordance with who we are, we quickly develop an awareness, an understanding, a conscious feeling (some would say an *inner knowing*) of incredible confidence, courage and compassion, coupled with a burning desire to make a difference that involves both our life and the lives of others. He goes on to explain that authentic happiness is in fact our *natural state*, but most of us aren't aware of it because we are totally confused, brain-washed and uninformed.

Please read on. This book takes you on a single journey ... *but it opens your life to a thousand joys!* You may well find it to be the most important book you have ever read.

The Publisher

Only love matters …

"I am going to say something I have never said before and this is the truth. I have no reason to lie to you and God knows I am telling the truth. I think all my success and fame, and I have wanted it, I have wanted it because I wanted to be loved. That's all. That's the real truth. I wanted people to love me, truly love me, because I never really felt loved.

"I said I know I have an ability. Maybe if I sharpened my craft, maybe people will love me more. I just wanted to be loved because I think it is very important to be loved, and to tell people that you love them and to look them in their eyes and say it."

Michael Jackson
(1958 – 2009)
American Pop Music Icon

(from an interview recorded in 2000 and made public
on *Dateline NBC* on 25 September, 2009)

PART 1

Cognitive Behavioral Therapy
and
Critical Thinking

"I do not feel obliged to believe that the same God who has endowed us with sense, reason and intellect has intended us to forgo their use."

Galileo Galilei
(1564 – 1642)
Italian Physicist, Mathematician,
Astronomer and Philosopher

Cognitive Behavioral Therapy

"It is your thoughts that make your life what it is today.
It follows that if you change the quality of your thoughts,
you will necessarily change the quality of your life."

The Author

Cognitive Behavioral Therapy (CBT) is based on modifying cognitions, assumptions, opinions and beliefs, with the goal of significantly reducing negative and destructive *emotions* and subsequent negative and destructive *behavior*. The approach follows from Rational Emotive Behavioral Therapy (REBT) which was developed by Albert Ellis (1913 – 2007) in the 1950s, and further refined by Aaron T. Beck in the 1970s.

CBT continues to be widely used today to treat various kinds of neurosis and psychopathology, including mood and anxiety disorders. It involves *critically questioning basic assumptions, understandings and beliefs* (e.g. what a person uses to evaluate and internalize a given external event and then come to some conclusion about it) that may well be illogical, irrational, incomplete, or indeed totally inaccurate.

Note that we are not talking about "positive thinking" per se as the primary solution here, the notion that you must think only happy thoughts. This is as dangerous a malady as having only unhappy thoughts all the time! The following example, perhaps an experience you have had yourself, illustrates the process.

Having failed an important exam, a person concludes and says to himself, "I'm dumb and useless, and will never get a college degree." This in turn lowers his self-confidence and belief in his abilities, affects his assessment of his future prospects, and even causes him to question his overall self-worth. All this in turn negatively impacts his mood, his level of motivation, his energy, and his belief that he will eventually succeed. He begins to study less, pay less attention during lectures, skip classes, argue with his professors, and leave important assignments to the last minute. His behavior is thus confirming his new-found belief ... that he is dumb and useless, and will not get that college degree he so desperately wants!

In therapy, this example is called a self-fulfilling prophecy or a "problem-pain" cycle (e.g. recall the "problem," relive the "pain"). The efforts of the therapist and client are to work together to reassess the particulars of the activating event itself (e.g. failing an exam) to see if *other conclusions* are just as plausible/realistic or indeed more plausible/realistic than the one initially adopted. If this "systematic thought evaluation process" (or S-T-E-P) helps the client to think and respond differently, to see that indeed it is possible to draw different conclusions from the same event, then his negative habit pattern of thought can be interrupted and his mood modified so that it is more empowering and productive. As explained, the main objective of CBT is to identify and debunk maladaptive cognitions, assumptions and beliefs that give rise to debilitating negative emotions that in turn can lead to dysfunctional and potentially destructive behavior (e.g. doing harm – either physically or emotionally – to either oneself and/or others).

Of note, sessions involving Cognitive Behavioral Therapy in some cases can have an *immediate* (e.g. after only a few days or weeks) and lasting impact; in other cases, it can take three to six months or, on occasion, up to a year. All this seems understandable, knowing that we are trying to dramatically change an entrenched habit pattern here, in this case one that represents a person's particular manner of thinking.

We know people's core beliefs about themselves and their world are formed, confirmed and firmly imbedded in their psyche during their early childhood years. These then lead to *automatic thought responses* to everyday events and are not easily over-ridden. Hence it is only through concerted effort and repetition – applying S-T-E-P over and over and over again – that new, more productive habit patterns of thought can be generated and, over time, become the new "norm."

J.K. Rowling, author of the phenomenally successful *Harry Potter* series of books, is a case in point. As a result of selling nearly 400 million books world-wide, she is considered today to be one of the richest women in England, with an estimated net worth of over $1 billion. However, times were not always so good.

In an interview published on 23 March, 2008, on the front page of *The (London) Sunday Times*, she confided that she had thoughts of suicide while suffering from depression as a struggling single mother. All this after separating from her first husband, a Portuguese T.V. journalist, in the mid-1990s. "(My) mid-twenties life circumstances were poor and I really plummeted," Rowling, now 42, said. She explained that she sought help from her GP and consequently spent nine months taking cognitive behavioral therapy. She added that she came out of it feeling fine.

The *Times* article goes on: "Cognitive behavioral therapy typically involves a series of sessions with a counselor and is designed to help patients control negative thoughts. The technique is recommended by the (United Kingdom) health department for depressive disorders, anxiety, bulimia, and post-traumatic stress disorder (PTSD)."

Rowling concludes her remarks in the article by saying, "I have never been remotely ashamed of having been depressed. Never. What's to be ashamed of? I went through a really tough time and I am quite proud that I got out of that."

The Process of Thinking

Using the example of the student just cited, here is a more detailed explanation of the **A-B-Cs** of the "systematic thought evaluation process" which lies at the very core of Cognitive Behavioral Therapy:

>   **A – activating event**. This refers to the objective situation (e.g. the external stimulus), the event, occurrence or specific incident that triggers a cognitive response in the first place.

>   **B – cognitive response**. This refers to how you interpret and come to some conclusion (e.g. thoughts!), often manifested in the form of "self-talk," about that event. This necessarily is a reflection of your personal belief system (PBS), and the particular habit patterns of thought you have adopted and use instinctively every day.

>   **C – emotional reaction**. This refers (in this example) to the distressing feelings – whether hurt, anger, fear, guilt or sorrow – that the thoughts in **B** automatically generate. Action (which may be more harmful than helpful) or inaction (inability to decide on a given course of action) immediately follows.

In other words, as you go about your daily routine, events (**A**) will invariably occur that cause thoughts (**B**) to be generated which in turn produce feelings (**C**) that correspond to these very same thoughts. Now, here is an important observation: The events that occur – in terms of type, frequency and intensity – are generally **totally <u>out of</u> your control**; the thoughts that you produce are **totally <u>within</u> your control**; and the feelings that follow are **totally <u>out of</u> your control** since they are a direct by-product of the particular thoughts that preceded them. Hence it is clear where you have to focus your attention if you want to change how you feel:

It is on the <u>thoughts</u> that you create in response to various events!

In this regard, the vast majority of your responses to situations that arise each day are spontaneous and automatic e.g. your responses are primarily habitual, meaning you don't give them any serious (conscious) consideration before they appear. But if you want, you can learn to *change* how you respond to various events (indeed *all* events) that occur in your life in order to better control the feelings that you generate. And necessarily as you do this over and over again, perhaps over three to four weeks, your new way of responding to events in turn becomes habitual, just like your old way was before. Clearly, this is the ideal situation as you are now in control of the so-called *new reality* you are creating and the *new feelings* that necessarily come along with it.

So, how can you change the way you think? We know all learning is a gradual and repetitious process, and involves passing through four levels of incompetence/competence. The first level is *unconscious incompetence*, where you lack a particular skill or ability but don't know it. The second level is *conscious incompetence*, where you lack a particular skill but now you know it (e.g. someone has pointed this out to you). The third level is *conscious competence*, where you "know that you know" how to do a thing particularly well. The final level of learning is *unconscious competence*, where you do automatically or instinctively what you are able to do well, and never have to think about it. At this point, your new behavior has become habitual – *it is fully ingrained* – and is carried out totally at the subconscious level. (Note that the word "learn" has both the words "ear" and "earn" in it, which tells us a great deal about the process that is involved!)

Returning to the **A-B-C** process, we see that the *thoughts* in **B** (whether positive or negative, rational or irrational) act as the connecting link or "bridge" between the initial *event or occurrence* in **A** and the subsequent *feelings* in **C**. This sequence of events is one of natural cause and effect, and clearly shows the process we all follow when we engage in the activity we call "thinking."

In this regard, it is key to note this critical fact: *Feelings* themselves (**C**) do not represent the absolute "truth" about any given situation. They are simply a reflection of the particular *thought* or thoughts that preceded them (**B**). So if you want to overcome hurtful feelings (e.g. suffering) in your life, you have only one recourse: *Knowing you cannot change your feelings by trying to change your feelings, you must focus instead on the thought or thoughts that caused those feelings in the first place.* **These things – thoughts – you <u>can</u> change!**

In reality, many of your "thoughts" in response to a given event all too often have a large, self-absorbed "egoic" component to them, a huge dose of "me!" … ("Why is this happening to me!?!!??? Why me? Why me?) … and this necessarily distorts your *interpretation* of the event and as a result how you *feel* about that event. This is not unlike being overly paranoid about things that happen to you in your life e.g. believing that the "world" is out to make your life a mess and you very miserable as a result. Of course, what actually happens is the exact reverse: You make yourself very miserable by the process just described and thus make your life a mess all by yourself!

Let me explain. We are all used to having positive, uplifting feelings that follow from a certain event or situation that we welcome. We readily accept such feelings as valid and realistic, as reflecting so-called "reality." ("Wow. Things are really great!") *But of course, they do not.* These feelings only represent how we have interpreted (e.g. evaluated and internalized) the activating event itself.

On other occasions, we react to a certain event or situation that we don't welcome with negative, depressing feelings. ("Uggg. Things are so terrible!") Again, we fall into the trap of accepting these feelings as being valid and realistic, and hence reflecting reality. *Of course, they do not.* Therefore to deal with feelings of all kinds, whether uplifting or depressing, welcomed or not welcomed, a person has to go back and focus on the often twisted, distorted and irrational *thoughts* that caused them in the first place.

Let's consider another situation. Assume Molly didn't win the competition to become the new creative director at the advertising agency where she worked. This is **A**. This activates her personal belief system and she concludes that she is incompetent, unappreciated and worthless. This is **B**. Consequently she is upset, disappointed and angry. This is **C**. Note that if her emotions are allowed to linger on unchallenged and unchanged, the odds are very small indeed that she will ever get promoted to such an important position.

The final part of the assessment process involves something called "reframing." After assisting the client to identify the irrational and inaccurate beliefs that are at play, the therapist works with that person to challenge the negative thoughts themselves, and to *re-assess and re-interpret* the situation in a more positive and realistic light. The client benefits from a more accurate and rational personal belief system as well as healthier and more effective coping strategies.

From this example, the therapist would help Molly come to realize that not succeeding at a single competition is not a life-threatening event, that it is not conclusive evidence on its own that she is incompetent, unappreciated or worthless. As well, Molly would be encouraged to use this as a learning experience to better prepare herself for future competitions.

For example, she could commit to improving her professional skills in general or her interview and interpersonal skills in particular. In other words, she could inquire about the areas where she was found to be weaker than the other candidates, especially the one who was ultimately chosen, and begin immediately to take specific steps – whether a self-study program, a training course or mentoring sessions – to improve on these.

Let me describe some challenges I faced in my own youth. My objective as I grew up was always to try to overcome whatever got between where I was and where I wanted to be. This way, I thought, life would be more interesting and a lot more fun. (To note, this has proven to be the case, at least for me.)

First, here is a comment by Winston Churchill (who had a serious speech impediment in his youth): "One ought never to turn one's back on a threatened danger and try to run away from it. If you do that, you will only double the danger. But if you meet it promptly and without flinching, you will reduce the danger by half. Never run away from anything. Never!"

As a youngster, I was shy, reticent and introverted. I had fine, almost snow-white hair. My nick-name was "smiley." In public school, beginning about Grade 3, I struggled in my studies and it was discovered I was dyslectic. So my dad and I got together every school night after dinner and started doing various exercises to help me cope (e.g. the multiplication table on flash cards). This helped a great deal.

Early in Grade 8, it was determined during my very first eye test that I couldn't see very well. I guess that is why I sat at the front of every class! So armed with a new pair of glasses, I won the prize for mathematics that same year. In Grade 9, I developed a serious speech impediment – I stuttered considerably for the next two to three years. Oh boy! What to do? So I joined the High School debating team for two years and traveled around to nearby schools to participate in contests. We even won a few, although I was often slow to make my points!

Then, early on in High School, it was discovered I had a photographic memory. After being found dyslectic, with poor eye-sight and a speech impediment, this was welcome news (although at the time I really didn't understand what it meant). Interestingly, this so-called "ability" is more common than most people think. About two or three percent of the general population have it in their youth but it tends to diminish later in life, usually beginning in one's mid-twenties. (Today, I can't remember what I had for breakfast yesterday!)

With this ability firmly in hand, as well as my new glasses and enhanced speaking skills, I went on to win the gold medal for "top student in the class" in each year of High School.

I share this bit of background with you for one simple reason. It is not to impress you in any particular way. Rather, it is to emphasize the importance of the *quality of your thinking* regarding challenges of various kinds that invariably you will face in life, and realizing it is possible through critical thinking, strong desire and sheer determination (as well as a certain amount of luck) to move ahead in spite of them.

Taking Responsibility for Your Thoughts

The need for each of us to accept more personal responsibility for every aspect of our life (beginning with the *quality* of our thoughts!) reminds me of this story about a construction worker. As he is opening his lunch pail to eat one day, he mumbles, "Peanut butter sandwiches, that's all I ever get are peanut butter sandwiches!" So his buddy says to him, "Why don't you ask your wife to make you something else?" And he replies, "I'm not married. I make my own lunch."

Isn't it the same with life? Each of us creates our own circumstances, we all "make our own lunch." Consider this: We have what we've got by doing what we've been doing, thinking the way we have become accustomed. It's simple enough. If what we want in the future is different from what we've got in the present, we have to change what we've been doing!

The following schematic shows the challenge we all face:

How Your Thoughts Generate Your Feelings
(clockwise from **A** through to **F**)

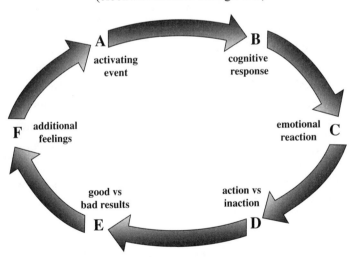

A activating event

B cognitive response

C emotional reaction

D action vs inaction

E good vs bad results

F additional feelings

Copyright © 2008 Walter Doyle Staples

*"You need to make it your business to feel good every day.
Otherwise, you will naturally drift off in the opposite direction and
accomplish little of importance in your life."*
The Author

Action versus Inaction

To understand this chart, follow the sequence of events from **A** through to **F** and carefully note what happens. (**A**, **B** and **C** have already been discussed in detail.) This is something that plays out several times a day in your life and invariably makes it either a very "good" day or a very "bad" one, or somewhere in between.

Some observations: First, inaction is a very real possibility if the cognitive and emotional response to **A** is negative (e.g. corrupted by "faulty" and irrational/illogical thinking). I submit that this is not an acceptable outcome. Second, there are several entry points where "intervention" is possible to re-evaluate **B** (e.g. opportunities to interrupt the pattern and change the conclusion that you have reached). For example, it could occur after **B**, **C**, **D**, **E** or even **F**. And third, if your additional feelings (**F**) are negative and totally discouraging (e.g. you expect to get only poor results no matter what you do), then this itself becomes another activating event (**A**) and the whole cycle repeats itself very much like a closed loop. Then you are on a merry-go-round that is picking up speed and it is very hard to get off.

Clearly, action, which begins with rational, logical thinking, is the only outcome that takes you somewhere you want to be, versus inertia, which keeps you exactly where you are and don't want to be. It is one of the key concepts in moving ahead and turning your life around quickly and permanently.

Interestingly, there is actually a "disease" associated with inaction. The word for it is "otiosity." Otiosity is the state or condition of being "otiose," meaning 1. at leisure; idle; indolent 2. ineffective; futile; sterile 3. useless; superfluous. I'm sure it is a term you don't want applied to yourself. (All definitions in the text are whole or in part from *Webster's New World Dictionary*.)

Chicago

There are always valid reasons why people fail at various aspects of their life. It all boils down to what people have come to believe *who they really are* – the "pictures" they have created in their head about how they "see" themselves that then dominate their everyday thoughts and feelings.

Several years ago, there was a "barbers" convention being held at a large hotel in Chicago. As a publicity stunt, the organizers decided to find a derelict in the slums nearby and spruce him up – give him a bath, shave, haircut and some new clothes – all the external trappings of a "new" person. Let's call him Charlie. They took Charlie's picture before and after, and had them displayed prominently in the local newspaper to show how much a shave and haircut could dramatically change a man. Charlie was a huge hit at the convention, drawing a great deal of attention. Finally he was *somebody* – at least somebody, he felt, *in the minds of other people.*

The day after the convention was over, however, something interesting happened. Several reporters wanted to interview Charlie but he couldn't be found. Can you guess where he was? At a friend's house? Looking for a job? Enrolling in barber school? Planning to start college? No, Charlie was found back in the slums, drunk and disheveled, where he felt he belonged, being precisely the person *he thought he was.* This begs the question: What could possibly be done to help Charlie break free from the prison he had built for himself?

How You "See" Yourself

This brings us to a description of "self-image psychology," which in essence says:

You become in your life the person you "see" yourself to be in your mind.

But how does this actually work? It's quite simple, really. You have developed a series of filters or perceptual frameworks – often called paradigms – that you use to see and interpret all the things that are going on in your life. These paradigms are a function of your individual beliefs, values, assumptions and opinions that you have acquired during your upbringing.

The master paradigm you have developed is called your "self-image." It answers the question, "How do I 'see' myself, in every conceivable aspect of my life?" You have specific "pictures" in your head that range from very positive to very negative that depict how you "see" yourself as a student, an athlete, an artist, a writer, a musician, a dancer, a lover, a negotiator, a public speaker, a parent, a teacher, a salesperson, a manager, and on and on. There are literally thousands of these "images-of-self" that together constitute your "self-image." This paradigm can be compared to a pair of invisible eye-glasses you wear every day. *And it is you who has created your very own prescription – your own "sense of self!"*

This "lens," of course, affects the way you see everything all around you including your "self," your future, and what you think you can or cannot accomplish in your life. The breakthrough comes when you understand that you *can* change the way the world looks to you – but first you must take the time to change the *artificial lens* through which you view it.

The simplest truths are often the most powerful; they need only be fully understood, accepted and internalized. What is the simple truth, then, that this book proclaims to all those who are hurting, who are looking for a way to move beyond despair and despondency to hope and happiness?

It is this: It matters not where you were born, who your parents are, how much education you have, what language you speak, what skills you have developed, or what successes or failures you have had. Nor does it matter what major challenge or challenges you may be facing in your life at the present time. It matters only who you think you are. *For if you change who you think you are, you automatically change who you are!*

Each day finds you at a certain place in your life. This has to do with many things including your physical, mental and spiritual health, your relationships with family and friends, your professional career and your personal finances. Sometimes, many of these aspects seem to be just fine while others are not. So you may simply want to fine-tune a few things. At other times, you may want to make more radical and wholesale changes, perhaps involving an important relationship or indeed the career path you are on.

Whatever is on your agenda, *the way you think* is by far the most critical factor. This is why the activity called "critical thinking" is such an important skill to understand and apply … or even perfect! Without it, you are lost and left to the mercy of chance and circumstance, such as these situations: "Gosh, I sure was lucky when I made that decision!" or "Darn, I sure didn't guess right when I decided to do that!"

The Great Wheel of Life

Let's look at how you organize your time and focus your energy on a daily basis. We have already briefly described the key areas of life in general, those aspects that when added together determine the overall quality of life you enjoy. The following depiction helps conceptualize the fact that there are six such key areas and each is like a spoke in a large wheel.

The Great Wheel of Life

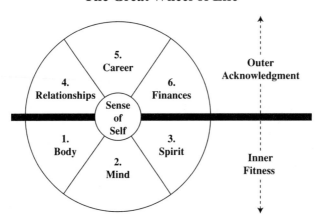

"Human beings, by changing the inner aspects
of their minds, can change the outer aspects of their lives."
William James

We know any wheel is only as strong as the central, supporting spokes that make it up. Hence if one or more of these is missing, the wheel becomes distorted in shape and invariably begins to wobble when put in motion. Like a car with a flat tire going down the road, you will hear a loud *whop! whop! whop!* that indicates something is seriously wrong.

Of course, if the distortion is significant enough, the wheel will totally collapse, as can happen with your life! Also note that your "sense of self" – who you think you are – lies at the very center (hub) of this wheel and necessarily affects everything that lies within the circumference of the wheel.

The three factors shown at the bottom of the circle are _internal_ that relate to your "person," namely: 1. your physical body; 2. your mental state; and 3. your spiritual nature. These three constitute what I call your "inner fitness" factors.

The next three shown at the top are _external_ factors that relate to the world outside of your personal "self," namely: 4. your relationships (e.g. family and friends); 5. your professional career; and 6. your personal finances. These three constitute what I call your "outer acknowledgment" factors. In other words, _the "state" or robustness of the last three factors is determined exclusively by the "state" or robustness of the first three._ Each of these six areas can be measured in any number of ways, and the results can range from terrible to excellent.

Here is the point: When you are on solid footing (e.g. your internal factors are all at or near the excellent level), this inevitably will be acknowledged or manifested in your everyday world, namely the three factors that are external to you. You very likely will have healthy, meaningful relationships, be progressing well in your chosen career, and your finances will all be in order.

The opposite is also true. Real-life examples are everywhere. If you ignore your physical and mental health, everything else in your life can suffer. The possible devastating effects of drugs (including a wide variety of prescription drugs, even some thought to be relatively benign such as sleeping pills) and/or alcohol on your body are well known to most of us. In situations that result in death, of course, there are often several factors at play and this undoubtedly is true regarding the following individuals: Marilyn Monroe (died 1962); Lenny Bruce (1966); Janis Joplin (1970); Jimi Hendrix (1970); Elvis Presley (1977); Freddie Prinze (1977); John Belushi (1982); Truman Capote (1984); River Phoenix (1993); Kurt Cobain (1994); Chris Farley (1997); Anna Nicole Smith (2007); and Heath Ledger (2008). At the same time, it appears in some cases that their lives were also impacted by substances such as those just described, including prescription drugs of one kind or another. (Source: Wikipedia)

Unfortunately, as it seems an easy solution, many people resort to drugs and/or alcohol to blot out or escape from their so-called "current reality." This could involve being tormented by what they most closely identify with, namely the world of form (e.g. _things_ – happenings, events and situations). In such instances, a torrent of constant and debilitating thoughts and preoccupations is bombarding their mind, and making them – and keeping them – on edge and often very unhappy. Examples: (1) "Because my last movie // my last song // my last performance just bombed, it's clear I'm a loser and my career is over." (2) "Everyone expects too much from me. I find the pressure just too much … I can't cope anymore." (3) "Because of my confrontational attitude, my marriage is over. Now I'm all alone and lost." (4) "Because of my drug and gambling addiction, I've lost my job and all my life savings. I will never recover. What do I do now?"

Since most people are not aware of proven and productive ways to deal with extreme stress, trauma or indeed a personal tragedy of one kind or another, some turn to harmful substances, hoping to maintain a certain sense of balance or "normalcy." While this approach may appear to provide short-term relief, it is often at the expense of longer-term grief. In other words, the so-called fix or "cure" that is being adopted frequently adds to and makes even worse the initial problem. Clearly, you cannot get rid of a problem by artificially altering your state of mind (e.g. using drugs and/or alcohol) on a regular basis and pretending it isn't there. *It is there,* and it needs to be dealt with. (See Annex 14, *The Wellness Workbook.*)

Another major concern in our society today is obesity, with up to a third of the general population being either overweight or obese, including children. A dramatic increase in diabetes, and the strokes and heart attacks that it can bring on, will likely be the result. As well, if you ignore your mental health – your ability to consider, think through and act on those things that are important to you – again, everything else in your life can suffer. Finally, if you lack spiritual knowledge and understanding, the primary source of inner strength, self-reliance and fortitude for some people, you may also be putting important aspects of your life at risk. As a recent example, consider how this has helped many people in Haiti cope with the effects of the devastating earthquake that stuck that country on 12 January, 2010.

We know events and happenings cannot and will not go perfectly all the time. Something called "Murphy's Law" – which says "whatever can go wrong, will go wrong and just at the most inopportune time" – invariably will show up at your doorstep as an unwelcome and uninvited guest. On these occasions, you will need something to carry you over the precipice, the great divide between dealing successfully with a major challenge or succumbing to it. In my own case, I had to succumb to challenges several times in my life (and endure the gut-wrenching pain that came with them) before I learned how to deal with them and move on.

The imperative, then, is to ensure that you are making constant, measurable improvement in the first three key areas, *namely body, mind and spirit* – which are the primary focus of this book – thus leading to a proper balance among all six areas such that each is nurtured and gradually improved upon. In this way, a synergistic effect is created and incredible momentum generated. The ultimate goal is to have each area produce its own amount of joy and fulfillment, in turn making its own significant impact on the greater whole, thus creating a very meaningful, rewarding and satisfying life.

Your Collective Consciousness

A problem we all have is how to better understand the "status" or quality of our thinking at any one point in time. So what can be done? Here is one suggestion.

You can gain clear and unobstructed insight into your opinions, beliefs and understandings about you and your world by closely monitoring what you say when you talk to your "self." This is that little voice inside you that never stops espousing on every subject under the sun.

An analogy is that you can squeeze an orange, collect the juice that comes out, then taste it to determine how bitter or sweet it is (e.g. you can decide that "bitter juice" equals "bad thoughts" and "sweet juice" equals "good thoughts"). Now consider your own situation. When life puts the "squeeze" on you, which it will invariably do from time to time, how do you react? Do you send out negative or positive signals in direct proportion to the degree of the discomfort? Or do you take everything in stride and deal with it from a position of strength and inner knowing?

As you go about your daily activities, you can listen and closely analyze what you say to yourself. It is often a two-way conversation that first takes one position on a given subject, and then another and another (e.g. it is not unlike listening to a heated debate between two people who each thinks he is right). This so-called "self-talk" (or internal verbalizations) gives you an indication of the *quality* of your thinking on a whole range of topics.

If you take the time to become aware of it and critically review it, it will show you to what extent you are using one or more of the following: ***Total absolutes, over-generalizations, over-simplifications, gross distortions, simplistic rationalizations or indeed false assumptions*** (see definitions in Annex 11, *The Wellness Workbook*) in the way you are now "seeing" (e.g. perceiving, understanding and accepting) the "state of affairs" in your world. You can never hope to move beyond total helplessness when you choose to engage in erroneous, irrational and illogical thinking. You are doomed to live a life of mediocrity at best!

Consider this simple question that you are invariably asked several times a day:

"How are you doing?"

How do you generally answer this question? Does your answer indicate that you think you are winning more than you are losing? Or is it the other way around or somewhere in between? Is it possible to come to any meaningful conclusion in this regard?

The question may be phrased a little differently: "How are you?" "How are things?" or "How is it going?" but each one is an interesting question nonetheless. It addresses the point of how well do you think you are doing in your life at the particular time you are being asked. And you usually have a lot on your mind at the time you are asked – you are supposedly preoccupied with more weighty concerns like watching the numbers on the elevator wall flip by or wondering how long it is until lunch – so you pay scant attention and give little thought to your answer.

Herein lies the value and insight represented by your response. Since you don't give any serious (conscious) thought to your answer before you give it – it's a spontaneous, knee-jerk reaction, like you are in a coma or trance – it comes straight from your subconscious mind. Hence it represents a great inner truth that often even you are not (consciously) aware of: Do you think you are moving ahead, marking time or going backwards in the greater scheme of things? Do you feel you are making progress towards a grander cause, that your life is indeed meaningful and fulfilling? Or do you feel like a scrap of paper blowing in the wind, at one moment happy, the next moment sad, depending on whether the wind is blowing in a favorable direction?

Like the countenance on your face, the gleam in your eye or the briskness in your step, your everyday response to this simple question is a window into your world. I am indebted to Dr. Robert H. Schuller, senior pastor of the Crystal Cathedral in Garden Grove, California, for helping me formulate the following illustration that sheds some light on this not-at-all-simplistic phenomenon.

Scale of the Human Spirit

Your overall notion of your "sense of self" exists and is always at work in your life at the subconscious level. In turn, it is manifested in your everyday feelings, behavior and self-talk. You can gain some insight into its current state and "status" – its relative vibrancy, if you will – if you listen to what you say to yourself and others.

For example, here are 10 possible responses (with number **1** being the least positive/empowering and number **10** the most) that people often use to answer the question, "How are you doing?"

Range of Answers:

1. **No answer.** The person is in shock, overcome by grief or tragic loss.

2. **"I'm mad!"** The person is consumed by anger.

3. **"I'm depressed."** The person is being controlled by negative thoughts and feelings.

4. **"Not so bad."** The person is barely functioning, watching things happen.

5. **"I'm OK."** The person is coping but remains very vulnerable.

… all these answers despite good health, wealth, love, status and excellent future prospects. Strange but true.

Or alternately, you may respond:

6. **"I'm good."** The positives temporarily outweigh the negatives.

7. **"I'm *real* good!"** And still at only #7; a strong element of control.

8. **"I'm terrific!"** Even greater control; potential for high achievement.

9. **"I'm fan-tas-tic!"** In control, making things happen.

10. **"I'm ... simply sensational!"** In control. In charge. Incredible!

... all these answers despite a crippling disease, despair, depression or even imminent death. Again, strange but true.

So, think for a moment about the answers you give on a daily basis and ask yourself:

1. Do your answers ever go from one extreme to another, depending on your particular mood and circumstances at a certain point in time? 2. Why? 3. Or are they always the same (whether very average, "I'm OK, I guess" or very uplifting, "I'm so good that it hurts, thank you!"), whatever your circumstances are? 4. Again, why? Give some serious thought to these basic questions.

Some people can be up, they can be energetic and alive even when things in their life are falling apart. Take a person who is terminally ill yet whose spirit is more vibrant than others who are in perfect health. Alternatively, a person can have everything – health, wealth, power, prestige and status – and yet be the most miserable person on the face of the earth.

Can this dramatic difference in outlook, in attitude, in understanding the nature of the "self" be explained by saying that some people live by a different standard, that somehow they are aware of a greater truth that others are not? What follows in the text will help you answer this important question for yourself.

PART 2

Practical Spirituality
and
Self-Image Psychology

"During the past 30 years, people from all the civilized countries of the earth have consulted me. Many hundreds of patients have passed through my hands. Among all my patients in the second half of life – that is to say, over 35 – there has not been one whose problem in the last resort was that of not finding a religious outlook on life. It is safe to say that every one of them fell ill because he had lost what the living religions of every age have given to their followers, and none of them has been really healed who did not regain his religious outlook."

Carl Jung
(1875 – 1961)
Swiss Psychologist

The Ultimate Insight

Through simple *awareness*, in stillness, the most basic
truth you come to understand about yourself is this:
You are love. *Only love.*

When you "allow" and "access" the stillness in you,
you also discover the following:

The *awareness* in you is the "it" of the universe.
The *stillness* in you is the "it" of the universe.
The *knower* in you is the "it" of the universe.

EXAMPLE

When the love in you recognizes the love that is in another
– what is our very essence –
that's "it" … that <u>awareness</u> is "it!"
The "it" is the Sacred.
And that Sacred is in you!

The Author

---

*"It is this belief in a power larger than myself and other than myself
which allows me to venture into the unknown and even the unknowable."*

Maya Angelou
American Poet, Historian and Author

The following are some of the key concepts that will be explored in PART 2:

ON *BEING*

Being defies simple words and description. It can only be *experienced*. This much can be said: *Being* is feeling the ever-present *I am,* of knowing at a higher level of consciousness that *you are*. This is the state of enlightenment, meaning being free of the illusion of the egoic (little) self, of believing you are nothing more than your physical body and the thoughts you think. It is only through *Being* that you can connect with your Source, your true essence, that which lies at the very center of all that is.

ON *INSIGHT*

Insight means the ability to "see into" and understand clearly the *nature* of a thing or things. In this book, this is what is attempted – to gain insight into the nature of man as well as the nature of the universe through the intellect and intuition. The former is when you analyze information critically, rationally and logically; the latter is what resonates with your soul and simply *feels* right. You are encouraged to conduct this same test on the information presented here. Some of it you may connect with, some of it you may not, and that's fine. Just spending time thinking about such ideas has to be considered progress, however. It is something you need to do if you want to wake up.

cont'd …

ON *WHO YOU ARE*

You "exist" as 99 percent pure fiction, not fact. Your Creator had the most important say in who you are, of course, but the rest is a story you yourself compose. How can this be? During your upbringing, you took in a vast amount of *subjective* information – the country, city or town you were born in, who your parents, teachers and mentors were, your language, religion, nationality, and so on. You then turned all this into *objective* fact and said, "Good! Now I know who I am!" The result is unfortunate and tragic, however, for by adopting a self-concept that is necessarily limiting, inaccurate and totally false, you end up living a lie! You never grasp the real nature of your true self, your actual Being.

ON *YOUR EMOTIONS*

Your emotions, for the most part, are contrived. You generate them yourself, continuously, in response to everyday events – whether it is anger, arrogance, hate, fear, guilt, jealousy, envy or regret. This occurs as you proceed to *judge* and *pre-judge* (a.k.a. prejudice) the world, and everyone and everything in it using your limited perceptual artifacts and mental capabilities. However, there is one emotion you seldom generate automatically in order to defend your (false) beliefs and justify your (distorted) view of the world: *It is unconditional love.* Yet, when called upon, this emotion comes forth naturally and effortlessly – spontaneously – and from a place you don't fully understand, appreciate or have any control over. It is the primary characteristic of your Source; it is the essence of your Being; it is in fact who you are.

*"We need to know that feeling 'hurt' or depressed on occasion
has a greater purpose behind it. It tells us that our thoughts are not
in alignment with 'truth.' Consider this: Feeling hurt physically sends us
a strong message – don't touch that hot stove! And feeling hurt
emotionally also sends us a strong message – our thinking is irrational or
illogical; it's all wrapped up in our ego. When we finally see what is going
on, we come to realize that <u>this suffering had to happen</u> to wake us up.
And once in this, the enlightened state, we're able to see beyond the petty
fray, the mundane minutiae of everyday life to a new frontier, a new
understanding. Now, with this as our vantage point, our new perspective,
we're better able to see our role in the greater scheme of things:
It is to help humankind rise up and prosper."*

The Author

An Explanation of Some Key Terms used in PART 2

1. What is meant by the term "Source?"

Your Source is not a person – it is an all-encompassing, all-pervasive *presence*. It is an energy, a power, an intelligence, it is everywhere and it is good! It is who you are, your essence, your reality, your true and only Self. It is that seemingly "unknowable" that lies at the core of all creation. Most simply, perhaps, it is that which provokes wonderment and awe. Many names throughout history have been given to this entity called your Source. Some call it "God;" others call it Abba, Adonai, Allah, Almighty, Brahman, Creator, Great Spirit, Holy One, Infinite Being, Jehovah, Kali, Krishna, Ra, Supreme Being, Tao, Transcendent Entity, Unity Consciousness, Yahweh, as well as many other names. You can call it Rachel or Ralph if you like. It doesn't matter what you call it, label it or conceive it to be; it is what it is.

2. What is your "ego?"

The ego is a derived sense of self, a notion or impression you have created in your mind that represents who you think you are. It is the ego in you that says to others, "I am different than you. I'm more important, more deserving, more capable ... I'm 'better' than you." It is the result of a *belief system* that our species has created over the long course of human history because of its need to survive. Primitive man lived in a very harsh and dangerous environment, and survival was his first order of business. Wild animals, other hostile tribes and often a brutal climate all conspired together to put him at risk. This instinct continues to drive the human species today even though many of the threats that existed in much earlier times disappeared long ago.

3. What is "real?"

Great thinkers throughout history have grappled with this question, and many have come to agree on the following: *"That which is real never changes."* So think about it: What about you and your world does not change? We know that everything in our visible world, the world of "form," changes. Each and every "object" has a beginning and an end, a birth and a death.

This of course includes your own "physicality" – your body. It shrinks, dies and decays, and becomes the simple dust you walk on everyday. Hence, by definition, your body is not real, your body is not the real "you." This begs the question: "If you are not your body, who or what are you then?"

4. What does it mean to live "authentically?"

Your Source is real, your Source is love, your Source knows only good, your Source is you. If you want to *be* love and *give* love, *be* good and *do* good, you need to align yourself with your Source. You must be it, for it is you. A peaceful mind begins with a caring heart. When you know what your Source is, understand that you are your Source, and then align yourself with this Source in everything you think, say and do, you can honestly proclaim to the world, "I see only perfection in every aspect of my life."

5. Why are Nature and the environment so important?

Humankind, from the earliest of civilizations to Native Americans to many environmentalists today, has held a firm and fundamental belief that there is a close and loving relationship between the "Father" and Mother earth, between God and Nature. It holds that to harm the land and fruits of the land is to harm God, and in turn, ourselves. After all, we are all one. As it says in the Bible, "In the beginning, God created the heavens and the earth …. Then God saw everything that He had made and it was good." (Source: Genesis, PART 1)

6. What is meant by "Being?"

Don't try to understand Being with your mind, accept only that you need to *experience* it for yourself. The closest thing in this world to God is *silence*. Being is experiencing Oneness when in that sacred place called "no-mind." It is the state of consciousness that is achieved by going into silence and being still (the process involved is described in detail in PART 3). "Being" involves living in the moment, in the Now, *being totally present in the present*, and experiencing his presence in that space. You move from a state of "conditioned" consciousness, meaning consumed by mind (e.g. all the thoughts the mind generates), to a state of "unconditioned" consciousness, meaning a place of no-mind (e.g. no thoughts). Equally, you could say that it involves a particular kind of "mindfulness" whereby you direct your attention to a place where there are no thoughts, no distractions and no concerns, only stillness and solitude. Through this approach, you enter a transformed mental state, and in turn have a transformed experience that is absent of all "noise" and other unnecessary distractions. By Being, you are able to understand the sacred truth about your Self beyond mind and the world of form. The objective is simple: Allow *what is* ... your true and only Self ... *to be* in all the fullness and richness that Being is.

7. What is meant by the term the "Now?"

The Now recognizes that in the world of spirit, there is no past and no future, in fact no notion of "time" at all; there is only the Now. Time, our fixation on what we call the past, the present and the future, is an illusion the ego has created in order to keep us under its control. Essentially, the Now is the continuous steam of "present-moments" that collectively represent actual human awareness. It's like a ribbon or tape that constantly comes and goes but always manifests itself in the present, in the Now. You cannot think at any point other than in the Now and never have. Of course, you can recall a memory from the past, but only in the present; and you can imagine or think about the future, but again only in the present. When the future does come, it can come only in the present, as Now. In other words, everything that has ever happened to you in the past happened in the Now and everything that will ever happen to you in the future will happen in the Now. Your only reality, then, is the Now. It is all there is. It is also the primary <u>door or portal</u> that allows you to access that place called no-mind. It is through Being – in the Now, in silence, in no-mind – where you will find your true and sacred Self.

8. What exactly is meditation and what role does it play?

Meditation is the primary way of calming the mind in the direction of no-mind. There are literally hundreds of ways of meditating that have been developed by various spiritual masters over thousands of years to do this (many well before the time of Christ), some quite informal, others very formal. Of course, you can calm the mind by using very simple meditative practices; you don't have to follow a complicated ritual. In fact if the process is too complicated, it can get in the way of the goal itself – calming the mind. Calming the mind can be achieved in the following specific ways: (a) by choosing to have no thoughts, not through any strenuous effort on your part but simply by surrendering to "what is" in the Now; (b) by practicing intense, protracted awareness in the present moment by looking at a flower, a tree, a mountain or the ocean, and _mindfully marveling_ at its incredible beauty, its actual Being; and (c) by focusing the mind on one or more (present moment) bodily-related functions such as your breathing, your heartbeat or the temperature at the very tip of your right toe. Alternately, if you just want to divert your attention away from the cascade of compulsive, ever-present and often unsettling thoughts you experience all the time, consider imagining what your eyes would see if they were turned around and looking back inside your head! Anything that takes you away from all the noise and preoccupations of your mind (and hence both the trivia and trauma of your everyday life) and into a place of stillness and solitude will have a beneficial effect.

9. What is meant by the term "object" consciousness?

"Object" consciousness refers to the manifested world, the world of "form," of physicality, of all the objects you are able to perceive through one or more of your five physical senses. If you look around you, this in fact is all you see. There is no end to all the things in your world, and they serve you to the extent you need or want them. A problem arises, however, if you identify yourself completely and unwittingly with these very same things. Your "story" could go something like this: "I am my house, my car, my jewelry … " or any or all of your various possessions. As well, object consciousness refers to the mind and all the thoughts that are generated by the mind. Thoughts are also things, and too many of them can overload your circuits and cause a mental breakdown or burnout. Constant, compulsive thinking with no pause for reflection and rejuvenation is not good for your mental health nor is it the best use of your mind. All too often people believe they have to think a great deal in order to achieve what they want to achieve, not realizing that this is usually not the case. When you are not thinking up a storm is usually when you are the most alert, the most creative, the most insightful, and certainly the most at peace.

10. What is meant by the term "space" consciousness?

"Space" consciousness refers to the unmanifested world, the world of "no-form," of no-thoughts, of no-mind, of no-sound, of silence. If you look up into the sky on a clear night, you will see the odd flickering light here and there, and a whole lot of "space." Most people tend to focus on the objects themselves that they see in space, wondering what they are, but forget about all the "space" in outer space itself. Perhaps this is because they think such space is just "empty" and has no meaning or relevance. Ironically, every single "object" in the physical world is also made up mostly of empty space – well over 99 percent empty space in fact – including your physical body. Clearly, space is very important and very relevant since it is by far the major ingredient in everything that exists in physical form. As well, we need to realize that a certain complexity arises when we try to describe what is the real "nature" of space, of emptiness (a.k.a. fullness!), of what is seemingly "no-thing" or nothing. We must be careful not to label it as this or that, however, because then we will understand it only in terms of being this or that. Rather, we should simply accept it as representing the great unmanifested, the "substance" of no-form, the essence of all creation. Needless to say, we will always remain ignorant of the true nature of "space" consciousness, for a very small part of "object" consciousness – the thoughts generated by our mind – is unable to understand the vastness of the universe. This dimension is simply beyond the ability of our minds to fully comprehend.

11. Where will my search for my Self ultimately take me?

First, don't look upon this as a search. To do so implies that you have to work hard at the process and have a specific end in mind; invariably, you will also have certain preconceived expectations about that end. A simple, calm and open-minded approach is more appropriate and more effective. *All that is necessary to begin is a small, gentle shift in your attention away from thinking you are someone, from having a compulsive need to be someone, to just Being.* Part of this is realizing that all things are inter-connected and inter-related, that Being in fact equals "inter-Being;" this means accepting that every "thing" on the planet, including every creature, every object and every individual is made up of the same basic ingredients or elements that are found in our physical world (e.g. hydrogen, oxygen, nitrogen, carbon, iron, magnesium, selenium, chromium, lithium …). In this sense, when you look at a rock, a flower, a tree, a bird, an animal or another person, you are in fact looking at yourself (or your "Self"). In the same way, when you show love, concern and respect towards any of these same things, you are showing love, concern and respect for yourself. *In this sense, all love in fact is self-love.* The result is a "we" versus "me" mentality or mind-set, a sense or "knowing" that we are not all separate entities, creatures or organisms, and therefore need special and individual treatment. We are all One. We are all made from the same "stuff" of One-ness.

12. Can you recommend certain individuals or teachings for further study?

If you wish to conduct research on your own into the topic of practical spirituality, here are the names of some noted religious figures and spiritual masters: **Abraham** (circa 2000 B.C.E.), who is widely regarded as the Patriarch of Jews, Christians and Muslims. The Covenant between God and Abraham forms the basis for Judaism, and is considered to be the first or one of the first monotheistic religions; **Buddha**, which literally means "the awakened one," whose teachings form the basis of Buddhism. Buddhism is based on the life of Siddharta Gautama (circa 563 – 483 B.C.E.), an Indian prince; **Lao-tzu** (circa 604 – 531 B.C.E.), author of the definitive book *Tao Te Ching* and founder of Taoism; **Adi Shankaracharya** (788 – 820 C.E.), the first person to consolidate the key principles of Advaita Vedanta, which is a Hindu philosophy that believes in the indivisibility of the Self and the Whole; **Jesus Christ** (3 B.C. – 30 A.D.), a Jew born in Palestine whose life and teachings form the basis of Christianity. There are many denominations of Christianity, the two main ones being Orthodox and Western Christianity; and **Mohammed** (570 – 632 C.E.), also spelled Muhammad, the founder of Islam, regarded by Muslims as the last messenger and prophet of God. Mohammed claimed to be a messenger of God in the same vein as Adam, Noah, Moses, David, Jesus, and other notable prophets. (Source: Wikipedia)

How to Live the Enlightened Life

It all begins with the erroneous notion of separation, the idea that there is a "you" and there is a "me," that you have your physical body and I have mine, that you are there and I am here, that you have your space and I have mine, that you are alone and I am alone. This can be extended to mean that I must look after and protect myself and my interests, knowing that you will try to look after and protect yourself and your interests, that I want to survive, prosper and succeed, just as you want to survive, prosper and succeed.

But each of us believes there is only so much to be had (or so it appears in the physical world). The things I want are also the things you want, which means I have to compete with you to make sure I get what I want at the expense of you getting what you want. This only leads to confrontation and conflict, to winning and losing. Look around and you will see just how much of this is going on in our world today, whether between individuals, various ethnic, tribal or religious groups, or indeed whole nations.

As Eckhart Tolle, author of *The Power of Now* has explained to us, there probably have been times in your life when things didn't go as you had hoped. As happened to him, this may have prompted you to mutter, "I'm not happy with myself," "I hate myself" or "I can't live with myself anymore." This is what people often say to themselves when they are down and depressed, and may even be having suicidal thoughts. At this point, however, a fortunate few have noticed a strange duality in their internal discourse. They wonder and ask themselves, "When I say, 'I-am-not-happy-with-my-self,' I seem to be talking about *two people or entities* at play here, first an **'I'** as well as a **'self.'** So, who is this **'I'** and what is this **'self'** anyway?"

A good question! In this text, you will see that there are indeed two entitles at play in your mind. One is your Source, your *true* Self, your essence, the "knower" – often referred to as God or "the Infinite;" the other is your ego, your *false* self, the constant "thinker," your tormentor, the great pretender, your so-called "little" self.

Your inner dialogue, then, is saying, "The **'I'** in me that is my true Self, is sick and tired of putting up with you, the other **'self,'** my false self, that

---

Practical Spirituality and Self-Image Psychology

part of me that is forcing me to think that I am separate, I am alone, I am vulnerable. Yes, I'm very tired of living out this charade. It's not the 'real' me that is living my life this way. This way, I don't experience any joy, any fulfillment; there is no peace, no love. It's so draining, so stressful, so depressing … it's all so unproductive. There must be a way out of this silliness, all this nonsense, all this insanity."

The ego is something we ourselves created during the long course of human history as a survival mechanism. Primitive man had to cope with other hostile tribes, a very harsh environment, and vicious animals that were looking for a quick meal. Man had to develop ways to protect himself, to survive these elements and threats. It basically came down to the "fight or flight" response: Engage the enemy and kill it any way you can, or run as fast as you can and hopefully escape to come back and fight another day.

And so the ego was "born." We created it, we did it all by ourselves (and in a very real sense, we did it "to" ourselves). And we have been living with it ever since even though many of the threats of these earlier times no longer exist today. In most cases, we have tamed the environment, brought wild animals under our control, but have yet to stop seeing "enemies" – other human beings! – all around us.

Here, then, is the reality. First, those with the biggest egos and who were willing to take the most extreme measures were the ones who survived. And second, because they did survive, you and I descended from them; we inherited their DNA. We are them in their most recent incarnation, complete with all their vanity, arrogance, greed, ignorance and neuroses. To note, the more peace-loving Neanderthals were killed off by the more aggressive Cro-Magnons about 30,000 years ago. (Source: Wikipedia)

Imagine prehistoric man acting totally in his own self-interest as he says to his fellow hunter-gatherers, "See that water buffalo over there? That's my water buffalo. Stay away from it. I want that water buffalo to feed myself and my family. My family and I are more important than you and your family. We intend to survive and I really don't care what happens to you. If you try to take that water buffalo away from me, I'll stop you any way I can: I'll trick you, I'll steal it from you, I'll fight you. In fact, I'll *kill* you. I'll do whatever it takes so that I get that water buffalo!"

The ego, then, is a figment of our imagination. It is an illusion, a mental construct we use to supposedly "protect" ourselves. The ego, acting on our behalf, says to others, "I'm more important than you; I'm better than you; I'm more deserving than you; I'm right, you're wrong; I need to win (and in the process make sure you lose)," and on and on. Your ego wants you to think of it as your great protector and benefactor when in fact it is not. It only wants to control you to further its own agenda, which it does by controlling the thoughts you think both at the conscious and subconscious level.

By controlling your thoughts, which invariably focus on either what you *desire* or what you _fear_, it is able to control your emotions and in turn the actions you take on a daily basis. In effect, you become it since it is "being" you; it is making you do what it wants you to do, pretending it has your best interests in mind.

When the ego is at work in your mind, saying all the things we have said it says ("I'm this and I'm that," etc., etc.), all at the expense of other people, this collectively is called "noise" or mental turbulence. The ego is a noise generator of monumental proportions. Noise suits the purposes of the ego very well: It distracts, it distorts, it corrupts and it weakens the person in whom it resides ... it prevents you from knowing your Source, your true Self.

The greatest fear of your ego is that you will discover the charade that it is perpetrating on you and how you "see" yourself, for if you turn down all the noise the ego creates, with its misguided musings and selfish mutterings, you will find yourself going more and more into silence. *Silence to your ego is the ultimate killer, for that is where you will find your Source.* And once you find your Source, there is nothing left for your ego to do. Its constant "chatter" will begin to dissipate and its power over you will begin to diminish. (Note: Although the odds that you can reduce your ego to zero are very small, indeed next to impossible, you can reduce it to a shadow of its former self.)

Your ego doesn't want to be marginalized in any way so it operates in constant survival mode. It will go to any extreme to ensure that this doesn't happen, even to the point of having you kill yourself which will result in its own death as well (e.g. just as a cancer itself dies when it kills someone). Whatever the cost, it will fight the good fight to the bitter end.

And so the battle rages on. It's a real war and one that takes place in your mind every minute of every day ... thought by thought by thought. So far, looking at all the carnage that is going on in the world around us, the ego is winning on many fronts but thankfully not on all. I like the wisdom contained in the comment, "We (as individuals) have to mend our mind before we (collectively) can hope to mend the world."

Let's consider human "consciousness" – our awareness of Now and being intensely *present* in the present – and see how it actually works. First, we need to understand that everything in fact happens in the Now. For example, you can think about the past, the present or the future but only in the Now. That is to say you cannot think about the past in the past or about the future in the future, for neither the past nor the future exists other than in the Now.

Since you cannot think anywhere but in the Now, Now in fact is all there is. It is filled with on-going, constantly-flowing, ever-present thoughts. If you carefully analyze what kind of thoughts dominates the Now in your daily life, you will find that a great many of them (over 99.99 percent in some people!) are egoic (e.g. ego-based) thoughts. Examples: "Poor me, I don't deserve to live like this; I don't deserve to be treated like this; I don't deserve to be so miserable, so poor, so unpopular, so unattractive ... I deserve *MORE* ... more of this and more of this and more of this!"

These are the messages you shout out to the world asking it ... sorry, *demanding* of it, to acknowledge and validate your importance, your worthiness, your abilities, your intelligence ... your *whatever*. This is the great noise factor and as you create it, others create it as well. In fact, the more you create it on your behalf, the more others will create it on their behalf, each side protecting its own turf, meaning their distorted and incomplete sense of self.

Until you understand and see that this is what the ego does, that this is the game it plays, that it really doesn't care about you, you will not be able to deal with it. *The trick is to consciously turn down the noise by recognizing the ego for what it is, then ignoring it to the best of your ability.* This is quite difficult to do at first – your ego has been running your mind for a very long time – but with practice and a lot of patience, it soon becomes habit.

One approach you can take as the incessant flow of ego-based thoughts impacts your consciousness is to say, "Please go away. You are of no use to me. You have caused me enough pain and suffering. I have better things to do with my life than listen to you." And you must say this with sincere love as well as firm conviction. Don't try to resist these thoughts or stop them from coming with any conscious effort. Just let them know you don't want to hear them anymore. The "welcome mat" that was once laid at the doorstep of your mind now says, "Go away!"

At this point, slowly but surely, the decibel level of the noise in your mind will begin to subside; you will enter that place known as silence and start to reconnect with your Source. New understandings and insights emanating from your Source will now impact your inner consciousness, as will their associated emotions that include peace, love, hope, harmony, joy, understanding, tolerance and compassion.

Quite a different dynamic follows: Instead of confronting people by judging them, criticizing them or labeling them in any number of ways, or even attacking them with your anger, you shower them with your kindness and your love, you honor them for their Being, you bestow upon them the respect and dignity that both they and you deserve. You accept them as your equal, you accept them as your brother and sister, and in this way you salute the God in them on behalf of the same God that is in you.

Practical Spirituality

Ask only this: "Who am I?"

Thoughts To Think About

The following represents a compilation of ideas, concepts and insights from the many lectures and seminars I have given and the books and essays I have written over the past 25 years. Together they represent a guide to peaceful, positive and purposeful living, one that is centered in the stillness and joy of our authentic selves. With this as your solid base, you will be able to live a dynamic, fulfilling and spiritually-balanced life, one of your own choosing yet one that is also chosen for you by God.

Spirituality is not served well by language of any kind; indeed, no serious subject is. All language originates from the world of form and hence necessarily has limitations contained within it. For example, how accurately and meaningfully could you explain to another person what a coffee latte or a peanut butter cookie really tastes like? (Hmmm. Not only alone but also when consumed together!) Or consider winning a gold medal at the Olympics, successfully climbing Mount Everest or falling madly in love? When people in these situations are asked, "How does it feel?" they invariably respond by saying something like, "It's an incredible feeling ... but I really can't put it into words." We in the West in particular are all too quick to put labels on everything we see and experience – another compulsion of the mind – and this can only lead to serious misunderstandings and unnecessary complications. (Isn't it strange – and arrogant – that the very moment we put a label on something, we think we *know* it?) I suggest you strongly resist this temptation and trust instead in your own ability to *experience* true "awareness," "understanding," "knowing," "joy," "bliss" and "love" on their own terms.

As you read this book, you probably noticed that you are being asked, perhaps for the first time in your life, to analyze in detail *how you actually think*. All too often you spend a lot of your time thinking in small, concentric circles (e.g. from A to F!) about why you are not living the kind of life you really want to be living, not doing in your life what you really want to be doing, and not getting the results in life you really want to be getting. You are stuck in a pattern of thinking that gets you nowhere, certainly not ahead, yet you don't know what to do to break free. You are locked in limbo, frozen in place, confined to a prison of your own making. It seems the best you can do is to ask this important and relevant question: "Where is the *key* because I want to get out of here?"

But how could this happen? Invariably, at some point, you will find that things are not progressing the way you think they should. You are disillusioned with life and unable to bridge the gap between *wanting* something and *doing* something in order to have it. Faced with this difficulty, you accept that you have to confront head-on personal failure and growing frustration. Clearly you understand your feelings about your predicament but are at a loss what to do about them. After all, having on-going feelings of disappointment and despair are not exactly conducive to taking decisive action.

As you seriously consider these ideas, you are going to find that there is one way and one way only to proceed, and it is this: You must embark on a journey of introspection and self-assessment to rediscover your true source of inspiration. *The process is all about coming to an informed conclusion about who you really are.* As you travel down this road, you will find that buried memories will come alive again, and bring renewed energy and excitement back into your life. As a result, you will become alive again as well.

If you agree to engage in this activity, the rewards you will receive will be in direct proportion to the amount of effort – time, energy and open-mindedness – that you invest in the process. The good news is that even a mind that is seemingly "hard-wired" (meaning very closed to change) can be modified if sufficient interest, determination and persistence are present.

Think of life as one long continuum of activity. The challenge you face is this: *Inertia* lies at one end of the scale and it creates monotony, sadness and misery in your life; *action* lies at the other end of the scale and it creates excitement, happiness and fulfillment in your life. The ideas in this text are designed to specifically minimize the former and maximize the latter. Our analysis will lead to the very *thoughts you think* on a minute-to-minute and day-to-day basis, and the ensuing feelings they generate. These feelings are a prime indicator of the quality of thinking you are using and in turn the quality of life you are living.

Consider the following:

Assume an exciting, inspirational thought strikes you: "I'd like to be an entrepreneur (or an engineer, a scientist, a doctor, a journalist, a history professor, a business executive ...). I have lots of good ideas. The newspapers are full of stories all the time about people who have succeeded at starting a new business. It sure would be exciting to try."

You then say: "But who am I to think I could succeed? I don't have what it takes. I don't have the education, the experience, the network of people, the necessary financing, the skills, the determination ... and I'm not the smartest person in the world, that's for sure." In other words, without any serious thought on your part, you quickly evaluate the possibility of succeeding at a certain endeavor, and conclude that you are not capable or deserving.

You then feel: Sad, down, perhaps even a bit depressed. All the fears and doubts you ever had rise once again to the surface and reinforce your evaluation of yourself. You quickly retreat back into your "comfort zone" where you know it is safe.

Here, there is no pressure on you. You don't have to prove anything to anyone, especially yourself. You just accept the low opinion you have of yourself ... it's the path of least resistance. After all, no one knows you better than you know yourself, so obviously your evaluation of yourself and your prospects for success are correct. (Wrong!) The result: You are immobilized, and your feelings of self-doubt and lack of confidence keep you exactly where you are. Hence nothing in your life changes very much, including your low opinion of yourself.

This thought sequence plays itself out in the minds of thousands, if not millions of people all over the world on a daily basis. On the surface, the conclusion that is reached appears very logical; on closer scrutiny, however, it does not. There is simply no conclusive evidence to support it, no matter who the individual is. *Any belief you may have about yourself and your abilities to succeed at any new activity needs to be tested in the real world through action – and often repeated action – and experience.* It begins and ends with two four-letter words ... "hard work!"

The most telling aspect of your life is your *relationship* with the Infinite or God. We know many people don't have a relationship with God because they don't "know" God. God can be known (of course, in a necessarily limited way) only through silence. Only through silence can you practice Being. Being is the process of reuniting with and hence coming to know your Source. It amounts to being *present* in the present and not distracted by incessant "noise" – all those repetitive, everyday, self-serving thoughts you constantly shout out to the world that say, "Hey, look at me. I'm special; I'm different; I'm important!" It is through knowing your Source that you come to know who you really are, for you are it and it is you.

Your Source knows only good; by being an instrument of this good, you are contributing to the collective wellness of all those close to you and through them, to all of humanity. Your life can be a life of miracles.

There is no such thing as "time" at the spiritual level. Time is something we humans created to help us keep track of noise and other silly distractions in our environment. To think that there is a yesterday, today and a tomorrow is a great illusion, for there is only Now, the present moment. For example, God is not doing anything today that he was not doing yesterday, nor will he tomorrow. That which is real never changes with time, and God is real. As well, anyone today can access any of the wisdom that ever existed throughout the ages; the great insights of any great thinker or spiritual teacher from the past, whether the Buddha, Jesus or Mohammed, are available in their original form today. The means to "know" God today are the same as they have ever been or ever will be; you need only begin the search and find the peace, joy and excitement that this brings into your life.

In the minds of some, there seems to be a great deal of confusion regarding "knowing about" God versus "knowing" God. You can come to know "about God" by reading the Scriptures or other religious books on the topic and going to church, a temple, a mosque or synagogue. "Knowing" God, however, and practicing his ways as a way of life is a very different matter and involves a very different process.

It's like the difference between a map and the actual territory. A map is not the territory; it's only someone's two-dimensional approximation of what that territory is like. You can never get to "know" God by reading a book about God or going to church and listening to someone speak about God, no matter how good that book is or how knowledgeable that speaker is. Similarly, you can never get to "know" the Grand Canyon by studying a map about the Grand Canyon or listening to someone speak about the Grand Canyon, no matter how good that map is or how knowledgeable that speaker is.

The proof of whether you "know" God or not is disarmingly simple: Have you adopted his ways as your ways in your everyday life? Are you God-like in your thoughts, feelings and actions? Do you live according to God's teachings ... or simply to further your own personal agenda?

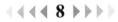

To be in the Now is to be in the continuous state of Being. Of course, in the Now you can think about the past, the present or the future. But in reality the "past" has never been and the "future" never will be. Both have "happened" (the past) or can "happen" (the future) only in the Now. Therefore there is never any need to rush for there is nowhere to go. To think you can arrive early if you rush or arrive late if you don't is an illusion. So just accept to Be – and this way experience silence, stillness and peace.

This state of Being is where all meaning in life lies. To rush, to anticipate, to hope, to fear, to regret, to be angry … all these things are only part of the noise and confusion you yourself generate. These thoughts distract you from what is important, they drain you of your energy, and they rob you of your joy. They are all a great illusion. To use the vernacular, they are simply part of an "ego trip" that you are (being taken) on and you need to get off.

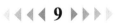

My ego says, "I know, therefore you don't." "I'm right, therefore you're wrong." "I have the power, therefore you don't." "I win, therefore you lose." Absurd, isn't it? So tell me … what does your ego say to you? If it's the same things, we are both victims of the same conspiracy! Shouldn't we smarten up and instigate a revolt?

◀◀◀◀ **9** ▶▶▶▶

Forget about your so-called past; it "happened" only to teach you important lessons to better equip you to "Be" in the Now. Forget about your so-called future; it will "happen" by default anyway as you practice Being in the present. Being, focusing on your eternal essence in each moment, is where

---

your joy is; it is the only way you can be fully alive. To do otherwise is to only know your ego better, and your ego has nothing to teach you. It has no joy, only pain, to share with you. Its only role is to prevent you from coming to know who you really are, from discovering your Source. Your ego is the great pretender. It wants you to think that you are it and it is you. In fact, its very existence depends on it.

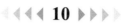

Only good things will always happen to you if your actions are love-centered (although at the actual time of the event, you may not agree with this statement). When you think this is not the case, you are only misinterpreting the message.

We get up in the morning, groom our physical bodies, don our physical clothes, and satisfy our physical hunger. We proceed to go to some physical place and compete and compare by playing silly games in the confines of our physical world to receive primarily physical rewards. At a certain level, we wonder why we do this all the time. Is this what we have been created to do? Is this all there is to our Being? Is this all a silly dream and we need to awaken from it?

One moment of insight is more valuable than a life-time of experience. So, consider the following and what insight you might gain from it.

People generally experience a wide variety of feelings as they go about each day, accompanied by a corresponding level of stress and anxiety. These feelings can range from simple discouragement and disappointment in some cases (e.g. low reaction) to desperation and despair in other cases (e.g. high reaction). If intense enough, the latter can lead to extreme anxiety, or even moderate to severe depression. Let's look more closely at this ailment, depression, for it can have serious consequences if not diagnosed early and properly dealt with.

Depression is the manifestation or emotional response to an observed incongruence between what you are *currently* "experiencing" (e.g. the thoughts/ cognitions you are having, and how you are interpreting and internalizing them) on a day-to-day basis (called your "actual reality" or reality one) and what you *want and think you should be* "experiencing" (e.g. events, happenings or outcomes), what is called your "preferred reality" or reality two. This apparent dichotomy often takes place at both the conscious and subconscious level.

Depression, which could be accompanied by feelings of extreme sadness and despair and/or various acts of aggression, will continue to haunt you in your life until you come to understand that both "reality one" and "reality two" are rooted totally in your ego, meaning your limited and inaccurate sense of self. It is the ego (which is in all of us, although we each manifest it to varying degrees) that distorts and manipulates your thinking, and in turn causes emotional upheaval and distress that in extreme cases can lead to thoughts about death and suicide.

This in part explains the huge increase in interest in practical spirituality in society today. For it is through spirituality that you come to see that "reality one" and "reality two" are both illusions. Hence both are irrelevant and meaningless, which means that the perceived difference between them is irrelevant and meaningless as well. Such realities are simply imperfect mental constructs based on false assumptions and erroneous beliefs, and a serious lack of understanding about how the mind works.

It all comes down to seeing and appreciating the role that the "One Self" plays regarding human consciousness and awareness as compared to the role that the individual "little self" or ego plays. The former is accommodating, accepting and inclusive while the latter is competitive, confrontational and exclusive. A clear understanding of who you really are is known as "reality three" and it is the only constant, true reality. How close you come to living out this reality on a daily basis is indicative of how close you have come to being awakened and enlightened, and experiencing the joy and peace this necessarily brings into your life.

Understanding how your delusions can confuse, trick and restrict you in your thinking has huge implications not only for your own behavior but for the behavior of groups, organizations and society at large. This topic is related to what is called "self-image" psychology, which in turn deals with the three key elements of the human psyche, namely (a) the self-concept; (b) the self-image; and (c) self-esteem. The latter, self-esteem – how much you really like, love, value or "esteem" yourself – determines to a large degree how you live your life: Your relationships; your work and career; your accomplishments, both personal and professional; and your physical and mental health. These together then determine the quality of your life in general in all its many and magnificent manifestations.

Your normal state of awareness can best be described as "unconscious" or asleep because you have no idea who you are. You are simply being consumed and distracted by a preoccupation with both mind and matter. You are oblivious to the Now, you are oblivious to Being, and you are oblivious to your Source. In this, the unconscious state, it isn't you who is using your mind. Far from it. It is the ego that is using your mind and for no useful purpose other than to satisfy its own selfish interests and demented desires.

The constant noise in your everyday life serves only to keep you separate from your Source. As technology and society increase in scope and complexity, this noise only gets louder and louder. You are then separated even more from your Source, you are focused even more on survival and success, and you live your life even more consumed with the illusion that you are alone, separate from everyone else, physical in nature, vulnerable to threats over which you have no control, and doomed to suffer and die.

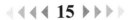

15

You have to give the ego some credit. It does its job (e.g. survival and so-called "success" at all costs) very well. It distracts, it distorts, it corrupts, and ultimately it destroys. And this is precisely what it was designed to do. So, once you know and accept this, what can you do to stop it?

16

Everyone seems to be in a great hurry to get somewhere. For a change, try to get nowhere. You can do this by going into silence. (Then you have really gotten somewhere!)

17

We all seem confused about who we are. We live out a dreaded duality, switching back and forth from thinking we are this to thinking we are that. At one moment, we think we are a human being having an occasional "spiritual" experience; at the next moment, we think we are a spiritual being having a certain "human" experience. So which is it? Or is it all just a dream and it doesn't really matter anyway? If it is, it means we do not matter as well and this cannot be the truth.

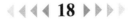

18

A raindrop is happy indeed when it enters a stream; it is even happier when it becomes part of a mighty river; and it is as happy as it can be when it then flows into a vast ocean. For to become One with your Source is to come home again, and home is where you know you are loved for simply being who you are.

19

Whenever I feel pain myself, any pain, or inflict pain on others, I have forgotten who I am. I am asleep and need to wake up.

20

Any peace process between individuals, groups or nations should follow these four basic steps: (1) actively engage; (2) seek to understand; (3) practice acceptance; and (4) offer unconditional love. The alternative is to confront, bully, repudiate or even try to exterminate. This results in you digging your grave and the other side digging theirs. Bravo! Another win for the ego ... and yet another loss for humankind.

21

You know, God is trying very hard to help us see the light, to find the right path. He has sent many great teachers over many years to inform and help guide us. If we don't listen to them, he introduces us to pain and suffering (of our own making, of course); if we persist in our ways, he gives us a look at emotional upheaval or indeed trauma (again, of our own making). He is really on our side. As his children, he is doing all he can to show us the way. Isn't it strange (and sad) that many of us still don't get it?

22

The way of the wise is as follows: Go into silence. Listen to God. Learn about his ways. Then practice these ways yourself.

The sun never stops shining yet we do not see it, feel it or appreciate it when clouds hide it from our view. We lack awareness of its *presence*. Similarly, God never stops radiating his love yet we do not see it, feel it or appreciate it when our ego-based thoughts hide it from our view. Again, we lack awareness of its *presence*. But in either case we should never forget the truth. Both are very real and both are omnipresent … they never go away. *Some things are eternal.*

Mere "thinking" in fact is not the highest state of mind. The highest state of mind is "no-mind." Ironically, thinking often leads us no-where and no-mind leads us very much some-where. It is unfortunate that most of us think too much too much of the time.

The ego lives only in "object" consciousness – the physical dimension of "form" – and wants you to do so as well. This is because the physical dimension is the world of opposites and extremes: Love – hate; good – bad; right – wrong; positive – negative; up – down; over – under; in – out; hot – cold; you – me, and so on. This way, the ego forces you to judge and label (and in the process, condemn) every thing and every one that you encounter. This can only be seen as entrapment, confinement, punishment, indeed a permanent death sentence. In fact, our predisposition to do this all the time is the collective curse of humankind.

26

Your so-called past is not something that is cast in concrete or etched in stone. It is only a series of memory traces that can be recalled, reanalyzed and reinterpreted in the Now and made anew. The process is called *"mental cleansing,"* and it involves taking your ego out of whatever happened to you and substituting only *love* in its place. New information, new awareness and a new-found sense of humility (self-love) allow you to do this. This is the way to free yourself from the bondage and pain of the past. Guilt, anger and regret about what you did or didn't do (or what others did or didn't do) in your life up to now melt away just as the sun melts the snow. This is freedom, liberation and enlightenment, and it opens the door to a whole new reality. It is one where you are not hurting anymore. As Norman Cousins (1912 – 1990) has said, "Life is an adventure in forgiveness." This necessarily begins with forgiving yourself. Interestingly, the Buddha defined enlightenment as the end of suffering. Ultimately, this is something everyone wants in his life: *No more suffering.*

"Ego-speak" is simply the playing out of thoughts in your mind that represent your basic fears and desires, all the things you think you need to complete what you perceive as your faulty and limited sense of self. For example: Do you want to be important? Your ego will gladly show you how. Do you want to impress others? Again, your ego will gladly show you how. But consider this: After your ego has shown you a myriad of ways to be important, impress others, show others how smart, how successful and how special you are, what have you really accomplished? Why do you feel you have to do this on a regular basis? (Hmmm Which part of you is doing all the doubting about your real self-worth here?)

When you reconnect with your Source, you will discover your essence. In so doing, you will reunite with wisdom you have always had but have simply forgotten about. It is like returning home again and knowing the place for the second time. But this time, you will never forget what it's like.

Consider this challenge: Select one day and agree to record all the significant thoughts you have that day. This is probably easiest to do if you take along a small digital recorder that you can talk into as you go about your usual activities. At the end of the day, write down all the thoughts you have recorded. Then take some time and carefully analyze these thoughts, one by one, and see which ones are (primarily) ego-centered e.g. inner directed, and which ones are (primarily) love-centered e.g. outer directed.

Be very honest with yourself (a.k.a. your Self) when you do this, for your ego will tempt you to overlook the truth. When you have finished, calculate what percentage of your thoughts that day represents "selfishness" versus "service," "judgment" versus "acceptance," and "condemnation" versus "judicious understanding, caring and compassion."

30

Here is an eternal truth to consider: *Perfection lies within you, all suffering lies without.* This is to say that as you observe your behavior and that of others in the physical world, you will see pain and suffering all around you. You proceed to innocently ask, "Why is this happening?" then realize that all is the work of the ego. Yet you know as you give more thought to the matter, you need only go inside into your essence and see the perfection that lies there. You know in this place there are no illusions, no complications, no misrepresentations, no untruths. There is only peace, hope, joy and gladness, and all are available in unlimited quantity to anyone who earnestly seeks them out.

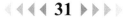

◄◄◄◄ 31 ►►►►

Love itself is not a "thought" – it is a feeling, a sensation, an emotion, an energy that you can only *experience.* In the physical plane, there is no love … there is only pleasure and its direct opposite, pain, and both are fleeting, meaning they come and they go. Being only temporary, both are illusions of the mind but few of us fully understand this. The evidence is the extent to which we go to pursue pleasure and avoid pain all the time. This way, we always "strive" but never actually "arrive." We never stop struggling, and hence never achieve the perfection that in fact we are.

◄◄◄◄ 32 ►►►►

God created each of us in his own image. He put a little of himself – his love, his grace, his power – in each of us. Unfortunately, this is the last place most of us think to look to find it.

◄◄◄◄ 33 ►►►►

We humans communicate with each other using thoughts and ideas generated by our minds … but we each have our own thoughts, our own ideas, our own minds. Hence we speak to each other from the perspective of being separate from one another. But when we communicate with each other at the spiritual level, from the place of "no-mind," we all speak the same language. For

---

there is only one language beyond the physicality of thoughts and things, and that is the language of love.

34

You must move beyond the mind, from "object" consciousness and into "space" consciousness, in order to fully appreciate and experience those things that clearly matter most in life: love; beauty; health; inner peace; joy; fulfillment; acceptance; harmony; and bliss. It is a matter of learning how to use your mind correctly and not allowing your mind (e.g. your ego) to use you for its own selfish and twisted purposes.

35

A fully engaged mind is the tool the ego uses to keep us enslaved. It is the world of regretting things past (pain) and aspiring to things future (pleasure), when in fact there is no past and there is no future. Time and mind are co-conspirators in this great illusion, and they are inseparable. Neither allows us to experience Being in stillness and in the Now.

36

The following is a traditional Native American story that has been passed down over many years. It is titled, *Two Wolves*. "An old Cherokee chief is teaching his grandson about life. 'A fight is going on inside me,' he said to the boy. 'It's a terrible fight and it's between two wolves. One is evil – he is anger, envy, sorrow, regret, greed, arrogance, self-pity, guilt, resentment, inferiority, lies, false pride, superiority, self-doubt and ego. The other is good – he is joy, peace, love, hope, serenity, humility, kindness, benevolence, empathy, generosity, truth, compassion and faith.' The grandson thought about this for a moment and then asked, 'Grandfather, which wolf will win?' The old chief simply replied, 'The one I continue to feed.'"

37

True awareness can be found only in the dimension of the timeless, through Being in the Now. Understanding the importance of the Now is key. First, it is all there is; and second, it is the place where you must go to understand your true nature. You can never hope to be fully alive and live a life of miracles (however big or small) until you know who you are.

38

It's interesting how we often fail to count our blessings, to appreciate all the positive and good things that are present in our life. This could include, at least for many of us: Our physical and mental health; homes to live in; clothes to keep us warm; food to nourish our bodies; jobs to go to; and the love of friends and family to enjoy and rely on. We live in caring communities, have access to civic and government services ... the list can be very long indeed.

But often we fail to focus on these things because the ego doesn't want us to. No wonder – *it cannot claim credit for any of them!* It's in the business of producing only pain and suffering, comparing and competing, judging and condemning. It wants to keep your focus on things only it has control over, namely all the silly events, petty encounters and meaningless distractions of everyday life. In other words, as long as you remain unconscious and unaware, it stays alive and well. In the process, it stays strong and active – *because it uses your energy to fuel itself* – and you remain weak and inactive, unhappy and unfulfilled.

The ego is a delusion. It is not you. It is not real. It did not create you. You created it. The ego began its life only when you did – when you were born; and it will die when the physical part of you – your body, also dies. But your essence will never die. It will live on. It is eternal.

When you "know about" God – by going to church and reading the Scriptures – you can talk eloquently about his ways and his teachings. Alternatively, when you "know" God, you are able to emulate his thinking and practice his ways. The former is theory and the latter is application. The former is the classroom and the latter is Life. Too bad so many of us fail to graduate!

41

When you surrender and allow what is to Be, you begin to understand and appreciate what has been hidden from you by mind and matter. In this place of silence, of stillness, a profound sense of peace and serenity overcomes and surrounds you … you feel great joy, great love and a real sense of bliss. In this way, you have reconnected with your Source, your eternal essence, with the Infinite that lies at the very center of all that is, including you.

42

Living hell is like a jail cell and not having a key; and so you die, living a lie, not knowing how to be free. In other words, if you are living your life

---

according to who you are not, how much joy can you expect? How much happiness? How much freedom? How much love?

◀◀◀ 43 ▶▶▶

You have to understand the power of guilt, the power it has to keep you paralyzed, immobilized, the power it has to make you miserable. Fear, anger, guilt, self-pity … all negative feelings such as these are major impediments to moving forward. You cannot engage in clear, logical thinking if your mind is hurting, wounded and in total disarray. Poor thinking necessarily produces poor decisions; and poor decisions necessarily produce poor results (e.g. more pain and misery!). And a wounded and weak spirit is unable to experience any real joy.

◀◀◀ 44 ▶▶▶

The mind is very much a memory trap, a worry trap and operates not unlike a pressure cooker. Pressure builds up and it can lead to an explosion. There is a way to decompress, to decontaminate, to cleanse, to heal the mind, however … go into silence. Enter the peace and tranquility of no-mind. Then wait patiently.

An incredible process begins to unfold. As you enter into no-mind, often for only a split second here and a split second there, you will find yourself recalling hurts from the past that are still lingering on as old, festering wounds. As this happens, analyze these memories in some detail and see where your ego played a role in how your pain was created in the first place. Now take the "ego-factor" out of the equation and substitute unconditional love, and see what is left.

What is left is nothing. The wound has been healed. The pain has been dissolved. You have forgiven yourself and the other party for the error of

---

(often both) your ways, for when on the wrong path, everyone is bound to make mistakes. Just as millions of other memories from your life have faded from your conscious awareness (because they contain no pain), so too will these memories fade away. *Remember, forgiving is not necessarily forgetting ... it is just letting go of the pain.* In the same way, go into silence and repeat the same process for thoughts that enter your mind as you think about the future, and what this might bring into your life. Whether these involve worries, fears or a myriad of selfish desires, these too will be cleansed and made anew when you remove your ego from the thought process.

◀◀◀◀ 45 ▶▶▶▶

When you remove your ego from your thinking, you are allowing what *is* ... your Self ... to *Be*. In the process, you have joined with your very essence, with the perfection that is within you ... namely unconditional love. With this as your foundation, as your paradigm for peaceful living, you are able to think more clearly, plan more effectively and contribute more uniquely. Then and only then are you able to act and perform recognizing the inter-connectiveness and inter-dependence of all things. The result can only be good when your thoughts are focused on the collective consciousness, on the collective whole, on the collective well-being of humankind.

◀◀◀◀ 46 ▶▶▶▶

Have you ever thought about what attracts you to Nature whether it is water, mountains, flowers or a forest? Why do you think we humans find it so appealing, so alluring, so calming? Perhaps it is because Nature is so "present-moment" – timeless and innocent, silent and still. Perhaps, as well, because it is so authentic. In other words, it never pretends to be anything other than what it is. In this way, Nature is a prime example of pure Being.

47

You should not be surprised or alarmed that unexpected and unwanted events (usually viewed as "problems") will continue to occur in your life, despite your best efforts to avoid them. They are simply part of life's journey. They can, in fact, be very helpful.

If you find yourself in a situation that is causing you on-going pain and suffering, it is simply telling you that you are not in tune with your spirit, with who you really are. I believe God has a plan for each of us and sometimes he needs to send us a wake-up call that says, "Hey, I know you are hurting … so don't forget about me!" We may hear this call on a specific occasion or it could be a constant, gentle whisper that never goes away. We need to know that our Father doesn't want to hurt us, he wants to heal us; he doesn't want to punish us, he wants to protect us (usually from ourselves!). He is forever wanting reunion with his creations and his voice will not go unheard. In this way, unwanted events, even very tragic ones, can be blessings in disguise because they bring us back to the path, back to his perfect plan.

48

Consider this: Light travels at 186,000 miles per second. Moving at this speed, it would take a person exactly 1.284 seconds to arrive at the moon since it is 238,857 miles away. That's about the time it takes you to snap your fingers. While traveling at this very same speed, however, it would take a person … *2.3 million years* to get to the galaxy nearest to Earth! It is called Andromeda. And we know there are thousands upon thousands of other galaxies *billions* of light years beyond that. (Source: Wikipedia) Clearly the phrase "the Infinite" is not only stranger than we *think* it is; it is stranger than we *can* think.

49

There is a timeless truth that needs to be understood, and it is this: The omnipotent spirit that created "all that is" also created you. The power at the very core of your Being is the same power that created the universe. Before becoming a fertilized cell in the womb of your mother, you were a spark of energy, a small speck of intelligence moving about in space, a small node of "Unity Consciousness" in a vast field of energy called the field of infinite possibilities. You were pure love in free form. Your essence was the Creator's essence, and of course it still is.

50

Evolution into what you are today began in the ocean. It was your first "home" in your new form, and it served you well. Then, one day, you walked gingerly out onto dry land to find food and warmth to sustain yourself. Being naturally curious, you wandered further and further inland, and soon forgot where home actually was ("soon" meaning a few million years!). After a while, you found yourself yearning to go back from whence you came, missing what you knew as your Mother. You had met many others like yourself who felt the same way. Yet many things were different now. You had evolved into a very different life form, in many ways a more advanced, a more "consciously aware" life form. You were in a completely new environment now and knew you could not go back ... or at least you *thought* you couldn't.

51

As a human coming into being, your conception began with the fertilization of a single cell. This cell then divided itself into two, four, eight, sixteen cells, etc., and on and on it went. And so it was that your cell count multiplied

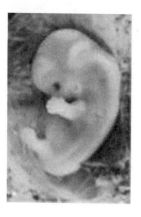

Human embryo at nine weeks gestational age. (commons.wikimedia.org)

exponentially as your physical body grew. (This process is similar to very simple, one-celled amoebic life forms that evolved into higher and more complex forms, some staying in the water, others moving onto land, and still others migrating into the air.) As you developed further in the womb, the human embryo retraced ancient life forms, looking first very much like a tadpole (see photo above), then a fish and finally a human being (e.g. Homo sapiens) as we know this species today. Hmmm. I wonder how we will look (physically) and think (metaphysically) after the next stage of human evolution, assuming we will somehow manage to survive the one we are now in?

◀◀◀◀ **52** ▶▶▶▶

You may wonder at the slow pace of human evolution. Why are we still so ignorant about so many things? Why can't we seem to get along with each other? Why do envy, distrust and hatred still abound in relationships between individuals, groups and nation states? Richard Christopher Carrington (1826 – 1875), an English amateur astronomer, puts it all in perspective with this explanation:

"Let us imagine that, by some magic, the whole Earth's history could be compressed into a single year. On this scale, the first eight months would be completely without life. The following two would be devoted to the most primitive of creatures. No mammals would appear until the second week in December. *Man, as we know him, would strut onto the stage at approximately 11:45 p.m. on December 31.* The age of written history would occupy little more than the last 60 seconds on the clock." (italics added)

Can you imagine that? The last 15 minutes on the clock! Incredible. Clearly our species is still in its infancy. And we have to wonder when and if we will ever grow up.

N.B. Although precise numbers are still being debated, scientists generally agree that our universe was formed about 13.7 billion years ago; that the Earth was formed about 4.6 billion years ago; that the first elementary life forms appeared on Earth about 3.8 billion years ago; that early dinosaurs roamed the planet about 230 million years ago; that human history began about 7 million years ago; and that "homo erectus" appeared about 1.7 million years ago (Source: Wikipedia) … and I date back to the early 1940s!

 **53**

Consider this beautiful blessing, this timeless truth: Your natural state of Being is pure bliss and unconditional love. So here is the relevant question: Why wouldn't you want to spend more time there?

 **54**

Let's look at what is called "neurosis." Neurosis is a mental disorder that results in any number of emotional disturbances that may include stress, anxiety, compulsions, obsessions, insecurity, anger, depression or guilt, as well as fears and phobias of various kinds. It is generally the result of a distorted, inaccurate or irrational perception of reality. Anyone seeking a cure for this affliction must begin by realizing, first, that such pain and suffering is always self-inflicted (no one can "cause" you to feel anything; you always choose – albeit often unconsciously and instinctively – to feel the way you do); and second, that such pain always has its origins in the "cognitions" (the thoughts and the inter-connectiveness of thoughts) being practiced by the individual. *The road to wellness is always to critically analyze and question the original thoughts and thought sequences themselves.* This will lead you directly to the source of any suffering (e.g. hurtful feelings) that you may be experiencing.

The fact is, everyone is a neurotic to some extent. No one perceives the world 100 percent correctly, no one thinks 100 percent correctly, and no one ever will. The critical question then becomes, "Are your current neuroses so debilitating that they are preventing you from being a happy and productive person in all the ways that you want to be happy and productive?" If so, you need to do something about it.

A neurotic person needlessly inflicts pain on himself by engaging in faulty and erroneous thinking. In other words, such a person "injures" himself both mentally and physically for reasons that are not necessary.

For example, a neurotic typically practices a particular manner of thinking over and over again, yet knows there is no possibility of a different outcome. The person's illogical and irrational thoughts are simply cycled and recycled, over and over again, resulting in only more intense and deeper feelings of misery and worthlessness.

For some, this type of thinking may give temporary relief. They bask in the illusion, at least for a time, that they are making progress because they are actively engaged in some kind of "activity." Eventually, however, it only creates more anxiety because they soon come to realize that they are right back where they started. (One definition of insanity is when someone does the same thing over and over again, yet still expects a different outcome. Using this as our gauge, how sane/insane are you?)

Imagine you are an airplane on the ground that wants to take off, but you don't know how. So you just taxi around the airport hour after hour thinking that it's bound to happen sooner or later. After all, you *are* an airplane! You *are* meant to fly! All of this "effort" of course is frustrating, time-consuming and very nauseating. It keeps you in the same place – a sort of living hell.

And in a very real sense, it is fatal. It drains you of your creativity, it eats away at your self-confidence and eventually it kills your dream (e.g. at some point, you will run out of gas!).

This is not a discussion about aeronautics, however. It is about going beyond inertia and the misery it creates in your life to personal empowerment and experiencing the fulfillment you really want in your life. It is about breaking free from your past and creating a whole new future. It may sound silly to some but this book is about following your dream, doing your "thing," being true to who you are. It is about being who you can and must be and doing what you can and must do, often for both seemingly selfish but ultimately altruistic reasons.

Here is an interesting quote from the book *Inner Peace, Inner Power* (1985) by Dr. Nelson Boswell that gives us further insight into how we think:

"Whether we are neurotic or not, we believe what we tell ourselves is reality, but often we come up with falsehoods, incomplete information, half-truths, and sometimes even nonsense. Our conclusions are often slightly or grossly slanted. We go around programming ourselves with our inner statements and messages, and we don't even hear ourselves. We don't sense the full meaning of what we say. We're not even aware that it is we who are programming our own minds. And then, when we're feeling down, angry, bitter or hopeless, we are not aware that it had to happen. We brought it upon ourselves …."

◄ ◄ ◄ ◄ **55** ► ► ► ►

All your moods are the result of your current thoughts or "cognitions." Your cognitions reflect the way you "see" things that are going on in your life – how you interpret and internalize these things. For example, the way you feel right now, *this very instant*, is a direct result of all the thoughts you have had in the past as well as those you are having right now. There is a direct and immediate one-to-one relationship.

If, at any time, you sense you are not feeling good (or indeed *great!*), take time and ask yourself, "What are the thoughts I'm having right now?" for these are the very thoughts that are generating these very feelings. Then assess whether your thoughts represent anything remotely connected to "reality" or simply reflect "the world according to your ego." If you find that your ego in fact is in control, you need to re-think the thoughts you are having. You will _always_ experience pain, whether sooner or later or a little or a lot, when ego-based thoughts are dominating your mind.

◀◀◀◀ 56 ▶▶▶▶

Whenever you feel down and depressed, your thoughts are consumed with an all-pervasive and all-consuming negativity. You are "seeing" yourself and everything in your world in a negative, depressing and often unrealistic way. And since your feelings are very real (at least they seem very real to you … heck, they may even be making you sick), you assume your thoughts that have caused this unhappiness must also be very real and hence "true" as well.

As a result, you come to believe that things _must really be_ as bad (in your life) as they seem to be (in your mind)! In other words, you have become "delusional" – through faulty, illogical and irrational thinking, you have come to believe something that simply is not true. You have jumped to a conclusion that is not valid, something very simple to do yet very profound in its consequences.

The negative thoughts that generate negative feelings almost always contain gross distortions, over-simplifications and over-generalizations, and bear little if any relationship to reality. Although your thoughts may appear totally valid on the surface, under closer scrutiny they do not stand up. So you quickly come to see that your sad and depressing thoughts are seldom based on an accurate interpretation of reality. All such thinking is simply "flawed and twisted" thinking, and must be recognized as such.

The solution is simple enough: You must take time and find some way to inject some much needed realism, objectivity, logic and common sense into the equation. This process is called "critical thinking," an exercise (described in detail in PART 1) whereby you systematically critique the way you are thinking in a very direct, very forceful and very probing way.

Let's be a little more specific about the "equation." You have an initial thought. OK. You come to some conclusion about it which then generates certain feelings (e.g. a mood).

Here are some relevant questions: Q1. What is the mood that is created? (positive/negative) Now go back to your conclusion that produced this mood and ask yourself: Q2. How *valid* is it ... is it an accurate depiction of reality? (Yes/No) Q3. Are there other possible conclusions you could draw from the same initial thought? (Yes/No) Q4. Of all the possible conclusions available to you, which conclusion might best represent reality? (this one/that one) Q5. Now, did the conclusion you accepted as the most valid cause you to take any action/inaction? (Yes/No) Q6. Has this action/inaction brought you the results you wanted? (Yes/No)

Depending on your answer to these questions, you should go back to the very beginning and re-examine your thoughts all over again, in some cases several times. This is the sort of analysis you should be doing *all the time*, whether concerning very good moods or very bad moods, experiencing very good feelings or very bad feelings – for feeling good for invalid, unrealistic or illogical reasons is just as unhealthy and dangerous as doing so for feeling bad.

Let's revisit the **A-B-C** "systematic thought evaluation process." Perhaps with more examples, it will be easier to understand how it applies to other important areas of your life.

We must accept that our "thinking," and the thoughts and feelings it generates, is the most important aspect of our lives. So let's look carefully at what appears to be "normal, logical thinking," at least on the surface, and see how so often it is not.

Obviously, nothing of any consequence can happen until you have a thought; and nothing very positive can happen until you have a series of thoughts that take you in the direction of your desired outcome. *Remember, when it is all said and done, the only real freedom you have is the freedom to discipline your thoughts!*

So let's analyze how you can do this by looking closely at the following equation that represents the universal thought process:

$$\text{Point A plus Point B equals Point C}$$

Point A is the "activating event" (**AE**) that starts everything in motion. It is an external stimulus that you perceive as you go about your daily affairs. This immediately causes what is called your "personal belief system" (**PBS**) to be activated at Point B, and it interprets and comes to some conclusion about the event. This in turn evokes a certain "emotional response" (**ER**) at Point C in you. Depending on what these feelings are (either extremely negative or extremely positive, or somewhere in between), this will cause you to act in a particular way or not act at all.

So our equation can now be stated as follows:

$$\text{AE plus PBS equals ER}$$

This equation is very important to understand because it represents how each of us actually thinks! It shows that something first triggers your personal belief system (**PBS**) to become engaged; this causes you to come to certain conclusions about the activating event (**AE**) itself; and finally, this causes certain "feelings" (**ER**) to be generated. It is a simple chain reaction of cause and effect.

This equation, when accepted and fully understood, shows that you have the ability to control your feelings and mood each and every moment of your life. This is a startling statement since 99.99 percent of the general population would probably not agree with it. Most people bounce from one emotion to another during the course of each day, going through a series of highs and lows, ups and downs, and it never occurs to them that they themselves are the ones who are creating all these feelings!

If these feelings are ones they don't particularly like, they often see themselves as victims of their circumstances, pawns on a chess table or puppets on a stage; they believe that the world is *causing them* to be stressed, depressed and miserable. They feel helpless in the face of a force they see as being much more powerful than themselves.

But they are wrong. And often, at a certain level, they know it. But they are not willing to accept personal responsibility for their own unhappiness, perhaps even misery. That would mean they would have to do something about it. It is so much easier for them to simply blame "other people" or "other things" in their immediate environment for their sorry state of affairs. For example, they may say, "Hey, there's nothing I can do about my situation in life. I've been dealt a lousy deck of cards, that's all. I deserve to be unhappy, miserable and depressed, so I may as well get used to it." Of course, you never do get used to it and you don't have to.

◀◀◀◀ **59** ▶▶▶▶

You have little or no control over the hundreds of events that take place and impact you on any given day. People can say unpleasant or hurtful things to you; your friends and family members can get sick or die; your relationships can falter or fail; and you can be stuck in a dead-end job or lose it altogether. In each and every case, activating events like these will trigger a variety of feelings in you, depending on how your personal belief system views, interprets and responds to them.

In this look at critical thinking – the core skill in Cognitive Behavioral Therapy – let's see how a typical thought sequence works.

You may have been in one of the following situations, with the male-female roles as depicted here or in reverse:

EXAMPLE 1. JUMPING TO A CONCLUSION AND SUFFERING NEEDLESS UPSET

AE: Your girlfriend didn't call you when she said she would. (you have no control)

PBS: You say, "She should have called and kept her word ... she's just trying to upset me." (you have 100 percent control)

ER: You say/feel, "I'm disappointed, I'm upset, I'm angry at her for being so thoughtless and uncaring." (automatic and self-generated)

Now let's see how a different belief system (PBS) changes the outcome.

AE: Your girlfriend didn't call you when she said she would. (you have no control)

PBS: You say, "Something must have come up that she didn't expect ... she wouldn't do this just to annoy or hurt me." (you have 100 percent control)

ER: You say/feel, "I'm fine. Things happen ... I just hope she's OK and will call me when she can." (automatic and self-generated)

Quite a different outcome based on a very different belief system, right? Of course if your girlfriend acted this way on a regular basis, you would talk to her about it and get more information (well, at least hopefully!). Maybe she really doesn't care for you and this is her way of letting you know. But in the case described here, assuming it is just an isolated incident, it doesn't make sense to needlessly upset yourself by jumping to a conclusion that is not justified by any facts you have at your disposal.

EXAMPLE 2. FAULTY THINKING AND NEEDLESS PAIN

Let's listen in on this conversation between Karen and Wayne, both in their mid-30s. They have been married now for about three months, following a divorce for each of them a few years earlier.

"Wayne, I don't like it when you don't cuddle up to me at night in bed. It makes me feel alone and unloved."

"Come on!" pleaded Wayne. "We cuddle up every night."

"No, we don't!" countered Karen. "We do for a few minutes but then you turn away and go to sleep with your pillow."

"My pillow? You've got to be kidding! Are you jealous of my pillow?"

"No, of course not. But my 'ex' did the very same thing. We'd cuddle up and kiss, or whatever. Then he'd move over to the other side of the bed and ignore me the rest of the night. And now I know why ... he didn't love me. That's why our marriage ended."

"I don't know about your 'ex,' Karen, but I love you. I really do. I'm just used to sleeping on my side of the bed, that's all. How can anyone be comfortable and go to sleep with his arms wrapped around someone else?"

"If you really cared for me, you would. I just told you how it makes me feel ... I may as well be in bed all by myself."

"But you don't have to feel that way, Karen. I do love you, you know I do."

"Now you're telling me how I should feel!" Karen shot back indignantly. "Why don't you respect my feelings? No one can change their feelings, you know!"

"Karen, I'm not denying that you have these feelings but I don't think you should be blaming me for them ..."

Poor Wayne. He tried to explain what he meant (e.g. *his* thinking and *his* logic concerning the matter), but to no avail. Karen was convinced that she was completely justified in having the feelings she had and she didn't appreciate someone telling her otherwise. And she was adamant that people couldn't just change their feelings (but of course they can). She also let it be known that a certain other person had better change his behavior in order to accommodate her feelings ... or else (or else he'd soon be an "ex" as well!) Now you can see how circular thinking gets you the same results ... *you end up with nobody sleeping beside you in bed all over again* (even though this person may very well truly love you)!

So let's analyze this conversation more closely point-by-point.

AE: Your husband, Wayne, doesn't cuddle up to you at night in bed. (you have no control)

PBS: You say, "Clearly he doesn't love me. My first husband did the same thing and he didn't love me. That's why our marriage ended." (you have 100 percent control)

ER: You say/feel: "I feel alone, I feel unloved. Wayne doesn't care about me or my feelings." (automatic and self-generated)

Karen is using her experience with her first husband to justify acting the way she does with Wayne. Here is the faulty logic. First, the premise that her "ex" didn't cuddle up to her meant he didn't love her is very suspect. What evidence does Karen have that gives certainty or at least some credibility to this statement? Second, Karen says that this is why her marriage to him ended. Again, what evidence does she have that supports this contention?

Finally, it is quite unreasonable for Karen to transfer her experience with one person to her current experience with Wayne, and assume that it applies perfectly. These individuals are two very different people and likely have very different reasons for acting as they do.

So let's see how Karen could modify the way she is thinking:

AE: Your husband, Wayne, doesn't cuddle up to you at night in bed. (you have no control)

PBS: You say, "Hmmm, I see that Wayne likes sleeping alone on his side of the bed after giving me a big hug. I guess it's just his way of being comfortable." (you have 100 percent control)

ER: You say/feel: "I'm OK with that. The important thing is that he loves me. And he deserves a good night's sleep as much as anyone." (automatic and self-generated)

◀◀◀◀ **60** ▶▶▶▶

Here is a quote from the book, *The Magic in Your Mind* (1961) by American author U.S. Andersen. It demonstrates an incredible degree of insight into what we are talking about:

"We exist in order that we may become something more than we are, not through favorable circumstance or auspicious occurrence, but through an inner search for increased awareness. To be, to become, these are the commandments of evolving life, which is going somewhere, aspires to some unscaled heights, and the awakened soul answers the call, seeks, grows, expands. To do less is to sink into the reactive prison of the ego, with all its pain, suffering, limitation, decay, and death. The man who lives through reaction to the world about him is the victim of every change in his environment, now happy, now sad, now victorious, now defeated, affected but never affecting. He may live many years in this manner, rapt with sensory perception and the ups and downs of his surface self, but one day pain so outweighs pleasure that he suddenly perceives his ego as illusory, a product of outside circumstances only. Then he either sinks into complete animal lethargy or, turning away from the senses, seeks inner awareness and self mastery. Then he is on the road to really living, truly becoming; then he begins to uncover his real potential; then he discovers the miracle of his own consciousness, the magic in his mind."

COMMENT: Note in particular his use of the terms "the awakened soul;" "the reactive prison of the ego;" "rapt with sensory perception;" "his surface self;" "animal lethargy;" "self mastery;" and "the miracle of his own consciousness." Thank you, Mr. Andersen!

◄ ◄ ◄ ◄ **61** ► ► ► ►

Let's look even more closely at what is called your "ego." The role your ego plays in your life is critical to understand, for your ego can cause you no end of grief if left unnoticed and unchecked. I would go this far on the matter and state the following:

> *Your ego lies at the very center of what causes all the pain and suffering you will ever experience in your life.*

The curse of the ego as it affects human behavior has been noted and written about for centuries. William Shakespeare is a well-known writer in this regard as he often incorporated this fact into the plot of his many plays. It was also noticed by the poet T.S. Eliot when he commented, "Most of the trouble in the world is caused by people wanting to be important." And Gehlek Rimpoche, a Michigan-based Tibetan Buddhist lama and author of *Good Life, Good Death* has gone even further, saying, "The true enemy is inside. The maker of trouble, the source of all our suffering, the destroyer of our joy, and the destroyer of our virtue, is inside. It is EGO." (his emphasis)

If you fail to understand your ego and how it impacts (distorts and manipulates) your thinking, you will "fail" (e.g. experience pain) in most aspects of your life. If you feel you want to engage in a heated debate about this statement, it is only because the ego in you is feeling threatened and wants to leap to its own defense! I implore you to deny it this opportunity.

In the meantime, keep an open mind on the matter and see if your view changes over time.

What is the ego, anyway? Where does it come from? What does it do, both what is positive and negative, productive and unproductive? These are key questions you must answer if you want to understand how you function and why you so often fail, or at least fall short.

"Ego" is defined as self-centered ... self-importance ... self-conceit ... self absorption. It originates from the Greek word meaning "little, separated self" as opposed to the collective "one Self."

The ego is a result of a "belief system" you have created (actually, what our species has created over several million years of evolution) and accepted during your life up to now. It is very important to understand that it is only a part of your *belief system*. This "system" or mindset is based on the erroneous assumption that you are separate from everything and everyone else; that you need to look after, protect and nurture your "self" in competition with, and exclusion of, everyone else; and that as an individual, you are somehow "special," meaning more worthy, more deserving and more important (and all that this entails) than everyone else.

Your ego is a very busy fellow, working tirelessly night and day with only one goal in mind: To masquerade as your best friend and protector, all the while keeping you separate from your true nature, your Source, the collective consciousness of all that is. This is a master deception, in fact the ultimate deception of all human existence: That you are alone and separate, and hence vulnerable, and can survive only if you put your interests first, well ahead of everyone else.

 **62**

In our feeble attempt to better understand our spiritual nature, most of us spend a lot of time negotiating with our ego. We discount, we debate, we concede, we compromise, and invariably we give in. And the ego willingly goes along with this because, as a result, it maintains control ... it still retains its power.

Consider these words by Lama Surya Das in his book, *Awakening the Buddha Within* (1997) about how to move beyond your first impulse, the ego:

"As you walk the inner path of awakening, recognize that it is most definitely a heroic journey. You must be prepared to make sacrifices, and yes, you must be prepared to change. Just as a caterpillar must shed its familiar cocoon in order to become a butterfly and fly, you must be willing to change and shed the hard armor of self-centered egotism. As compelling as the inner journey is, it can be difficult because it brings you face-to-face with reality. It brings you face-to-face with who you really are."

Here is a question: "Where are you looking for meaning?" The vast majority of people look for the most important things they want in life – acceptance, love, prosperity, health, happiness, peace of mind, meaning and personal fulfillment – *outside* themselves. Let's give these "things" a specific name. We'll call them … high level spiritual needs. People look and look and look, but don't really find what they are looking for. So they end up disappointed and frustrated, even angry both with themselves and others. This leads them to ask some serious questions: "What's wrong? Why isn't life giving me all that I want? Am I not capable, worthy and deserving?"

Clearly you have been taught, through social conditioning and environmental programming, to believe – wrongly! – that you can find what you want in your life outside yourself. This is another paradigm, literally a framework or "mental construct" which is a certain way of thinking to which you have become accustomed and addicted. As such, it is firmly ingrained in your mind and won't easily go away. It does seem very logical, at first, to look at what you can actually see that is physically (in "form") all around you for all the things you want. After all, this "stuff" is right there, right in front of you. You can clearly see it, you can often touch it and you can easily relate to it. But alas, what you see is only an illusion, a temporary state of affairs that is constantly changing, constantly evolving (e.g. physical things that you can see and touch are always "trans-forming").

The problem continues when you look to the physical world to define yourself, to determine who you really are. For example, you may say to yourself and others, *"I am what I do* – I am a teacher, a laborer, a truck driver, an accountant, a home-maker;" or you may say, *"I am what I own* – I am my car, my clothes, my jewelry, my bank account, my house;" or you may say, *"I am my body* – I am my skin, my lips, my eyes, my legs, my hair." But you would be wrong in each and every case. For who you are has nothing to do with the physical world. The world at large has no idea who you are … that isn't its job. It's yours! And once you understand this, you'd better wise up and look in another place, in another direction, say … *inside* yourself. After all, if what you want in life cannot be found "out there," the only other place to look is "in here!"

◄◄◄ **65** ►►►

"Materialism" is the doctrine that says physical things and physical matter (all that is in "form") are the only reality and that everything else in the world including "thought," "will," "spirit," "love" and "wisdom" can be explained and interpreted only in terms of matter; it is the belief that comfort, wealth, pleasure and success are the only and the highest goals you should strive for; it is the tendency to be more concerned in life with material things and physical objects than with spiritual thoughts, hopes, fears, feelings, insights, and ethical and moral values.

Why do we, especially in the West, engulf ourselves in a culture of materialism? Is it just another form of escapism? If so, what are we trying to escape from? Some would say we are escaping from accepting our divinity because if we accepted it, we would have to live up to it – and most people aren't prepared to do that. Why are we individually and collectively such willing participants? What are we accomplishing by participating (in many cases, *indulging*) in this? Why do we encourage our children to go down the same path? Is it that we don't know any better? Are we simply involved in a silly game of "monkey-see, monkey-do," and just let the game go on?

Our preoccupation with the physical world, with what we can perceive with our five senses, is a major problem for society today. Why? Because you cannot get what you want most in life through the frantic and uncontrolled accumulation of more and more things! (On your deathbed, do you plan to brag about how many pairs of expensive shoes you bought during your life-time, how many juicy lobster tails you ate, how many bottles of premium wine you drank, or how much you paid for your favorite putter or driver?)

◀ ◀ ◀ ◀ **66** ▶ ▶ ▶ ▶

The following strictures indicate how several of the world's major religions view excessive consumption:

- Buddhism: – "By the thirst for the riches, the foolish man destroys himself as if he were his own enemy."

- Christianity: – "Watch out! Be on your guard against all kinds of greed; a person's life does not consist of an abundance of possessions."

- Confucianism: – "Excess and deficiency are equally at fault."

- Hinduism: – "When you have the golden gift of commitment, you have everything."

- Islam: – "It is difficult for a person laden with riches to climb the steep path that leads to bliss."

- Taoism: – "One who knows he or she has enough is rich."

Source: Smith, Douglas V. and Kazi F. Jalal (2000).

As a species, we have been very successful at exploiting technology, especially in the last few hundred years. Sir Isaac Newton, the English mathematician, alchemist and philosopher, introduced the world to the scientific method, namely how to discover so-called "reality" by using rational, logical, linear, left-brain thought, with reality meaning "what actually is," including how the universe works. The many marvels that our minds have come up with are almost too numerous to mention: Jet aircraft; television; spacecraft; cell phones; nuclear reactors; the computer; solar energy; the Internet; etc.

Is our proven prowess to mold our environment to our liking leading us to believe that we can solve all our problems ourselves? Albert Einstein once commented that humans cannot hope to solve all the problems they have created by using the same mind that created them. Take a moment and think about this as it may apply to you and your so-called "problems."

Newton lived from 1642 to 1727. It has been said that he discovered more of the essential core of human knowledge than anyone before or after. Chet Raymo, a U.S. science columnist and author of *The Path: A One-Mile Walk Through the Universe* (2003), has said this of Newton:

"He developed the theory of infinite series, and showed that it was possible to treat the Infinite and the Infinitesimal with mathematical rigor. He refined concepts of space, time, inertia, force, momentum, and acceleration, and formulated laws of mechanical motion. He invented the *Theory of Universal Gravitation* and applied it to celestial and terrestrial motions. To facilitate his calculations, he devised what is now called the differential and integral calculus." And note that Newton accomplished all this before he was 24 years old!

Incredibly intelligent people such as Newton don't come along very often. But even Newton was unable to explain where matter originated or who/what devised all the laws of physics and mathematics in the first place. Clearly, we are sadly lacking in our ability to fully understand and master the physical world.

For example, man has never created something from nothing. Think about it. Everything we have designed, built and use today was possible only because we found a host of raw materials already on the planet, whether we use wood for making paper, fine furniture and buildings; sand for making glass, cement and silicon chips; or gold for making expensive jewelry, dental fillings and coins. Never have we humans created something from absolutely nothing, and we never will. As a result, many believe that there is an intelligence at work in the universe that was around long before we arrived and set things up so we could play the often silly and amateurish game called Life.

Pierre Teillard de Chardin (1881 – 1955), the respected French theologian and paleontologist, made this interesting statement some years ago:

"We are not a *human* being having a spiritual experience;
we are a *spiritual* being having a human experience."

Think about it … have you ever bruised a knee? Have you ever scratched an itch? Do you regularly cut your hair? Do you regularly trim your fingernails? Have you ever bled from a cut? Have you ever suffered from a sunburn? Have you ever broken a bone? Have you ever hungered for food or water? Yes? Then you are human.

Alternately, have you ever been sad? Have you ever been happy? Have you ever cried? Have you ever laughed? Have you ever been a voluntary giver … and felt great? Have you ever been a voluntary taker … and felt grateful? Have you ever regretted something you did? Have you ever hungered for love and basked in being loved? Yes? Then you are spirit.

As spirit, you necessarily have a number of spiritual needs that you are striving to satisfy. You want to love and be loved; you want to accept and be accepted, to have hope, happiness, peace of mind, fulfillment, meaning, and a real sense of purpose. You want to feel worthy, to be relevant … to *know* that you are important. Nothing more, nothing less.

And so, a question: How many of us are spending all our time and energy trying to satisfy our spiritual needs from a physical world? The answer: *Practically all of us!* But clearly a physical world is *incapable* of satisfying spiritual needs. Think about it: How much can a rock love you, even if it is a three carat diamond? It cannot. Or a mansion in Hollywood? Or a Ferrari sports car? Or a Rolex watch? Or a private Lear jet? The physical world mocks us with the phrase, "Seek me out and you will find." But this is an illusion. We have to look at our essence, our spirit, our "Godliness" you might say, to meet our most important needs.

 ◀◀◀ **69** ▶▶▶

We discussed earlier how humans have been preoccupied and perplexed with trying to answer the question, "What is *real?*" Our answer: *That which is real never changes.* So think about it ... which part of you and the world you live in never changes?

Most people hold to the belief that what is "real" is what they can observe using their five physical senses: What they can see, hear, smell, taste and touch. But of course everything they sense this way – boats, buildings, bridges, bicycles and boulevards – as well as their physical bodies, is slowly turning into dust. Yes, you and I are made up of simple dust. Your body is composed of the same basic elements that comprise everything in the physical world: A little oxygen, a little hydrogen, a little nitrogen, a little mercury, a little carbon ... you can purchase them in the quantities that are in you at your local pharmacy for about 10 dollars.

In other words, everything you observe in the physical world with your physical senses, including your own body, is not real because it is constantly changing. It is in a constant state of flux. It is simply moving from one "form" to another "form," albeit in many cases at a relatively slow pace. Who you are, then, cannot be your physical body. It is your eternal spirit, since this is the only part of you that is not changing, and hence is the only part of you that is actually real.

For example, you witness to your chagrin how your physical body regularly ages and begins to decay. But as all this physical aging takes place, does your spirit whither and dissipate as well? Do you love any less? Are you any less kind, less generous, less compassionate, less forgiving, less merciful ... do you feel any less *alive* inside? Of course not. Many would say that these qualities actually increase in you as you get older. But clearly they have been in you all along. It's just that with age and maturity, you are more aware of them and have chosen to make use of them more often.

◄ ◄ ◄ 70 ► ► ►

Every living species on the planet cognizes its "own universe" in its own unique way. A snake uses infra-red, a bat uses ultra-sound, and a honey bee uses ultra-red to determine its so-called "reality." And each is able to survive as a result. In turn, humans use their own perceptual artifacts (eyes to see, ears to hear, nose to smell, tongue to taste, and skin to feel/touch) to determine their reality, basically the nature of the physical world. And they too are able to survive as a result. (well, in most cases!)

And your ego – that thinks because you are human, you are superior to other living things – tells you that your sensors are more accurate and hence your version of reality is more reliable, more "correct," more "real." But you know from personal experience that your sensors are often inferior to many animals and birds at seeing, hearing and smelling. In fact, it has been said that human beings are able to "perceive" less than one percent of one percent of all that is actually out there.

So here is the situation. One species sees this world; a second sees that world; a third sees another world ... a fourth ... a fifth ... etc., etc., each seeing its world and each believing that what it sees is reality. But there is only one true reality, and *none of us* is actually "seeing" it. Clearly we all have imperfect sensors.

We can now understand that what is real cannot be perceived by physical means, regardless of the species involved. The sun never really sets or rises; the Earth is neither flat nor solid nor round; and you can never actually sit still because you live on a planet that is rotating on its own axis, circling around the sun, and also flying off into outer space at several thousand miles an hour. Yet your physical sensors would lead you to believe none of these things.

If you looked into an electron microscope, you would see initially that matter is made up of molecules, atoms, electrons, protons, and many other small atomic and sub-atomic particles. As you looked closer and closer to find the smallest, the most minute building block of nature, you would find that there are no more particles. There is just empty space. In fact, *all matter is made up mostly of empty space*, about 99.99 percent. You therefore come to understand that the basic building block of matter is "non-matter." This non-matter is simply referred to as the "void." Someone looking at you and who was able to see the "real" you, would first see something as expansive as the night sky, with emptiness everywhere, with only the odd star flickering here and there representing highly dispersed atoms. The same applies to any physical object, no matter how compact or "dense" you may think it is, such as the mineral called lead.

Everything in the universe is made up of the same matter, it is all made of the same old *stuff*. There is only so much oxygen, so much hydrogen, so much nitrogen, so much carbon, so much manganese, so much silicone … everything in nature is made up of the same basic building blocks of nature including your brain, bones, blood, cartilage, skin and hair. As some astute observer once said, "This is that, that is that, you are that, I am that, and that's all there is!" All this stuff is simply being recycled between you and every thing and every one else in the universe. Incredibly, some scientists have concluded that every living person on the planet today has one million atoms in him or her at any given time that were once in the body of the Buddha, Jesus and Mohammed.

Consider these facts. As you breathe and eliminate waste, you recycle your atoms. You have a new liver every six weeks, a new stomach lining every five days, all new skin once a month, a new skeleton every three months, and on and on it goes. In fact, in less than one year you replace 98 percent of all the atoms in your body. And you replace 100 percent in two years. So to think that you are a body and only a body requires you to ask, "Which one? Which model? Is it the 1990 model, the 2000 model, the 2010 model, or this year's latest edition?" So you see that various parts of your body have a different "shelf-life," some quite short, some quite long. But whatever the time-frame, all of it is changing all the time.

Now it gets even more interesting. There is a part of you that has no shelf-life at all – it is timeless, changeless, immortal. Each model, each new edition of "you" carries forward "memories" from past experiences. Each new model remembers how to laugh or cry, love or hate, feel joy or sadness, as well as tie your shoelaces, brush your teeth, take a shower, ride a bicycle, peel an orange, toss a salad, barbecue a steak, and drive to and from work. But since you first learned all these things, every single cell in your body has been replaced, in most cases many, many times.

It seems there is an invisible intelligence, some type of "knowing" that is in you beyond your basic physicality, beyond your simple form, beyond the world of the changing. And this intelligence is in *everyone* on the planet, not just a chosen few. This invisible intelligence is often referred to as your essence, your spirit, your divinity, or your soul. You can choose from any of these terms or select another one that you feel more comfortable with (after all, it isn't what you call it ... it is what it is!).

Now consider this: How many other types of "knowings" might be in you that you don't remember because you have temporarily forgotten about them? I suggest that the most important memory you want to reconnect with is who you are, for this and only this will lead you to discover why you're here.

Clearly, the spiritual and physical are not separate from one another but are very much part of each other. One represents the invisible memory or intelligence (formless) that is the "real" you while the other represents the visible carrier or host (form) – your body – of the memory itself. You have chosen to show up in the form you now have because you found it convenient for your present purposes, whatever they may be. And once your present purposes have been met, you will necessarily move on and return from whence you came.

In other words, you have come from "no-where" to "now-here" to do what you need to do; and soon you will return back to "no-where" once again, wherever that may be. Note that the letters for both of these "places" are exactly the same, just as the very essence that represents who you are is exactly the same, no matter where you are.

Carl Jung wrote a book some time ago titled, *Modern Man in Search of a Soul* (1955). In it, he postulated that most human beings move through various stages of personal development. He listed and described in some detail five specific levels of "maturity" as people get older (e.g. as they become more "aware," they move to a higher level of consciousness). The age groupings shown here necessarily vary greatly among individuals. The following description is based loosely on Jung's ideas:

FIRST

Age 0 – 10: Adolescence. You are at the stage of the "child," the age of innocence. You are dependent, impressionable, vulnerable and compliant, meaning you are pretty much under the control of other people and the circumstances in which you find yourself. You are quite helpless and easily victimized. During this period, you are very much in the process of being molded to conform to societal wishes, beliefs and norms (e.g. various values and virtues, as well as vices).

SECOND

Age 11 – 25: You are at the stage of the "athlete." You take great pride and get a lot of your meaning from your physical appearance you attractiveness, your beauty, your strength, your physical prowess. You sculpt your body in a gym, you tan your body in a studio, you cleanse your body in a spa, you coiffure your hair in a salon Your "sense of self" is very much entered around this part of you and you try to stretch out this period of your life as long as possible. At various times as you age, you may take vitamin supplements, protein drinks and steroid pills; or more aggressively, you may undergo plastic surgery, face-lifts, tummy-tucks, hair transplants and breast implants. But of course your body slowly deteriorates no matter what you do and eventually disappears into simple dust. Since this part of you is always changing, it is not "real."

THIRD

Age 26 – 50: You are at the stage of the "warrior." You take great pride in competing, in winning, in accomplishing, in succeeding – you "strive to arrive" – in proving to yourself and others that you are smart, capable, superior and uniquely "special" compared to everyone else. You strive to accumulate material objects (both in quantity and quality), fill important positions in your career, achieve goals that you have set for yourself … all this then defines for you "who you are." And of note is the fact that you may often go to great extremes to achieve these things: You may lie, cheat, steal, even go to the point of becoming over-stressed through over-work and put your very life at risk. This stage can be characterized by aggressiveness, manipulation, plotting and scheming, often accompanied by a whole lot of ranting and raving in general. "Warriors" do whatever they need to do to win.

Up to this point, you are motivated mainly by *fear* in your life … fear of not being secure, not being accepted, not being loved, not being respected, not being able to prove that you are capable and deserving, not being acknowledged as "special" by others for being better/faster/smarter than those with whom you compete. You then undergo a slow evolution, sometimes very slow, into being more love-motivated in your thinking and behavior. You move from your concern being primarily for "me" (meaning only yourself, as is the case with many young children) … to "we" (small and large groups including family and extended family) … to primarily "others" (meaning everyone but yourself). In the extreme, your focus is directed totally at others, including those you don't even know and likely will never meet. This includes others who have yet to be born.

At the extreme end of the scale in one direction is a person's fixation with "getting everything and giving nothing" … while at the extreme end in the other direction, it is about "getting nothing and giving everything." Then again, some people like Mother Teresa and Saint Francis of Assisi held a firm belief that is even more "radical" than either of these two extremes: *It is that you get everything by giving everything away!*

FOURTH

Age 50 plus: You are at the stage of the "statesman/humanitarian." You see well beyond the (little) self and feel an intimacy for all living things. Your primary concern is for the greater good, the collective whole. Increasingly, you volunteer your services, participate in community activities and actively support charities of various kinds.

FIFTH

Age 50 plus: You are at the stage of the "spiritualist" and see yourself "at one" with the collective consciousness of humankind. You have moved beyond simple duality (the Self versus the ego) to complete identification with the divine. You are fully awake, you are fully aware, you are fully alive. You are at one with the "uni-verse," a term meaning "one-song."

◁◀◀◀ **72** ▶▶▶▷

Clearly there is a point where a person sees beyond his individual nature and private needs and wants. Here, such a person is "at one" with spirit, hence is totally "need-less" and "self-less" in his thinking and behavior. We will call this level "Unity Consciousness." Buddhists would say that if you were at this level, you could ignore all the others, that in fact there is only one level of true consciousness. They would say that the other levels are only temporary diversions/distractions along the true path to Oneness or nirvana.

"Nirvana" in Buddhism is the state of perfect blessedness achieved by the extinction of individual existence and by the absorption of the soul into the supreme spirit; it involves the elimination of all earthly desires and passions.

The late Maharishi Mahesh Yogi (1918 – 2008), the founder of Transcendental Meditation, was once asked the following question by a news reporter at a public event. "Maharishi, wise people everywhere know that 'As you sow, so shall you reap.' And mystics are fond of saying that we are all one. If there is literal truth to these sayings, then whatever you do to another person you must be doing to yourself. Therefore, as you have said, violence has no value to solve problems. My question is, how literally can we take these sayings that we are all one? We seem to be separate, but is there some higher reality that we are not perceiving? Are we like individual cells in one body?"

The Maharishi answered, "Exactly like that. I think your inference is grand. All are one. The example will be of a tree – so many thousand leaves, thousand branches, thousand flowers, fruits and all. They are all different on one level – they are one on another level. They are one on the level of the sap – they are different on the level of the expressions of the sap."

◄ ◄ ◄ **73** ▶ ▶ ▶ ▶

Let's look at the word "love" (note that *transcendent* love, *familial* love and *romantic* love will be discussed further in PART 5). Love is defined as 1. a strong affection for or attachment or devotion to a person or persons 2. in theology, love is God's benevolent concern for mankind and man's devout attachment to God 3. the feeling of benevolence and brotherhood that people should have for each other.

Love is not only an emotion. The state of love is a transcendent quality that goes beyond any emotion. Rather, love is the singular creative force for good throughout the universe. The "language" of the soul is the language of love. To love is an active, very personal experience that taps into the soul's essence. Yes, love does induce emotions of many kinds and of varying intensity, depending on the circumstances. As this text will show, only love is real and only love endures. It is the ultimate expression of our true nature.

Does love have an opposite? No, the spiritual plane does *not* have opposites. The absence of love is simply non-love. Everything in the physical plane does indeed have opposites: Up, down; left, right; backward, forward; over, under; hot, cold; on, off; good, bad; war, peace; before, after; open, closed; wet, dry; light, heavy; right, wrong, and so on. Thinking this way, many people believe that fear or hate is the opposite of love. It is in the physical plane. But in the spiritual plane, fear and hate do not exist. Only the ego-based mind knows these emotions.

It is the same with "light." Most of us think that the opposite of light is darkness. But there is no such thing as "darkness" per se; darkness is simply the *absence* of light. Hence darkness in fact does not exist. So everything that is not love is non-love (meaning the absence of love), and this we (meaning the ego) manifest in many forms including fear, anger, greed, guilt, hate, jealousy and resentment, all the usual litany of human failings. Ultimately, love is what each of us is seeking. It is all we want for it is all there is.

It serves no useful purpose to "know about" love simply on an intellectual level. It has to be *experienced*. For example, you can be taught everything there is to "know about" baseball – its history, its rules, the current standings, and everything in the record book. You can watch it forever yet still never, ever really "know" it. You have to experience baseball (actually play it to win but sometimes lose) to really "know" what it is. It is the same with love. You have to *be* love (Unity Consciousness) and sometimes *not* be love ("self"-consciousness) to fully understand and appreciate it.

Many believe that our greatest challenge as human beings is to discover who we are and why we're here. We find the answer to the first question when we come to see that we are not as we first "appear" and begin to look in another place. We find the answer to the second question only after we find the answer to the first.

There is such a thing as building up (maximizing) the ego for the ego's sake and tearing down (minimizing) the ego for divine purpose. Most people spend all their life doing only the former and relatively few ever get around to the latter. Building up the ego for the ego's sake ignores love and tries to impose your "will" (e.g. the illusion you have that you are special and separate from everyone else) on others; alternatively, tearing down the ego for divine purpose involves being love and recognizing a greater power at play in all things and in all situations.

The task at hand is about discovering this basic "truth." The change you need to make involves seeing a "STOP" sign at some point on the road you are now on and pausing to think about how you are living your life. If you conclude that you are on the wrong path, you must make a U-turn in the middle of the road and head off in exactly the opposite direction. All the great spiritual teachers have told us that this is the way. And that's fine. But sooner or later we have to figure this out for ourselves.

The path to higher awareness and enlightenment is a difficult one but it certainly is achievable. It is possible for the average individual to manifest qualities that reflect his divine nature. Sogyal Rinpoche in his book, *The Tibetan Book of Living and Dying* (1992) explains the process of enlightenment and getting on the true path this way:

"In the modern world, there are few examples of human beings who embody the qualities that come from realizing the (true) nature of mind. So it is hard for us even to imagine enlightenment or the perception of an enlightened being, and even harder to begin to think that we ourselves could become enlightened…. Even if we were to think of the possibility of enlightenment, one look at what composes our ordinary mind – anger, greed, jealousy, spite, cruelty, lust, fear, anxiety and turmoil – would undermine forever any hope of achieving it…. Enlightenment … is real; and each of us, whoever we are, can in the right circumstances and with the right training realize the (true) nature of mind and so know in us what is deathless and eternally pure. This is the promise of all the mystical traditions of the world, and it has been fulfilled and is being fulfilled in countless thousands of human lives." (N.B. The word "true" has been added in brackets for clarity.)

World religions of all kinds have traditionally played a central role in society by providing spiritual guidance leading to hope, healing, harmony and personal enlightenment. Their ultimate goal is basically the same:

To help people reconnect with their essence, reclaim their inheritance, and help remake the world. Their sacred teachings show remarkable similarities in tone and insight, as the following quotations clearly demonstrate:

- "God is the sun beaming light everywhere." Tribal African; African Religions

- "The radiance of the Buddha shines ceaselessly." Dhammapada; Buddhism

- "God is light, and in Him is no darkness at all." 1 John 1:5; Christianity

- "In the lotus of the heart dwells Brahman, the Light of Lights." Mundaka Upanishad; Hinduism

- "Allah is the light of the heavens and earth." Koran; Islam

- "The Lord is my light; whom shall I fear?" Psalms 27:1; Judaism

- "The light of Wakan-Tanka is upon my people." Song of Kablaya; Native American Religions

- "The Light of Divine Amaterasu shines forever." Kurozumi Munetada; Shinto

- "God, being Truth, is the one Light of all." Adi Granth; Sikhism

- "Following the Light, the sage takes care of all." Lao-tzu; Taoism

While there are aspects of different religions that often divide us, they also offer a *universal spirituality* that can unite us. Ignorance of this very fact has lead to much needless violence and many atrocities throughout history.

 ◀◀◀ **77** ▶▶▶

Many of us are victims of the curse of "instant gratification," the desire to have all the things we want sooner rather than later. This means that we are quick to give in to temptations we think will complete our perceived faulty and incomplete sense of self. (Whether it is our desire for food, sex, a mental high or material objects of various kinds, the operative phrase of the current generation is, "I want it now!") Of course, we all want to feel good, worthy, valued, respected, important, loved ... it is in our nature to want these things. And so our ego says, "Come, trust me, and I will give you everything you want."

But the ego's way is at the expense of other people, the environment and the collective whole; in fact, it is against our own self-interest. This is the wrong way. *The great irony is that our Creator has given us these very same things; they are "in-born" within us.* Being created in his image, we are good, we are worthy, we are valued, we are respected, we are important, we are loved. We don't have to yearn for and frantically chase after these things ... we already have them! In this sense, we are all chasing an illusion and necessarily getting nowhere. We are living a tragic mistake, a mistake both in perception and understanding.

Let's look at human nature as we know it and witness it in action every day. The following 10 characteristics (it would be easy to come up with many others) are indicative of the way we have evolved over many thousands of years. In fact, it is probably true that if we were not this way historically, we would not have survived and gone on to perpetuate others just like ourselves. Imagine a species that may have existed a million years ago that was totally self-less and motivated only by kindness and love of humankind ... how long do you think it would have survived in that environment – 200 years; 20 years; 2 years; 2 months; 2 weeks; 2 days; 2 hours; 2 minutes?

We see that most if not all of these characteristics represent our more primitive, primordial side – that side of our nature whose main purpose was to ensure our physical survival in earlier times. At the same time, we need to understand that some of these characteristics do serve a useful purpose and can be the basis for good today.

Here are the 10 characteristics:

We are all **ambitious**. We want to "advance" – be more, do more, have more and better, whether wealth, fame or respect. We are all **opportunistic**. We tend to take advantage of situations to further our own self-interest. We are all **stubborn**. We are obstinate; we refuse to listen or comply, preferring to stick with the status-quo. We are all **ignorant**. We don't know all there is to know about any one thing in particular or about everything in general, and never will. Hence each of us lives our life in a huge void of uncertainty. We don't know who we are, why we're here or where we're going. It's no wonder, then, that we live according to something we are not. We are all **greedy**. We have an excessive, even compulsive desire to have or acquire; we want more than we need or deserve. We are all **lazy**. We have a tendency to put in the least effort in order to get the most results. We are all **fearful**. We have a preoccupation, a concern, a feeling of anxiety, apprehension or agitation, sometimes even terror, relating to danger, evil or pain, whether imaginary or real. We are all **selfish**. We put our own interests first, well ahead of others, to an extent that is neither fair nor right nor moral. We are all **vain**. We have and project an excessively high regard for ourselves: Our ideas, our opinions, our abilities, our appearance, our possessions, and so on. We are all **vengeful**. We want to return an injury for an injury by inflicting punishment and pain on others for what they have done to us.

If you are offended by this list, as some people initially are, just ask yourself, "Have I ever exhibited this particular quality *at least once* in my life? Have I ever been ambitious, opportunistic, stubborn, ignorant, greedy, lazy, fearful, selfish, vain or vengeful at least once?" I already know your answer. Now we both know that each of these qualities is in you (in varying degrees in everyone), whether you want to admit it or not.

So, how could some of these characteristics be the basis for good? How could they add to the collective wellness of humankind? Well, you could be ambitious, opportunistic and stubborn, and use these same characteristics to help others live healthier, longer and more productive lives. Think of all the medical researchers who have spent years, sometimes their entire careers, to come up with cures for debilitating diseases such as diabetes, tuberculosis and leprosy. Or inventors. Where would our society be today without modern telecommunications and transportation equipment and systems? Whether modern agricultural practices, new medical devices, new materials and their applications … all were developed to serve a very real need (although, in some cases, simple greed may have been a motivating factor as well). And characteristics such as ambition, opportunism and stubbornness will continue to drive people to use their ingenuity, creativity and innate intelligence to better the human condition.

When other, totally selfish motives are at play, however, you need to ask the question, "Why? Why have you exhibited many or all of these traits at one time or another in your life, albeit some more frequently and more passionately than others?" Specifically, "What is your personal 'pain-story,' your justification or rationalization for acting this way?"

Again, may I introduce to you … *your ego!* The ego's power and influence has been at work in the human psyche since the beginning of time. Simply stated, it *owns* you, or at least it thinks it does. And most of us would have to readily agree since we haven't seriously considered the possibility of something else as the driving force in our life. For example, "we think, we feel and we do" each day without really thinking about the force or forces that are directing all of this; most of us do whatever we do instinctively and just hope for the best. Your ego represents an elaborate belief system that is in your genetic make-up, your DNA, that first and foremost has said to you and is still saying today, "Survive! Look out for number one! Nothing is more important than your personal safety, comfort and welfare!" And survive both you and I did.

To know you must survive implies you must be at risk. If you think you are at risk, you come to believe you must compete. (Sure it's a struggle, but what choice do you have?) In order to compete, you must be prepared to fight or flee. If you fight, you might lose; if you flee, you might be caught. Fear, then, is one of the main driving forces behind everything you think and do.

After telling you to (1) survive, your ego then directs you to move up the ladder to the next level and instructs you to (2) seek safely, security and freedom from fear; (3) seek acceptance, friendship and love by associating and fraternizing with others; (4) seek recognition, status and self-respect; and finally (5) prove to yourself and others that you are unique, capable and worthy of high achievement. Having gotten you this far, your ego tells you with great fanfare that you have finally "made" it … you are now on top of the world! And, of course, it takes full credit for getting you there!

The "ego" in you is always focused on building up the ego for the ego's sake (e.g. What's in it for me?) and is incapable of considering more altruistic pursuits. The ego's goal is only self-aggrandizement. This needs to be kept in mind when considering the above description which loosely describes Abraham Maslow's hierarchy of human wants and needs as first postulated in his book, *Towards a Psychology of Being* (1968). His ideas are usually depicted as part of a large pyramid with five distinct levels: "<u>Physiological</u>" needs are at the very bottom, rising to "<u>safety</u>" needs, "<u>social</u>" needs, "<u>self-esteem</u>" needs, and ending with "<u>self-actualization</u>" needs at the very top. Maslow's theory in this regard is central to helping us understand our basic desires and motives for wanting "more" in our life. In this regard, the key question we must ask ourselves is: "What is my real motivation for wanting more?" Is it simple self-interest (selfishness) or self-lessness? Or can the former also lead to the latter? Hmmm. What do you think as it applies to what you are trying to achieve in your life?

Later in life, Maslow postulated that his "pyramid" should not stop at self-actualization needs at the very top, that in fact there is another, much more important factor that he had left out. This he called "<u>transcendence</u>," meaning the spiritual level. Maslow's transcendence level recognizes our natural desire to act morally and ethically, with compassion, humility, empathy, kindness, benevolence and generosity. Without taking into account this spiritual or trans-egoic side to our nature, he felt we are simply living as instinct-driven animals or pre-programmed machines.

The primary factor that initially gave credibility and power to your ego, and continues to do so today, is that you were born as a single entity. You discovered that you came in a certain package or "container," so to speak, a body with finite walls that were made of soft, delicate skin. You arrived in this body very much separate from everything and everyone else. Very quickly, in fact *instantly,* you found yourself all alone. This, at a time when you were the youngest and most vulnerable, is a very scary realization indeed!

But then it gets even worse. Your very own "physicality," your physical form, allows you to use only physical sensors to perceive what you see as only a physical world. Now as you look out and observe all that is going on around you, your "separateness" is confirmed. Yes, you are separate. Yes, you are alone. Yes, you are at risk. Yes, you must compete. Yes, you must fight. And yes, there is good reason to be afraid. (Yes, those train tracks do come together somewhere off in the distance!) We are all "wired" – 6.8 billion people – to think this way; we are all driven instinctively to want more and more out of life and eventually get to the so-called "top." Knowing this, should it be any surprise that there are so many problems in the world?

The ego evolved as a necessary survival mechanism for individual human beings during the long and grueling course of human history. And it did its job very well, at least for those of us who survived. The irony is that today it has become more of a death wish. We must find some way to overcome or *transcend* it (e.g. not just "tame" it or try to control it) as it now clearly threatens both our individual and collective selves. As we humans develop more and more efficient and innovative ways of killing each other (e.g. IEDs, cluster bombs and unmanned, missile-carrying aerial drones), and more and more invasive ways of degrading and destroying, in fact *raping* the planet (e.g. open-pit mining, clear-cutting of forests and bottom-trawling of the ocean floor), there is an urgency today in this regard that has never been greater in human history. Whether we are up to the challenge or not, only time will tell. Some think it is already too late.

◀◀◀ **80** ▶▶▶▶

We have just described the 10 personality traits or characteristics that are a product of your ego. In contrast, let's look at other traits that are "beyond" your ego, in fact that are totally unknown to your ego, examples of what we will call "supreme virtue." They are prime examples of your essence or true nature. It may be that we don't see them on display in the world as often as we would like but when we do, we usually take special notice of them. These traits or qualities go by such names as:

Honor; respect; compassion; empathy; humility; honesty; truthfulness; virtue; courage; industriousness; justice; righteousness; fairness; generosity; service; responsibility; forgiveness; mercy; and unconditional love.

This list is by no means complete but it's a good beginning. Let's briefly see what some of them mean:

Honor: A keen sense of right and wrong; adherence to actions and principles that are considered right. **Respect**: To feel or show honor or esteem for others; consider or treat others with deference or courtesy. **Compassion**: To feel sorrow or deep sympathy for the troubles or suffering of others, with an urge to help. **Empathy**: The projection of one's own personality into the personality of another in order to understand him better; intellectual identification of oneself with another. **Humility**: The state or quality of being humble of mind or spirit; absence of pride or self-assertion. **Honesty**: Refraining from lying, cheating or stealing; being truthful, trustworthy and upright. **Truthfulness**: Sincerity, genuineness, honesty; the quality of being in accordance with experience, facts or reality. **Virtue**: General moral excellence; right action and thinking; goodness of character. **Courage**: The ability to face anything recognized as dangerous, difficult or painful; quality of being fearless or brave. **Industriousness**: The putting forth of earnest, steady effort; hardworking; diligent.

We now see how you can live authentically, meaning in a genuine and real way as opposed to a false and hypocritical way. You need only manifest the divine essence that is within you. To live authentically is to live in agreement with fact or actuality, in a manner that is consistent with who you are. When you are authentic, and only when you are authentic, can you be useful to a higher cause (in other words, play this game called "life" with much more insight, much more skill and much more passion). This involves love: Love of self, love of others and love for all of humanity. The only alternative is to stay trapped into trying to prove to the world that you are a "somebody," indeed a *special* somebody. The irony is that you don't even know who this "somebody" is that you are pretending to be. It's like every day is Halloween and you don a different costume that you think best suits the occasion: "Hey,

do you like me like this? No? Then how about this? Or this? Or this? …
please, like *some* version or variation of me!"

"Hypocrite" means 1. an actor, one who plays a part 2. a pretender; an
imposter 3. a person who pretends to be what he is not 4. one who pretends to
be better than he really is or pious, virtuous, etc., without really being so.

When you live thinking you are a human being having an occasional
spiritual experience (e.g. adopting virtuous behavior only when it suits or
pleases you), you have to ask yourself, "Are you really what you portend to
be?" (e.g. is being spiritual only a part-time job?) At a deep subconscious
level, you know you are not – you are living falsely, dishonestly and
inconsistently; *in fact you are living a lie.* Yes, a lie that you have been
led to believe by authority figures, caretakers and well-wishers of all kinds
who constantly told you to do this and this and this, but do not do that and
that and that (e.g. believe this but don't believe that; act like this but don't
act like that; go to this church but don't go to that church; enjoy doing this
but don't enjoy doing that …). And you have never seriously questioned
all their dictates. After all, these people were much older and wiser than
you, and supposedly had your best interests in mind … shouldn't they
know?

All professional actors live a lie when they perform on a stage and take on
the persona of someone they are not. And it is a very difficult and stressful
undertaking, to which most of them would readily attest. Now consider
spending all your waking moments pretending you are someone you know
you are not. This results in a serious case of "cognitive dissonance" … you
are aware that there is a disconnect. You say to yourself, "I don't like this
game; I'm not very good at playing this game; I don't want to continue
playing this game." You show your displeasure by resorting to the usual
primitive behaviors that result from disappointment, frustration and anger:
You lash out, you criticize and you complain. In other words, you demonstrate
all the usual mean-mindedness, even invectiveness, that is indicative of the
fact that you are not happy.

For completeness, we should take a look at what "happy" actually means.
After all, many people think that to be happy is their primary purpose in life.
But happiness is not something that can be had by itself. It is a by-product,
a feeling that results from "being" and "doing" what is in accordance with

who you are (e.g. when you are in a state of continuous validation of your true identity, living as your true Self).

"Happy" means having, showing or causing a feeling of great pleasure, contentment, joy, gratification.

You cannot be happy or have happiness directly – you cannot buy it, steal it, eat it, drink it or touch it as a thing in its own right (although many thieves, con artists, fast food addicts, alcoholics, drug addicts and sex addicts would have you believe otherwise). *You can only have it, feel it and show it by acquiring it indirectly.* Happiness is an energy, and is not a result of anything "physical" in this world. You can <u>never</u> hope to put your hands around it, caress it and say, "Wow! Look, I finally have this thing called happiness."

Here is a observation by Margaret Young, the popular American singer of the 1920s: "Often people attempt to live their lives backwards; they try to have more things or more money, in order to do more of what they want, so they will be happier. The way it actually works is the reverse. You first must be who you really are, then do what you need to do, in order to have what you want."

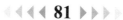

Man has always been in search of happiness. William James identified this universal trait long ago when he wrote, "If we were to ask the question, 'What is life's chief concern?' one of the answers we should receive would be: 'It is happiness.' How to gain, how to keep, how to recover happiness is in fact the secret motive of all that we do, and all that we are willing to endure." And William Butler Yeats, the Irish essayist and poet, added this insight: "Happiness is neither virtue nor pleasure nor this thing nor that, but simply growth. We are happy when we are growing."

As a human, you are a creature of habit. You like to hide out in your comfort zone, that place where you feel safe and sound. The comfort zone is like your security blanket that you wrap around yourself. To accept that you can and should live to a higher standard is a very scary notion for most people. There are several reasons for this: First, it requires you to accept the possibility that you may not be currently living as you should; second, it requires you to consider accepting additional responsibility and undertaking some serious thinking, study and self-assessment, things people seldom readily agree to do; and third, you must confront the fear of failure, the possibility of not succeeding at this task should you decide to go down this road. It's no wonder, then, that so few embark on this journey into the unknown. But it's really not the "unknown," of course, since you are simply returning "home." It is different, but only at first. Soon, very soon, you come to realize that this is where you belong.

◀ ◀ ◀ 82 ▶ ▶ ▶ ▶

"Be consistent; live in harmony." Here, then, is the path you want to take. Let's see what "consistent" and "harmony" actually mean.

"Consistent" means 1. firm 2. coherent 3. being true 4. being in accordance with 5. being in harmony.

"Harmony" means 1. congruity 2. fitting well together 3. agreement in feeling, action, ideas and interests.

Doesn't this sound like a better way to live to you? Think about it. How can you ever hope to be happy if you are not living consistently and in harmony with who you really are?

Author Gary Zukav explains what he means by "authentic power" – the alignment of the "self" with our soul, in his 1989 book, *The Seat of the Soul:* "When we align our thoughts, emotions and actions with the highest part of ourselves, we are filled with enthusiasm, purpose and meaning. Life is rich and full. We have no thoughts of bitterness. We have no memory of fear. We are joyously and intimately engaged with our world."

All real growth involves the attraction and internalization of divine energy and the manifestation of its power and relevance. The objective is always service – the giving of gifts for the common good.

So how should you go about living your life? There are two principal ways you can gain some insight into what you should do and how you should behave. One way is to watch others who you admire and then try to emulate (e.g. copy or duplicate) their behavior. This option is called "modeling" since you are using a model (an actual "picture" or image) as a prototype for your own actions. And it works quite well. Athletes use it, actors use it, and singers and dancers use it. Of course, this approach has its limitations. First, you may not be witnessing what the other person is doing in a perfect way. Second, you may not have the natural talent and ability that the other person has, and hence cannot do exactly what the other person has done. Third, a perfect model for what you want to do may not exist, or at least may not be readily available to you. And fourth, you may not possess the same motivation, self-discipline and intensity as the model does.

The second way involves creating a "picture" in your mind of the precise behavior you want to exhibit. This approach is called "creative imaging" because you are relying on your imagination to define the specific behavior you want to adopt. This approach also has its limitations. First, some people are not very good at forming mental pictures – they may be more verbal and less visual in the way they think. Second, mental pictures are less specific in nature; at best they are an approximation of the behavior you want to emulate. And third, as in modeling, you simply may lack the natural talent and ability, as well as the motivation, self-discipline and intensity you need in order to do what you are visualizing in your mind.

Most people, of course, make use of both these approaches in their daily life. Consider the evolution of a child. A child's mother (or father) may be a teacher, a nurse or a singer. A child's father (or mother) may be a policeman, a fireman or an actor. We all know children who grew up and adopted the same career paths as one of their parents – they ended up doing what they witnessed on a daily basis.

We also know children who became as adults what their imagination created for them. Walt Disney was interested in cartoons when this art form was still in its infancy. The Wright brothers were interested in airplanes when none had yet been built that actually flew. Thomas Edison was interested in electric light at a time when only candles were available. Alexander Graham Bell wanted to use copper wire to transmit the human voice over long distances when such an idea was considered totally absurd. Yet, through trial and error and total faith in themselves and in what they wanted to do, they all succeeded.

Clearly, then, whether you rely on various role models that are available to you or the creativity of your own mind, you can achieve a very high level of competency if you really believe in the thing you want to do. This applies to all areas of human endeavor: Art, literature, engineering, sports, business, entertainment, and of course practicing spirituality and integrating it into the kind of life you want to live.

In this regard, some key questions come to mind: Is there a spiritual teacher with whom you are familiar, admire and would like to emulate? Is there a unique contribution you would like to make to others – and ultimately to yourself, since we are all One? Where does your real, intense, waiting-to-be-manifested *passion* lie? The only way to answer these and other questions like them is … *go into silence and listen attentively to what it tells you.* As the Buddha has wisely counseled us, "Your work is to discover your work, and then with all your heart to give yourself to it."

◀ ◀ ◀ **85** ▶ ▶ ▶

The physical world operates on the basis of cause and effect. It's the master law of the universe. It says that for every action or effect, there is first a prior cause. In the human system, your *thoughts* are the cause, and your *behavior and circumstances* are the effect. Hence we see that life is really a mental adventure, not a physical journey. It is your thought processes (the cause) that you must focus on and improve upon if you want to change key aspects (the effects) of your life.

The following quote from one of my earlier books summarizes the process: "You are today where your previous thoughts have brought you; you will be tomorrow where your current thoughts take you."

If you want to exercise more control over your thoughts in order to become more competent, more productive and more fulfilled, you must understand how your mind works.

To emphasize an earlier point, the total accumulation of data involving everything that has ever happened to you in your life is referred to as your personal belief system, your "reality" or the "truth" as you know, understand and accept it to be. It serves as your frame of reference as you continue to experience new things in life and represents the total "programming" your mind has been subjected to, voluntarily or involuntarily, up to now.

For example, *who you are at this very moment,* whatever you happen to be doing, is what your mind *believes* you are. Your ability to solve a problem, perform a task or reach a specific goal all depend on your mind's stored beliefs about your strengths and weaknesses in each of these areas.

The breakthrough comes when you realize that many parts of the belief system you now have are *at least partially and often totally unreliable* since they are based on information that is inaccurate, insufficient or irrational. Few of us really "know" that much about anything, even in this modern age, especially about our own inherent talents and abilities that have rarely (if ever!) been fully tested. People acquire their beliefs from their prior experiences – or more correctly, from their *interpretation* of these prior experiences. Therefore any particular belief you may now have is more of a subjective opinion than an objective fact. Only by the critical reassessment of long-standing beliefs can you change them and move ahead with your life. This necessarily involves doing some serious thinking, in fact some serious re-thinking!

Let's look at beliefs (in particular, yours!), how you got them, and how they influence the way you think, feel and act on a daily basis. You have many different belief systems at work in your life that you use to observe, understand and define yourself and the world you live in. In many cases, you have become totally comfortable with them and therefore no longer question them or even know that they exist.

For example, you very likely have come to like certain people and not like others; to like certain foods and not like others; to like certain cars and not like others; to like certain books, movies, clothes, jewelry and jokes, and not like others. It could also be said that not only have you become comfortable with these personal frames of reference, you have become a *slave* to them. They are forcing you to limit yourself to "thinking inside a box" of a certain size. If you feel compelled to challenge or dispute this statement, this is proof by itself that you are limited in how you think.

Consider your master paradigm, the belief system you now have that defines for you so much of your basic make-up: Who you are; why you're here; what you stand for; what strengths, talents and natural abilities you have; how you should behave; what dreams and aspirations you should have; and so on. In other words, you have adopted a certain "mind-set," a certain "sense of self," a certain "self-identity," a certain "self-concept," a certain "notion" of who you are – how attractive, how capable, how acceptable, how lovable, how intelligent, how productive, and therefore how important and how worthy you are. *This is how you have allowed your brain to be programmed up to now.* And guess what? This book is going to ask you to question your master paradigm and change it, even change it dramatically in some important areas.

To ask you to change your personal belief system – how you see yourself, your world and your place in it – can be (but need not be) an extremely challenging, even daunting task. So let's remember before we proceed that we have all had to make both minor and major paradigm shifts in our life about our beliefs concerning many things. Here are a few simple examples:

- On 14 October, 1947, Chuck Yeager became the first person to break the sound barrier in an airplane. Many thought this would never happen.

- On 6 May, 1954, Roger Bannister became the first person to run the four-minute mile. Many thought this would never happen.

- On 20 July, 1969, Neil Armstrong was the first person to walk on the surface of the moon. Many thought this would never happen.

- In the early 1990s, Japan entered an economic recession after almost 40 years of rapid economic growth. This recession went on for more than a decade, and well into the new millennium. Many thought this would never happen.

- On 11 September, 2001, a group of terrorists flew two commercial aircraft into the twin towers of the World Trade Center in New York City, destroying both structures and taking more than 3,000 lives. Many thought this would never happen.

- On 10 October, 2002, shares in Nortel Networks (a much-prized high-tech stock) closed the day on the New York Stock Exchange at 67 cents. It was valued at over $124.00 (or 12,400 cents!) only 24 months earlier. Many thought this would never happen.

- During the last quarter of 2008 and first quarter of 2009, some economists estimate that between $10 trillion to $15 trillion "evaporated" into thin air as a result of the global banking and credit crisis. Many thought this would never happen.

Add to this list the fact that when you look down a set of train tracks, they appear to come together somewhere off in the distance. But when you get on a train and travel that distance, you find that they do not. In other words, what you "see" on the physical level is not always real!

So perhaps the task at hand – changing your concept of who you are, why you're here and what you can do with your life is not quite as daunting as first thought. I like this comment by the American writer Elbert Hubbard (1849 – 1912): "The recipe for perpetual ignorance is to be satisfied with your opinions and content with your knowledge."

So, how satisfied and content are you as you read this text?

As part of my research into human behavior, I identified 10 core beliefs that are representative of all peak performing men and women. Many people have approached me over the years concerned about their own core beliefs and how it affected their level of self-esteem, happiness and personal performance, so I made a special effort to provide them with the following guidance that first appeared in my book, *Think Like A Winner*™ (1991).

Of all your beliefs, the most important are your core beliefs, for they are absolutely critical to your future. You possess thousands upon thousands of beliefs about every aspect of your life. You have an opinion or belief about designer clothes, government officials, dolphins, Caribbean cruises, Pepsi versus Coca Cola, ice cream, leather furniture, UFOs, artificial flowers, classical music, polo ponies, jumbo jets, fly fishing and honey bees. But none of these particular beliefs is likely to have a major impact on your life. *The same cannot be said about your core beliefs.* For core beliefs are basic to your very being and are primary determinants concerning the direction your life takes.

Recall the expression, "We are engineered for success (by our Creator) but often programmed for failure (ultimately by ourselves)." And it is absolutely true.

When you were born, you didn't know anything about anything, and hence didn't have a whole range of beliefs about anything either. Your mind was simply a blank slate. Then you experienced something of life, and began to learn things about yourself and your world. And if you validated this same information often enough in your later experience, you accepted it as "true" and it became part of your reality profile.

The problem is that as you grew up, you allowed yourself to be conditioned to a large extent by your environment to believe many things about yourself and your world that are simply not true. This should be no surprise. You adopted the majority of your beliefs at a very young age, at a time when you were not that well informed about many things. You simply were not in the best position to make important decisions that would stay with you for the rest of your life.

I offer the following set of core beliefs as one that is available to you. Of course, you must have one set of core beliefs or another, hence it is only prudent that you adopt one that empowers and energizes you rather than limits and deflates you. Consider each of these beliefs carefully, and imagine what your world would begin to look like if you held the same beliefs and made them a part of your life today.

1. Winners are _made_, not born.

At birth, you were given a magnificent computer for your personal use but no software of any kind to run it! You lacked the particular beliefs, knowledge and insight you needed to succeed in life. But this you can acquire at any time, if you choose to do so. Success is a journey, a trip that only you can take one step at a time.

IMPLICATION: Life is really a "do-it-yourself" project. Adopt the philosophy, "If it is to be, it's up to me." Surely you didn't think some-one else was going to do it for you! And of course, you wouldn't want anyone to.

2. The dominant force in your existence is the _thinking_ you engage in.

Life is an inner game. All causation is mental. You succeed from the inside out. You become what you think about all day long.

IMPLICATION: Be very careful about the thinking you engage in. For as you think, so you become.

3. You are empowered to create your own _reality_.

Your five senses perceive the world in the best way they can. But it is your brain that interprets this input and gives it its meaning. Would you rather have something or someone else decide its meaning for you? Of course not.

IMPLICATION: Be aware of the reality you create. Does it make sense to have drawn the conclusions you have about yourself based solely on the current evidence? Absence of evidence of something is not necessarily evidence of its absence.

4. There is some _benefit_ to be had from every adversity.

Adversity is a great teacher. It tells you that something doesn't work. But in the process of finding this out, you learn something. And this is the great benefit – so long as you change your approach and "keep on keeping on" until you get the results you want.

IMPLICATION: Focus on the benefit, not on the failure.

5. The personal belief system you now have is _total choice_.

You have a belief about almost everything in your life. But none of these beliefs is a total absolute, either about you or your world. A belief does not necessarily reflect knowledge; more often than not, it reflects a _lack_ of knowledge. For example, everyone once thought the world was flat – until Columbus came along and proved otherwise. One approach is to believe what you want to believe about yourself and the world you live in, then go out and prove that you are right!

IMPLICATION: Select core beliefs that empower and help you move ahead rather than ones that limit and deflate you, and hold you back.

6. You are _never defeated_ until you accept defeat as a reality, and decide to stop trying.

Defeat and failure are relative. They are only part of life's magnificent journey. They have no meaning or relevancy, unless you decide to give them meaning and relevancy.

IMPLICATION: Never give up and you will dramatically improve your chances of succeeding. Give up and you will surely fail. Remember, winners never quit and quitters never win.

7. You already possess the ability to *excel* in at least one key area of your life.

Studies have found that everyone is potentially a genius – at something! So it remains for you to apply yourself and find out what this area is! Genius is only the ability to think in unconventional ways. When everyone thinks alike, no one is thinking at all. Choose this unconventional and energizing thought: Believe you can become outstanding in your chosen field of endeavor. If you do, you will be in the top one-half of one percent of the general population.

IMPLICATION: Find out what you are good at. Often it is something you love to do, that gives you the greatest satisfaction and sense of importance. Otherwise, just *decide* what it is you want to excel at. Then go out and do it!

8. The only real limitations on what you can accomplish in your life are those *you impose on yourself*.

It's up to you to decide if any limitations on your potential exist. No one can label you a failure without your consent. Remember: The world forms its opinion of you primarily from the opinion you already have of yourself.

IMPLICATION: The only way to discover your limitations is to go *beyond* them. Assume no limitations. Who are you to know, anyway? So get on with the task at hand!

9. There can be no great success without *great commitment*.

If you are going to become outstanding at anything, you have to … *work* at it. You have to pay the price. You get nothing by doing nothing. You get out of anything only in proportion to what you put in. And there is no limit to what you can put in! Hmmm. I know of no one who has ever drowned in his own sweat … do you?

IMPLICATION: Commitment is a function of your belief and desire. Work on these two, and commitment that is unwavering and indestructible will automatically follow.

10. You need the support and cooperation of _other people_ to achieve any worthwhile goal.

No one functions in a vacuum. You have a family, work in an organization and live in a community. Many people with different specialties must come together in the pursuit of a common objective. It necessarily follows that the better the support and the better the cooperation, the better the results will be.

IMPLICATION: Find out how to establish and maintain effective, trusting and productive interpersonal relationships.

Start programming these core beliefs deep into your subconscious reality – your inner consciousness – and they'll begin to be manifested in your life. Simply put, consciously believing and "seeing" is the key to achieving.

 ◀ ◀ ◀ **87** ▶ ▶ ▶ ▶

The following is an experience I had a few years ago while attending a seminar by Marianne Williamson, author of the best-selling book, _A Return to Love_ (1992). I found the event very uplifting and exhilarating.

The date was Saturday, 20 June, 2003. The place was The Church of Today (now called Renaissance Unity) in Warren, Michigan, about 45 minutes north of Detroit. I had not been back in the area for about six years. I had lived in Grosse Point Farms, near Detroit, for a year in 1996/97, and had attended several events at this church during that time. The occasion for my return was a 12-hour workshop by Marianne Williamson on _A Course in Miracles_®, a 10 AM to 10 PM marathon. There were about 250 people in attendance, with women outnumbering men about seven to one. (Please visit "www.acim.org" to learn more about the book, _A Course in Miracles_®.)

After a warm applause that greeted her, Marianne began talking. Here is a small sample of her opening comments that day:

"Everyone will be either your crucifier or your savior according to how you act and react" … "When you close your heart to another, that's when you feel pain because you are acting separate from your Source" … "When you're not loving, you have forgotten who you are" … "You have this computer file in you called 'my inner divinity' that you cannot delete" … "Look for the innocence in others (God) and not their failings (ego)" … "How many of us are trying to get from others what we can get only from God?" … "When you act with anger or detachment, this is not where you are bad, this is where you are wounded" … "God does not wish to judge you, he wants to heal you" … "No matter what the ego says, God will have the final say."

"Good!" I thought, "She's going to deal with real *substance*." It was clear this was not going to be a day that dealt with weird abstractions, mundane theory, simplistic niceties or over-used clichés. It was going to be hardball! – the how and why to change what you think and do every minute and every day of your life. The workshop only got better as it went along. It was 12 hours of quiet revelation, a clearing of the mind, a cleansing of the spirit. I knew I was at the right place. And I knew I desperately needed to hear what this person had to say at this point in my life.

To make sure we didn't leave that day without something to think about, Marianne read the following from her book, *A Return to Love*. I still think about it and continue to be inspired by it today. Here is what she said:

"Because thought is the creative level of things, changing our minds is the ultimate personal empowerment. Although it is a human decision to choose love instead of fear, the radical shift that this produces in every dimension of our lives is a gift from God. Miracles are an 'intercession on behalf of our holiness,' from a thought system beyond our own. In the presence of love, the laws that govern the normal state of affairs are transcended. Thought that is no longer limited, brings experience that is no longer limited."

By sharing with you some of what Marianne said to our group that day, as well as introducing you to the wisdom contained in *A Course in Miracles®*, I hope I can stir in you some of what was stirred in me.

Plot, scheme, deny, hide, manipulate, fabricate, deceive, delude, deprive, condemn, cheat, judge, criticize … all these are the depraved and destructive workings of the ego.

Whenever you experience on-going frustration, unhappiness or anger in your life, understand that this is a sure sign you are not in harmony with what is. You are using your mental faculties to try to mold the world to make it conform to how you want it to look. But the "world" is just too big a thing to take on all by yourself. Besides, when you try to do this, you have the process totally backwards. Decide what you earnestly want in your heart first, then let the world come to you and enter that space you have just created. When the two meet, miracles, both big and small, always happen.

Here is a quote from the book, *Jonathan Livingston Seagull* (1970) by Richard Bach:

> *"The only difference, the very only one,*
> *between those who are free and the others,*
> *is that those who are free have begun to understand*
> *what they really are and have begun to practice it."*

This is one of my favorite books of all time (and it contains only 127 pages). I recommend it to you. It is about a very brave and daring young seagull named Jonathan Livingston Seagull who *thinks* he is an eagle.

Here is my take on the story. We know all seagulls who think they are seagulls do what other seagulls do; and we know all eagles who think they are eagles do what other eagles do. So Jonathan, believing he is an eagle, acts accordingly. He hovers at great heights, he soars above mountain tops and he dives at frightening speeds, all the dramatic and often dangerous things that eagles do. Of course, his fellow seagulls think he is completely mad and kick him out of the flock. But is he really mad?

Think about it. Because he thinks he is an eagle (e.g. it is what he *conceives* and *believes* himself to be), and for this reason only, Jonathan is able to do pretty much all the things that eagles do. What a great metaphor for you in your life!

You now know what you have to do: Decide who you want to be and what you want to do. Do you want to hover at great heights and soar above mountain tops? Do you want to be the best you can be? Do you want to do something significant and contribute something unique to help others in the world who are suffering?

You can! It only requires that you formulate the appropriate pictures in your head, then begin to act on them with immense passion, unbridled self-confidence, unlimited determination, sharp focus, and an unwavering commitment to succeed.

◄ ◄ ◄ **91** ▶ ▶ ▶

If you were God and had all the powers available to you that God has – to radiate, to illuminate, to communicate, to educate – what would you do with your life? What pleasures would you gladly forsake? What initiatives would you eagerly undertake? What contributions would you earnestly make? Ahhh, yes, if only you were God. (OK, if you want to notch it down a bit … if only you were *God-like!*)

Where do you think most of the stress, anxiety, fear, despair or depression in your everyday life comes from? I suggest it comes, first, from not living in the Now, in the present moment. You do this by spending most of your time thinking about and regretting the past or imagining and worrying about the future. If your focus is always away from the Now, away from the present moments that together add up to your very life, how much joy and how much love can you expect to have? (See Annex 10, *The Wellness Workbook.*)

Second, stress is invariably added to your life when you are not living it authentically, in alignment with your Source. When your mind is consumed by the ego, run by the ego, and pursues goals and outcomes that the ego decides it wants for you, you are living your life in accordance with something you are not. Again, how much joy and how much love can you expect to have when you do this?

Most of us willingly and eagerly conspire with our ego to get all the things we want, all the while not knowing we already have everything we need. Clearly this is a recipe for unhappiness, and ultimately on-going suffering.

We all want to achieve various goals in our life, for "creating," "doing" and "achieving" are all very much part of who we are. For this reason, it behooves us to understand the creative process – how we manifest our thoughts into "form" – for this will make us more effective and more successful in all our undertakings. The following describes in some detail what I call "The Five

Great Wonders of the Mind," previously described in my book, *In Search of Your True Self* (1996).

1. The first Great Wonder of the Mind.

You *think in pictures* that are activated by words.

This is how your mind actually works. You represent ideas in your head by way of PICTURES! Primitive humans communicated their ideas and experiences to others for thousands of years by drawing pictures in the sand or on the walls of caves. Only relatively recently in historical terms have humans created various languages and alphabets to symbolize these "picture" messages.

Pictures are things you put in your head. You think in pictures your every waking moment – you even dream in pictures at night.

EXAMPLES

Think of the word – WEDDING. What do you see? Do you "picture" the joy, the excitement, the beautiful bride, the happy faces of parents and giggling children? How do you feel? Think of the word – FUNERAL. What do you see? Do you "picture" the sadness, the sobbing, the sense of loss, the solemn faces of loved ones? How do you feel?

Or consider what pictures pop into your head when I ask you to recall – your first dance, your first date, your first kiss, your wedding night? Isn't it true, pictures always flash into your head when you hear a certain word? And various feelings and emotions always tag along to complete the picture. Note that the emotions you evoke are totally dependent on the pictures you have.

2. The second Great Wonder of the Mind.

You *always act out* the pictures in your head.

This represents the <u>success system that never fails</u> in humans. It is how you have been designed, how you think, how your mind and body actually work together. Notice I did not say this happens sometime, half the time or whenever it suits you. *I said always!* In fact, you "cannot not" act out the pictures in your head. The mind is a goal-seeking mechanism – it's called teleological or psycho-cybernetic. It takes a picture and transforms it into its physical counterpart, just like a digital camera.

CLICK! Act it out. *CLICK!* Act it out.

Let me ask: How do you "see" yourself at something you believe you are not very good at? Are the pictures in your head and your performance at the task exactly the same? (You are supposed to say yes.) Now compare this to how you "see" yourself at something you know you are very good at. Again, are the pictures in your mind and your performance at the task exactly the same? (Again, you are supposed to say yes. Thank you!) Does this surprise you?

EXPLANATION: If you "see" yourself performing poorly in your mind, you tend to perform poorly when you act out these same pictures. If you "see" yourself performing well in your mind, you tend to perform well when you act out these same pictures. You always manifest in your behavior the pictures you hold foremost in your mind. Simply put, you become in your life the person you "see" yourself to be in your mind. As has been mentioned before, this statement is the essence of "self-image" psychology.

Here is how U.S. Andersen explains this phenomenon in his book, *The Magic in Your Mind* (1961).

"There is within us a power of complete liberation, descended there from whatever mind or intelligence lies behind creation, and through it we are capable of becoming anything and doing anything we can visualize. The mental stuff of which we are made is of such kind and quality that it responds to the formation of images within it by the creation of a counterpart that is discernible to the senses. Thus any picture we hold in our minds is bound to resolve in the material world. We cannot help ourselves in this. As long as we live and think, we will hold images in our minds, and these images develop into the things of our lives, and so long as we think a certain way we must live a certain way, and no amount of willing or wishing will change it, *only the vision we carry within*." (italics added)

3. The third Great Wonder of the Mind. Here is the good news!

You can *change the pictures* in your head to whatever you want!

What is your most powerful tool? There is only one in your arsenal of weapons that makes you unique among all living creatures on the planet, that taps into your potential and determines the course your life takes. Any ideas? Yes!

It's your – *imagination!*

One of your most important abilities is your ability to choose your thoughts. Imagination is the tool by which you can free yourself from the bondage of the sensory world. You see, the world is a "neutral" place. It really is. It is you who gives meaning to anything and everything you perceive. There is no anger, no fear, no stress, and no disappointment in the world. There are only angry, fearful, stressful and disappointing feelings, and you create them all by yourself. What you decide you "see" is what you get. And so it is – you control the pictures you put in your head, either positive or negative, empowering or deflating, and thus create the world as you "know" it and accept it to be. As Anatole France (1844 – 1924), the respected French writer once said, "To know is nothing at all, to imagine is everything."

Your ability to use mental imagery has evolved over time to the point that you can form pictures in your mind in complete variance to the physical world around you. Let's see how easy it is to create pictures in your head. With your eyes open or closed:

IMAGINE! Can you see yourself – standing in front of the Statue of Liberty on Staten Island, looking up at the grand old lady as she holds the torch of freedom so high and so proud?

IMAGINE! Can you see yourself – driving across San Francisco's beautiful Golden Gate Bridge in a bright, red convertible, your hair flying about in the warm, summer air?

IMAGINE! Can you see yourself – in a sparkling white sailboat in Jamaica's Montego Bay, skimming across the bluish-green water at 14 knots, the towering sails stretching and billowing in the strong ocean breeze?

Now I want you to get excited about what you just did. You just performed a series of miracles! You created pictures in your head of things you probably have never seen or done before. But you were there! You gave these pictures color, you gave them sound, you gave them meaning … in fact, you gave them LIFE!

Now, can you see that if you change the pictures you put in your head, you change the way the world "looks" to you?

Let's demonstrate. "See" yourself …

- performing superbly while responding to a series of questions during an important job interview, with all the interviewers nodding their heads in approval and agreeing with your answers. How do you feel?

- making a perfect sales presentation to an important new client, and closing the folder with the signed contract securely inside. How do you feel?

- giving an inspiring, motivational speech to 300 sales professionals, and they all rise in unison to give you a rousing, standing ovation. How do you feel?

The trick is to keep clearly in mind the desired outcome you want. Your mind will then ensure that you act and perform in such a way that you will bring this picture into reality.

You see, YOU are the director, the producer, the scriptwriter and the principal actor on the stage of your life. To paraphrase William Shakespeare, "Life is but a stage, and we are all actors on it." You first create a sort of fiction in your imagination. *And fiction with sufficient fixity of thought becomes fact!* You have only to "see" it in your mind and follow it up with positive, purposeful action if you want to make it happen in your life.

You always act out the pictures you put in your head. Remember the words of Earl Nightingale (1921 – 1989), originator of the best-selling audio program *The Strangest Secret:* "You are what you think … you become what you think about." It's like flicking the channels on the internal television screen of your mind:

FLICK. Channel one. Old movie.
FLICK. Channel two. Horror story.

FLICK. Channel three. Some negative pictures from the past.
FLICK. Channel four. Some positive pictures from the past.
FLICK. Channel five. Some negative pictures about the future.
FLICK. Channel six. Some positive pictures about the future.
FLICK. Channel seven. Aha! You see yourself achieving your primary purpose in life.

It's incredible. It's all so bright, so beautiful, so colorful. It's full of sound and animation – it all seems so real! What excitement! You rerun it a few times to get the picture just perfect. Wow! It's so clear. Isn't it interesting – the more clearly you see your future, the more control you have over it … or is it the more control it has over you?

There is no limit to your ability to think in pictures. You can imagine yourself doing anything perfectly in your mind. And it is a miracle since there isn't a doctor, a psychologist or a neurosurgeon anywhere on Earth who knows how you do it.

Now here is an interesting finding: It has been determined in experiments that a picture imagined earnestly, vividly and in every detail in your mind can have 10 to 60 times more impact on the brain than a real-life experience. In other words, a picture you purposely create in your head *by choice* has the potential to be far more powerful than a picture from the outside world that is imposed on you *by chance*! So who is in charge of your life? *You are!* But to be in charge, you have to know how to take control.

The process of visualization is then perfected by taking repeated action until the desired physical results are consistent with the ingrained mental image. For example, you become an excellent public speaker by giving as many speeches as you can. You become the best scorer in soccer by shooting at the goal as often as you can. You become the best hitter in baseball by hitting as many balls as you can. Practice, practice, practice. Practice may not result in perfection, but it does result in gradual and predictable improvement.

You can also organize pictures in your head – "frame" them – in certain ways to give a different effect. Specifically, you can change either the CONTEXT of a given picture or its CONTENT.

Assume you see life as one big Nintendo war game. The following may be some of your impressions:

"Everyone is taking shots at me; things seem to be exploding all around me; I see things as big, bright, clearly defined and moving very fast. It's all so … "

One context you could adopt is:

CONTEXT 1. – "… intimidating. The world is changing too fast. I'm not sure how much of this I can take!"

The very same impressions could lead you to adopt another context:

CONTEXT 2. – "… challenging. The world is an exciting place to live. Lots of fun, lots of action, and lots of opportunities. I like it!"

The first context could well be the reaction that older, less venturesome people would adopt whereas the second may apply to younger, more adventurous people. Clearly the mental reactions – and hence the feelings – in each case would be significantly different.

As well, you could modify the CONTENT of the present picture to get any desired effect. For example, you could:

FREEZE THE FRAME. Note that everything comes to a complete halt. CUT THE SOUND. Now everything becomes eerily quiet. BLUR THE PICTURE. Everything becomes fuzzy and confusing. Next, make everything black and white, and smaller and smaller until all you see is a little black dot that slowly fades away and disappears into oblivion.

Clearly, each of these mental adjustments changes the effect and impact of the vision itself. So we see that it is the way you organize what you see in your mind and the way you choose to interpret the things you see that determine their ultimate meaning to you.

4. The fourth Great Wonder of the Mind.

The mind _cannot tell the difference_ between fact and fiction.

In other words, your mind doesn't know the difference between a picture you put in your mind by *choice* versus one that gets there by *chance*: A classmate's rebuke, your father's put-down or the "loser" label pinned on you by a close friend.

In light of this, you might think your mind is dumb, very dumb. Can you imagine a device as sophisticated as your brain not knowing the difference between fact and fiction? I can. A million-dollar computer doesn't know the difference between fact and fiction. It acts only on the information you give it – right or wrong, true or false, desirable or undesirable – then it provides the correct answer, not sometime, not half the time, not only when it feels like it – *but always!*

Assume you want a computer to add 4 plus 4 but you type in 4 plus 3 by mistake. Guess what? You get 7 for an answer, right? But the computer did exactly what it was supposed to do – it added the two numbers given to it perfectly. The computer is a perfect instrument. But it needs to be given what? Yes, the right data! And so it is with your mind. If you give it the right data – *the right pictures* – it will always act out these pictures perfectly. You have a "success system" in you that never fails! You need only recognize it and accept it for what it is, then use it purposely to your advantage.

Imagine going to a movie. At the conscious level, you know the movie is just a movie, right? It's pure fiction. It's all staged and scripted. Actors and actresses are merely acting out roles assigned to them. But what does your subconscious mind do? It accepts the information as though it were real! And because your mind cannot distinguish between fact and fiction, your body reacts emotionally to all the scenes – you get excited, you become afraid, you laugh, you cry. It's all fantasy … but to your brain and central nervous system, it's all very real!

Or imagine this scenario taking place. You are driving along the highway. You have gone a few miles, perhaps driving a bit too fast and made "running" stops at two stop signs. Your seat-belt is not fastened. All of a sudden, you notice in your rear-view mirror that a police car is quickly overtaking you, with its red, white and blue lights flashing on the roof. Let me ask you: What pictures begin to appear in your head? How do you feel? Are you a little tense? Nervous? Is your stomach starting to tie itself up in tight little knots?

So what happens? The driver of the car is Douglas Kelly, your old high school buddy. He says he has tried to call you at home several times to ask – if you wanted to buy two tickets to the Policemen's Ball! Well, it wasn't what you thought it was, was it? Isn't it amazing how your imagination can really mess you up if you allow it to?

Imagine you were zipping along on a train, looked ahead and concluded that the train tracks came together, and therefore the train you were on was certain to crash. So your ever-present survival instinct tells you to immediately jump off, knowing this is the only way to avoid serious injury or possibly death. Obviously, such drastic action is not required.

But this is what a lot of people do in their life. They jump off a given path they are on to avoid what they perceive to be a negative outcome. The key word is "perceive." Obviously you are limited physically from seeing things in the world as they actually are. So you have to rely on something else besides your physical sensors to keep you on track and moving ahead.

Back to pictures. As an exciting new picture begins to turn into reality in your life, another miracle begins to unfold.

5. It is the fifth Great Wonder of the Mind.

The mind can _imagine things for you_ that you cannot begin to contemplate.

Isn't this incredible? After you put the first picture in your head, a part of your mind starts to put even more fantastic pictures there that normally you are not capable of doing. It is as though your mind is tapping into a source of knowledge, energy or intelligence that you consciously cannot. *And of course, it is!* Hidden prompters come out of nowhere, be they words, pictures or flashes of insight, and literally force you to think in new directions, expand your horizons and test your outer limits.

For example, if your goal is simply to get up in front of a small group of people and make a short presentation in a professional manner, your conscious mind will help you do it. But another part of it will also force you to consider speaking in front of 1,000 people and sweeping them off their feet! Once you focus on a given outcome, your mind proceeds to bring into your life the people and circumstances that will allow you to reach further than you ever thought possible, and in ways you cannot fully understand.

Consider Richard Branson, Michael Dell or Bill Gates, all founders of very large and successful corporations. They all started out with a little dream that grew bigger and bigger through hope and inspiration not all of their own making, which in turn brought them to a level of success beyond their wildest dreams.

Back to the Five Great Wonders of the Mind. Which one seems to you to be the most incredible of all?

After a little thought, I think you will agree that it is … **number 3**. You can change the pictures in your mind to whatever you want. *Clearly it is the only one over which you have total control!* It means that you can imagine yourself doing whatever you want in your life, and the subconscious mind automatically accepts the input as real and begins to act on it to bring it into reality. It's also because number 3 will trigger number 5 to kick in, and you are well on your way!

You don't know for sure what natural talents and abilities you have, so little has been tried. They lie hidden, untested, waiting to show themselves. But to expose them, you need to replace your self-doubt with self-confidence, inaction with action, complacency with urgency. You can excel at something, and very probably at many things – even achieve at the genius level – but it's up to you to take the initiative and find out what these things are. There are opportunities all around you. Seize one that is of great interest to you, one that has *heart* for you, and see what kind of a contribution you can make that is unique to you and consistent with the goals you have set for yourself.

◀◀◀ **95** ▶▶▶

I believe it is possible to tell how successful you will be in your life by asking the following five questions, and then critically assessing your answers. They are in no particular order … except I would put the last one first!

1. What are your goals?

2. Who are your friends?

3. How do you spend your spare time?

4. What books are you reading?

5. What values do you live by?

 **96** ▶▶▶

Consider the following guided visualization to demonstrate how creative you can be, as well as the emotional effects that such an outlandish adventure like this can have on you. (CAUTION: Note that this is an *imaginary exercise* done while sitting in a chair!)

Close your eyes. Imagine you are standing all alone on the roof of a skyscraper in Manhattan at one o'clock in the morning. You are 110 stories above street level. The view is incredible – you can see the lights of New York City in all directions, from Brooklyn to the Bronx. There are red lights, yellow lights, green lights and flashing neon signs so large that they are visible from 10 miles away.

Now carefully walk over to the edge of the roof and look down. Can you see the headlights of all the cars, buses and taxis streaking up and down the street? You are 1,500 feet up in the air. Now there is a small ledge around the roof to prevent people from inadvertently walking right off. It's about two feet high and one foot wide. Put your right foot up on this ledge, very carefully, then slowly lean over and look down once again. Can you feel a slight shiver go through your body?

Next, take your left foot and slowly lift it up beside your right so that now you are standing all alone on this narrow ledge. Wheee! You feel a gentle summer breeze blowing at your back. Everything seems so quiet, so peaceful, so surreal. Right?

Now all of a sudden … WOW! You jump right off the ledge and fly away! Imagine that you are Wonderwoman or Superman, and you can fly anywhere you want. So you fly off first in this direction and then in that direction, and even hover over the Empire State Building for a closer look. Eventually you land right in the middle of Central Park, full of excitement and bristling with energy. Open your eyes.

Isn't it amazing? Just as your imagination can immobilize you, it can also free you to do things you never thought you could! When you see yourself achieving a goal – *any goal* – in your imagination often enough, you begin to believe you can achieve it in real life.

The implication here is clear. You don't have to rely solely on your past experiences to determine your level of self-confidence and self-esteem. You can add as many new successes as you want – by *imagining* them over and over again in your mind! They then are duly recorded and added to your memory profile for future reference. In this way, they become part of you and help you achieve whatever goal you have set for yourself.

Mohammed Ali, the former world heavyweight boxing champion, once made this comment: "The person who has no imagination can't get off the ground. He has no wings. He cannot fly."

By using your imagination in a positive and purposeful way, you gain control over what you think about. And we know what you *think* about ... *comes* about. Now <u>*you*</u> are the programmer, <u>*you*</u> are the designer, <u>*you*</u> are the creative force behind the reality you create in your life!

We all need a big, challenging goal to provide meaning and purpose to our life. It gives us something to aim at, to work towards and look forward to.

A goal is a target to shoot at. If you don't have a target to shoot at, how can you score any points? And if you can't score any points, how can you measure any progress? And if you can't measure any progress, how can you get excited about any aspect of your life? You have to find a way to put some points up on your scoreboard!

I believe life is like a poker game. Your ability to play the game is directly related to the number of poker chips you have in your pile. If you have only five chips and everyone else around you has 100, guess who has the ability to take more risk? The universe rewards action, and action requires taking risks. You have to have sufficient self-esteem – enough poker chips – to break out of your comfort zone. Have you noticed that we are a nation of cheerleaders? But we're always cheering for someone else! We don't give enough thought to scoring "points" for ourselves. We don't purposely go about adding to our own pile of poker chips.

Take an ice hockey game. There are five players on each team gliding around on skates fitted with narrow steel blades, and each one is carrying a long, wooden stick that he often uses to whack his opponents over the head. All the players are covered from head to toe in heavy padding so that no one, not even their wives or children, can recognize them. The objective seems to be to knock everyone down on the opposite team, then use every means possible to get this little round, black object – called a "puck" – into the other team's net. Each net is guarded by a guy who has an even bigger stick, and wears a mask that is all painted up to scare away anyone who dares to come near.

Every once in a while, someone manages to shoot the puck into the opponent's net. Instantly, everyone in the crowd goes wild … we yell, we scream and we whistle! But with all the head-gear and padding that each player is wearing, no one even knows who scored the goal! Meanwhile, all the players on the successful team mill around, trading high-fives, and patting each other on the back. They spend several minutes basking in their miraculous accomplishment.

At the end of the game, players from both teams are whisked off in their sleek limousines to celebrate into the wee hours of the night. And what happens to us poor schmucks in the crowd who actually *paid* to come and watch these guys play? We have to elbow our way down the stairwells, try to find our car in a sea of vehicles, scrape the snow and ice off the windows, pray that the engine starts, then spend the next hour or so getting out of the parking lot and onto the main highway to get home. A great way to spend our free time, right? *Wrong!*

You have to ask yourself, "Have I got my priorities straight?" You need to start putting some points up on your own scoreboard, and spend less time cheering for other people who are having fun doing what *they* like to do, and getting rich at your expense. And today is the perfect time to get started!

◄◄◄ **98** ►►►

If you are not sure what *pictures* you have in your head that depict the "sense of self" you have created for yourself, and are curious to know what they are, just look at your life and what you have manifested up to now. If your life is all about collecting, protecting and indulging in material objects and things to add comfort and enjoyment to your personal life, then you are a materialist. You are living in "object" consciousness. If, on the other hand, your life is all about sharing, caring and giving, and helping others who don't have many of the things that you do, then you are a spiritualist. You have investigated, experienced and been impacted by "space" consciousness. Most people of course have some combination of the two factors at play in their life, often in very different proportions. There is no need to judge one group or the other in this scenario, however, for both are on the same path. Perhaps the most that could be said is that the first group is at the beginning of the path and the second group has traveled some distance down that path.

◄◄◄ **99** ►►►

Let's look at the key elements that together describe "self-image" psychology and how it works.

It is very important to realize that you think in a "three-dimensional" format. Every thought you have has an "idea" or verbal component, an "image" or conceptual component, and an "emotional" or feeling component. And each plays a specific role.

Imagine that someone says the word *beach* to you. The idea component that creates initial awareness is simply "beach." The image component is whatever pictures you conjure up in your mind at the sound of the word.

All the meaning lies in the image. For some, it may include large expanses of clear, white sand, waves breaking on the shore, and people sunbathing or throwing Frisbees. The emotional component, which represents the mind-body connection, is what you feel or sense as a result of these images. In the case just cited, the emotions may include feelings of fun, frivolity and freedom. Others may imagine an isolated beach stretching off in the distance for several miles without a person in sight. Their emotional reaction would probably include feelings of peace, solitude and tranquility. All the feelings you evoke are dependent on the particular images you conceive. If you were knocked unconscious by a massive tidal wave – a tsunami – as a child, for example, your feelings about a beach may well be radically different. It's probably a place you prefer to avoid!

In the same way, you record information in your mind about all your experiences in a three-dimensional format: Verbal; conceptual; and emotional. This information is collected through your five senses to form the basis for your personal belief system or your understanding of you and your world as you now "know" it and accept it to be. Scientists estimate that there are one hundred billion cells known as neurons in the average human cerebral cortex. They are capable of storing more than 100 trillion bits of information. All your memory elements are recorded in three dimensions, the three components of everything you have ever thought or experienced. This way that you think, *in images and three dimensions*, is critical to understand as we begin to discuss the self-concept, the self-image and self-esteem.

Birds sing, dolphins frolic, cats purr, dogs bark, deer roam, eagles soar, squirrels scamper about ... but why? How is it that they are all so happy and so authentic? I suggest it is because these creatures aren't confused about who they are. They don't go about pretending to be something that they are not. There is no great debate going on in their mind about their true nature, their essence, their self-identity, their reason for being here. They know exactly who they are and what they're supposed to do. And so they just "be" and "do." They keep on task. They live their life consistently and in harmony with their Being.

There is on-going research and discussion today about the role "self-esteem" plays in the lives of people, both young, middle-aged and the elderly. Of specific interest is the effect that either high or low self-esteem has on various aspects of their personalities, performance at school or work, as well as their overall mental health. In this regard, we need to understand how fragile a person's level of self-esteem can be when it is based primarily or exclusively on the ever-changing, ever-unpredictable world of form. If something goes wrong in a person's "physical" world, the world of "objects," such as a job loss, a divorce, personal bankruptcy, a serious illness or death of a loved one, this person may have little or nothing to fall back on to see him through. Such tragic events in fact are what drive many people to finally change how they view the world. Having no place else to look, they begin to look "within" for meaning and healing, for understanding and acceptance.

Note that people with low self-esteem can think either too much or too little about themselves. If they act in a superior fashion and demonstrate aggressive behavior towards others, as some do, they are usually just making up for a limited and incomplete sense of self. In other words, they are pretending to be a "somebody" in their interactions with others, all the while believing (secretly) that they are a "nobody" in their heart. In this sense, they are acting in a superior fashion as a defense mechanism to compensate for feelings of inferiority and unworthiness.

To better understand what lies at the very core of "self-image" psychology, we need to discuss in more detail what I call the three "pillars of the self." They include:

1. the self-concept; 2. the self image; and 3. self-esteem

Understanding what these terms mean will help you better understand how you have come to "see" yourself (often in ways that bear little or no relation to reality), and in turn, how much you like or love yourself, whether a little, a lot, or not at all. Needless to say, this is very important stuff! It may well be something you have given little or no thought to during your entire life.

The **self-concept** answers the question, "Who am I?" To do this, the question necessarily becomes, "Who do I think I am?" because you are really being asked for your opinion on the matter. It refers to the whole range of beliefs you have acquired/accepted during your life up to now that relates directly to your own sense of identity.

Your **self-image** necessarily follows from your concept of your "self." It is the belief system you have adopted that answers the question, "How do I "see" myself ... in the many facets of my life?" – what kind of mother, what kind of father, what kind of student, what kind of lover, what kind of worker? How well do I read, do I write, do I sing, do I dance, do I paint? How good am I at languages, at mathematics, at drawing, at mechanical repairs, at remembering names, at telling jokes, at playing a musical instrument, at managing people, at setting and reaching important goals?

It's interesting to note that educational researchers first discovered in the 1950s that a person's self-image is a far more accurate predictor of academic performance than I.Q. In fact, your self-image determines your performance in every aspect of your life. We all know very talented people in music, sports or the arts who weren't able to fully develop their ability because of a poor self-image, while others with much less talent went on to have successful careers because they weren't inhibited by feelings of low self-esteem.

This leads us to **self-esteem** and the importance of self-love. Self-esteem is the _emotional_ component of the self-concept and self-image, and represents the real core of human personality. It is generally agreed by psychologists that *self-esteem is the most critical element affecting all human performance.* It answers this question, "How do I feel about myself – how much do I truly like, love, respect and value myself ... in all the ways I currently 'see' myself?"

Here, then, is a very important fact: Your self-image (which is made up of a series of pictures or "images of self") may be high or it may be low, it may be consistent or inconsistent with reality, but your self-esteem is always true to these very same pictures that you are currently holding in your mind e.g. ones that you believe depict who you really are!

> In other words, the <u>pictures</u> that collectively represent your self-image are at the root of how much you like yourself. *So if you want to change how much you like yourself, you have to change how you "see" yourself – the pictures you have in your head.* More positive pictures produce more positive self-liking that leads to more positive behavior.

Thus we see that "how much you like yourself" is directly related to "who you think you are" – your concept of your "Self." It is either your inner catalyst or your inner brake; it either propels you forward or it holds you back. It is the most important single statement you can make about yourself as a person.

With regards to the three pillars of the self, it is also clear that the "self-concept" and the "self-image" are the most critical parts to focus on since they are the only parts over which you have any control. The "feeling" component, which collectively determines your level of self-esteem, is *automatic*. It is totally dependent on all the pictures you have accepted that you believe represent the "real" you.

Here is what three world-renowned experts have said about critical aspects of your psychological make-up: Your personal belief system; your self-image; and your level of self-esteem. Note that all three are closely related and interdependent, and each plays an important role in your life:

"The self-image is the key to human personality and human performance. But more than this. The self-image sets the limits of individual accomplishment. It defines what you can and cannot be. Expand the self-image and you expand the area of the possible. The development of an adequate, realistic self-image will seem to imbue the individual with new capabilities, new talents, and literally turns failure into success."

Maxwell Maltz, M.D.
Author, *Psycho-Cybernetics* (1960)

"There are positive correlations between healthy self-esteem and a variety of other traits that bear directly on our capacity for achievement and for happiness. Healthy self-esteem correlates with rationality, realism, intuitiveness, creativity, independence, flexibility, ability to manage change, willingness to admit mistakes, benevolence, and cooperative-ness. Poor self-esteem correlates with irrationality, blindness to reality, rigidity, fear of the new and unfamiliar, inappropriate conformity or inappropriate rebelliousness, defensiveness, over-compliant or over-controlling behavior, and fear of or hostility towards others.

"The higher our self-esteem, the more ambitious we tend to be, not necessarily in a career or financial sense, but in terms of what we hope to experience in life – emotionally, intellectually, creatively, and spiritually. The lower the self-esteem, the less we aspire to and the less we are likely to achieve. Either path tends to be self-reinforcing and self-perpetuating."

Dr. Nathanial Branden
Author, *The Six Pillars of Self-Esteem* (1994)

"What is self-esteem? It is how a person feels about himself. It is his overall judgment of himself – how much he likes his person. A person's judgment of self influences the kinds of friends he chooses, how he gets along with others, the kind of person he marries, and how productive he will be. It affects his creativity, integrity, stability, and even whether he will be a leader or follower. His feelings of self-worth form the core of his personality and determine the use he makes of his aptitudes and abilities. His attitude towards himself has a direct bearing on how he lives all parts of his life. In fact, self-esteem is the mainspring that slates each of us for success or failure as a human being."

Dorothy Corkill Briggs
Author, *Your Child's Self-Esteem* (1988)

◀◀◀◀ **103** ▶▶▶▶

In the greater scheme of things, you and I are simply tiny particles of intelligent energy existing in an infinite void whose very essence is pure love.

You live in an area known as your "comfort zone." Its parameters are totally defined by your self-image and your level of self-esteem. Your comfort zone is your safe haven – it's your security zone. It's why you keep doing the same things the same way over and over again. Your comfort zone dictates that you avoid all risk that is above and beyond what your current self-image is able to support.

So what do you do? You retreat, and do what is safe and non-threatening. You engage in what is known as "habitual behavior." Such behavior is evident in your everyday habits – how you fold your arms, how you cross your legs, what food you eat, what friends you have, what books you read, what places you visit, what challenges you accept – everything you do in your life.

Test yourself. Fold your arms. Some people do it one way, others the other way. Whatever you do, you are used to doing it the way that is most comfortable for you. OK, now undo your arms and fold them the other way. Do you find this considerably more uncomfortable? Try the same thing by crossing your legs the usual way, then the other way. Same sensation?

The comfort zone represents all the things you have done often enough to feel comfortable doing them again. Whenever you try something new, it falls outside the limits of your comfort zone. In this area, you feel fear, anxiety and apprehension, the undesirable feelings that are associated with being "uncomfortable." When you anticipate feeling uncomfortable about doing something, you usually succumb to the fear and forgo the thought. You simply return to old thoughts, feelings and actions that are more acceptable, more … well, more comfortable!

The concept that "you shouldn't try new things" came from your childhood protectors – parents, teachers, adults and other well-wishers of all kinds. They often used fear as a tool to ensure your physical well-being: "Don't touch that hot stove!" "Don't play in the street!" "Don't talk to strangers!" And their warnings succeeded in most cases in getting you safe and sound to where you are today. So this approach – instilling fear of trying new things – has served a certain purpose. A problem often arises later in life, however, when you cling to your old ways, despite the fact that as an adult you are much better equipped to tell the difference between what is dangerous and what is not.

If you want to change and try something new, you have to accept being uncomfortable, sometimes *very* uncomfortable, for a while. Then – *surprise!* – after repeated effort, uncomfortable becomes comfortable! And in the process, you expand your comfort zone. You will experience this yourself by repeatedly folding your arms or crossing your legs in the more uncomfortable way over a certain period of time, usually about 21 days.

Most people are comfortable with the prospect of a significant success where the probability of failure is minimal. For example, betting $1 on a lottery ticket where the prize is $1 million is an everyday occurrence. There is no anxiety connected with doing so ... only faint hope! On the other hand, most people are not comfortable with the prospect of a major failure. Very likely, no one would buy a lottery ticket if 10 percent of all the losers were to be rounded up the very next day and sent to Siberia! Playing the lottery may not be the best example to understand basic human motivations that lie behind real-life choices that people make. Nevertheless, regarding the achievement process where the prospect of significant success is offset by the prospect of significant failure, a general rule applies: You can hope to be successful in a big way only if you are also comfortable with the prospect of failing in a big way.

◄◄◄ **105** ►►►

Statistics are published regularly in the U.S. and Canada that measure various parameters and trends that apply to our society. They are indicators of the behavior of people, and how well they are coping with and adjusting to on-going challenges in their lives. Topics addressed often include the levels/rates of teenage pregnancy; drug abuse; smoking, especially among teens; child and adult obesity; high school drop-outs; divorce; robberies; rape; suicide; and so on. On occasion, the results are encouraging but more often, they are not.

In February, 2008, the U.S. Centers for Disease Control and Prevention (CDC) reported an alarming rise in the number of suicides among middle-aged Americans in the five years from 1999 to 2004. In women aged 45 to 54, the level spiked by 31 percent. In Canada, the rate has risen significantly during the same period for men aged 40 to 60.

Of course, there are many factors that come into play regarding suicide. They include genetics, upbringing, life experiences, culture, education, as well as climate and geography. Adding to the complexity, there is also the important role that the self-image and self-esteem play. Take a look at the list just cited and you will see that many criteria – genetics, upbringing and culture – are pretty much out of your control. Not so for your self-image and self-esteem. Regarding these, you have a great deal of control, in fact *total control*. It's just that – perhaps – nobody has told you!

The deepest human need is for self-respect, self-worth and self-liking. It is all tied into our self-concept, our sense of personal identity. Without high self-esteem, we certainly cannot perform at our optimum. In fact, many people begin to self-destruct – they break down both physically and mentally – when they don't feel good about themselves and lack meaning in their life. It follows that anything we can do in a positive way (e.g. not at the expense of others) that makes us feel more important, more worthy and more capable will directly increase our level of self-esteem. It remains for each of us to explore this outlet, go down this path, and make something of our lives.

◀◀◀ **106** ▶▶▶

As has been discussed, a successful approach called Cognitive Behavioral Therapy – itself a form of "critical thinking" – has been used for over 50 years by leading psychiatrists and psychoanalysts all over the world to help people suffering from either mild, moderate or severe depression. Unfortunately, depression is one of the most prevalent yet most difficult diseases in our society to treat. Many people don't even want to admit that they are depressed because of the stigma (e.g. embarrassment and shame) that is associated with it. Therefore they decide to just tough it out and "keep on keeping on," hoping that things will get better all by themselves. Since the disease is often never admitted to, it is seldom properly treated, leaving people to endure their pain all alone and in the silence of their own mind.

The *Toronto Star* reported some interesting results in the first country-wide survey on mental health in Canada (with a population of about 31.5 million at the time) in an article dated 4 September, 2003. It found that 2.6 million people (1.4 million women and 1.2 million men) reported having symptoms of mental illness (e.g. about one in 12 people). Symptoms were related to anxiety, bipolar disorder, schizophrenia, major depression, eating disorders and suicide attempts. Of this number, almost half or 4.5 percent reported symptoms or feelings associated with major depression. Mental illness was found to be 18 percent for people aged 15 to 24, 12 percent for those aged 25 to 44, 8 percent for those aged 45 to 64, and 3 percent for seniors 65 and older. Unfortunately, fewer than half sought out any treatment.

Also note this important finding. The results of a 16-week study at the University of Pennsylvania on the effectiveness of cognitive therapy were published in the April, 2005, issue of the (U.S.) journal *Archives of General Psychiatry*. The study involved 240 people with moderate to severe depression. One group of 60 people received cognitive therapy; another group of 120 received antidepressant medication (usually Paxil); and a third group of 60 received a placebo. The finding was that *cognitive therapy when provided by experienced psychotherapists was just as effective as antidepressant drugs* in the initial treatment of moderate to severe depression.

According to the researchers, patients in the cognitive therapy group attended two 50-minute sessions each week for the first four weeks of the study; one to two sessions a week for the next eight weeks; and one session a week for the final four weeks. After eight weeks of treatment, the response rate was 50 percent in the medication group; 43 percent in the cognitive therapy group; and 25 percent in the placebo group. After 16 weeks (or about four months), the response rate was 58 percent for patients in both the medication and cognitive therapy groups!

The researchers concluded by saying, "It appears that cognitive therapy can be as effective as medications," a finding that is contrary to the current guideline of the American Psychiatric Association that says most moderately and severely depressed patients require medication.

◀◀◀ **107** ▶▶▶

We have seen how each and every picture in your mind has "attached" to it a certain number of feelings – some good, some bad, and many others somewhere in between. And these feelings in turn directly affect many important aspects of your behavior such as your motivations, self-confidence, creativity, initiative and energy level. Your self-esteem, then, lies at the very core of who (you have decided/accepted) you are. Clearly, you first get to "define" yourself by selecting the various pictures that depict how you "see" yourself; you then have to live with this "self" that you have created.

So the secret is out and it is this: *The "pictures" you have of yourself in your mind at any given point in time determine your level of self-esteem at that same point in time.*

It's clear that the key to having "more" in your life – more hope, more fulfillment, more confidence, more peace, more prosperity, more freedom, more courage and more passion is available to you: *It lies in the pictures you choose and accept as representing the "real" you!* These pictures in turn become what your subconscious mind focuses on and acts upon. Indeed, you are what you think; you become what you think about all day long ... whether for better or worse, richer or poorer!

◀◀◀ **108** ▶▶▶

One of the greatest failings of our species is the erroneous belief that our "essence" lies *outside* of us, when in fact it lies *within*. In other words, it is "in-born." ("On that day, you will know that I am in our Father, and you in me, and I in you." 1 John 14:20) With this serious error in perception as

---

our mind-set, we spend most of our life undertaking a laborious search "out there" to find out who we are, all the while not thinking to look "in here." (Hmmm. I can hear God frantically saying, "Hello! Hello! Open *this* door. I'm in here! I'm in here!") Our search is necessarily fruitless and fatiguing, and our life can be quite frustrating as a result. For how can we do all that we need to do and all that we are able to do if we lack an understanding of our very essence, of our incredible power?

Consider this. Science is only now catching up to spirituality. Scientists have discovered that a single cell found in a microscopic piece of skin, flesh or cartilage has the DNA of the whole species contained within it whether a human being, a plant or an animal. In the last few years, we have seen the first cloned sheep (Dolly, born on 5 July, 1996), followed by a mouse, a pig, a cat, a rabbit, a cow and quite recently, a horse. (Later, on 23 April, 2009, scientists announced they have cloned a puppy that even glows in the dark! They named him "Ruppy," short for Ruby Puppy.)

In other words, the son or daughter created exactly as the father or mother. Think about it. A fertilized cell of a living organism can replicate all parts of the original organism; the "intelligence" of the whole is contained in the smallest particle of the whole.

◀◀◀◀ **109** ▶▶▶▶

Once you have discovered revelation and meaning in the area of the unmanifested, something quite remarkable begins to unfold in your world. With a firm base in what is called "presence" (one might say this means being "grounded" in your Sacredness), you start to see that this influences in a very meaningful and significant way the other part, the manifested part, of your life (e.g. the myriad of external events and happenings of your day-to-day existence).

"Something" from the world of the unmanifested begins to flow into the area of your every-day reality. This doesn't necessarily change what happens to you, although this too is possible. It does change, however, your *perception* of what is happening to you, and therefore how you respond and react to it.

It has been said that life is **10** percent what happens to you and **90** percent how you react to it. Or that life is **10** percent what you take and **90** percent what you make of it. Now let's take a moment and think about this.

First, "things" will always happen in your life; that is simply what life is all about. Second, we have seen that each occurrence, each event, in and of itself is _neutral_ until you assign some *meaning* to it, which in turn creates some *feelings* about it. (Recall A, B and C in PART 1.) Third, it is therefore clear that you actually create **100 percent** – not just **90** percent – of your daily "experience" all by yourself! When you understand this, accept it and act on it, your life cannot help but be more meaningful, more peaceful, more serene, and certainly much more impactful. In a very real way, you are in charge of the reality you create – *all of it* – should you agree to take on this responsibility.

So what is this "something" that we have been talking about here? This something, this invisible force that migrates from the unmanifested to the manifested part of your life, is really … love. Love originates in the world of the formless, in stillness; so if you want to bring it into your everyday reality, you have to have developed this part of your consciousness. To "see" (figuratively) with love requires you to see without thought, without judgment, without fear, without anger, and without any intention, goal or specific outcome in mind.

Look at the teachings of Mahatma Gandhi, Martin Luther King Jr. and the Dalai Lama. You will see that their beliefs and philosophy about life and how to live it to the fullest are consistent with this approach: Practice only love; humility; respect; understanding; and compassion.

◄◄◄ **110** ►►►

The sun is about 4.6 billion years old. It is a huge mass of hot, glowing gas burning through nuclear fusion reactions. The temperature at the center of the sun is about 15.6 million degrees Celsius. In another 8 billion years, it will run out of fuel. In the meantime, it is steadily getting brighter and brighter, and increasing in temperature. In 3 billion years, it will be hot enough to burn away all the earth's oceans and lakes. Four billion years after that, the sun will have used up all its hydrogen. At this point, it will be a giant red star 2,000 times brighter than it is now, and hot enough to melt all the earth's mountains and rocky areas. When finally out of fuel, the outer layers of the sun will collapse inward towards its central core, eventually becoming a small, dense, cool star called a white dwarf. As it cools, it will stop emitting light. Scientists know this is what is happening, that one day the whole solar system as we know it will be completely wiped out. (Source: Wikipedia)

◀◀◀ 111 ▶▶▶▶

One "conditioned" mind will always have difficulty communicating with another "conditioned" mind. However, two minds communicating in stillness – the state of "unconditioned" consciousness – have instant rapport and an acute sense of Oneness.

◀◀◀ 112 ▶▶▶▶

See if you can relate to what Marianne Williamson says in her book, *A Return to Love* (1992):

"The world has taught us we are less than perfect. In fact, we have been taught that it is arrogant to think we're deserving of total happiness. This is the point where we're stuck. If anything comes into our lives – love, success, happiness – which seems like it would be suited to a 'deserving' person, our subconscious mind concludes it can't possibly be for us. And so we sabotage. Few people have wronged us like we've wronged ourselves. No one has snatched the candy away from us like we've thrown it away from ourselves. We have been unable to accept joy because it doesn't match who we think we are."

◀◀◀ 113 ▶▶▶

When you grow in consciousness and begin to see the exciting world around you in new and different ways, you develop a larger and clearer vision of yourself (e.g. your Self), and what you can accomplish in your life.

◀◀◀ 114 ▶▶▶

Whatever understanding you have of yourself, this is what you become. You can become anything you want because the world exists through the power of beliefs. There is nothing fixed or limiting about a human being. All the power of the universe is inside you. Simply put, *you are who you _think_ you are,* and this you have the power to change at any moment.

◀◀◀ 115 ▶▶▶

The God of the universe must have a lot of things on his mind. But he took time out to create you and necessarily has a plan in mind for you. Through gentle searching, this plan will become evident to you. Once you know his plan for your life and begin to act on it, it will help you focus your efforts, plan your time, direct your decision-making, add meaning and peace to your life, and most importantly, prepare you for an eternity with him.

◀◀◀ 116 ▶▶▶

Here is a quote from *A Course in Miracles* ® that talks about what is "real" and what is "truth."

"Truth is unalterable, eternal, and unambiguous.
It can be recognized, but it cannot be changed.
It applies to everything that God created, and only what He created is real.
It is beyond learning because it is beyond time and process.
It has no opposite, no beginning, and no end.
It merely is."

◀◀◀ 117 ▶▶▶

There is an incredible *presence* or *knowing* that lies deep inside each of us. We often hear its pleadings, its gentle whisper calling us home, wanting to reunite us with the joy, peace and love that it represents. But we seldom heed its call. Perhaps it's because we are afraid of it; after all, it is unknown to most of us. Or perhaps we think we can heal ourselves, that we are strong enough or smart enough to overcome anything that ails us.

We all have issues from the past by which we feel trapped or limited. These can be manifested in our daily life in many ways including fear, anger, guilt, regret or grief. Certain preoccupations may also be at play. We may lack confidence in our ability to live our life the way we think we should; indeed, we may want to live a life completely different from the one we are now living. We may wonder why there isn't more love, hope, meaning or sense of purpose in our life today. We may be suffering from the recent loss of a loved one, a debilitating addiction, a marriage break-up, or indeed the loss of a job we've had for many years. Or perhaps it is the fear of our own death that frightens us the most; we know we are all going to die sometime.

As all this is happening, we soon find we cannot heal ourselves all by ourselves (e.g. by purposeful, conscious effort), yet we often live in ignorance or denial of this very fact. Perhaps we feel unworthy, weak or inept because we are unable to do this. We may even feel ashamed of our seeming incompetence. After all, we *do* solve a large number of problems of various kinds every day. So our ego, never too far from our innermost thoughts, tells us to just labor on, learn a little more, try a little harder, become a little smarter – but no matter what, *never surrender!* – all representing false hope, wasted effort and poor logic. The result is, and can only be, on-going pain and suffering. What a dilemma! Yet what an opportunity to grow if we would but wake up!

◀◀◀ 118 ▶▶▶

In 1925, Carl Jung took an extensive trip to Central Africa, visiting Kenya and Uganda. Later, in his semi-autobiographical memoirs titled *Memories, Dreams, Reflections* (1961), he recounted what he saw and experienced, which to him felt like a revelation of the creative significance of human consciousness:

"To the very brink of the horizon, we saw gigantic herds of animals: gazelle, antelope, gnu, zebra, warthog, and so on. Grazing, heads nodding, the herds moved forward like slow rivers. There was scarcely any sound save the melancholy cry of a bird of prey. This was the stillness of the eternal beginning, the world as it had always been, in the state of non-being: for until then no one had been present to know that it was this world. I walked away from my companions, until I had put them out of sight, and savored the feeling of being entirely alone. There I was now, the first human being to recognize that this was the world, but who did not know that in this moment he had first really created it.

"There the cosmic meaning of consciousness became overwhelmingly clear to me. 'What nature leaves imperfect, the art perfects,' say the alchemists. Man, I, in an invisible act of creation, put the stamp of perfection on the world by giving it objective existence. This act we usually ascribe to the Creator alone, without considering that in so doing we view life as machine calculated down to the last detail, which, among the human psyche, runs on senselessly, obeying foreknown and predetermined rules. In such a cheerless clockwork fantasy there is no drama of man, world, and God; there is no 'new day' leading to 'new shores,' but only the dreariness of calculated processes."

Conclusion

Armed with these new insights and understandings, each of us has the opportunity for a new approach, a new beginning, a new way of living. Love is God's greatest gift to humankind and we are expected to act responsibly in this knowledge and in its use. I pass this challenge on to you in the hope that I have done my part, however small, however incomplete, however imperfectly, to assist you on your own journey.

PART 3

Mindfulness Meditation
and
Suggested Exercises

*"Take 15 minutes ... go into silence ... and try to see the
many facets of 'Oneness' ... of a simple, stoic frog
... sitting patiently ... on a shiny, green lily pad."*

*"Where do you think all great thoughts
– of wonder, revelation and hope –
come from, both big and small? From silence, of course.
Can it be any surprise, then, to discover
that this is where God also resides?"*

*"STS: This means one thing on the back-end of a Cadillac
and quite another at the forefront of your mind.
In the latter case, it means your 'spontaneous tears of sorrow'
as you witness all the needless pain and suffering
that is taking place in our world today."*

The Author

Mindfulness Meditation

*"We could say that meditation doesn't have a reason or doesn't
have a purpose. In this respect, it's
unlike almost all other things we do except perhaps making
music and dancing. When we make music, we don't do it in order
to reach a certain point, such as the end of the composition. If that were
the purpose of music, then obviously the fastest players would be the
best. Also when we are dancing, we are not aiming to
arrive at a particular place on the floor as in a
journey. When we dance, the journey itself is the point,
as when we play music the playing itself is the point.
And exactly the same is true in meditation.
Meditation is the discovery that the point of life
is always arrived at in the immediate moment."*

Alan Watts
(1915 – 1973)
American Writer, Thinker and Interpreter of Zen Buddhism
Author, *The Way of Zen*

Dealing with the "S-A-D Factor"

As discussed, a major problem in our modern society today is the S-A-D factor, namely stress, anxiety and depression, and how to deal with it. In fact, anxiety is recognized today as the number one health concern in the world as reported both by noted international organizations such as the World Health Organization (WHO) as well as by individual countries themselves. Experts estimate that up to one-third of the general population is affected – either short-, medium- or long-term – by a significant mental or emotional challenge of one kind or another during their life-time.

Unfortunately, a large number of us are getting "stressed out" on a regular, repeat basis. This is causing havoc in both family settings and our places of work, as well as placing huge demands on national and local healthcare workers (including pharmacists, psychologists, psychotherapists, psychiatrists, nurses, social workers and other mental health professionals) who have to deal with the situation on a daily basis. The cost to governments and companies in lost productivity alone is staggering, and amounts to tens of billions of dollars each year. All this at a time when many skilled workers and experienced managers of all kinds are in short supply due to the retirement of many who are part of the baby-boom generation. The oldest in this group, born between 1946 and 1964, are now approaching their mid-sixties.

Regarding the workplace and the incidence of depression, anxiety and use of alcohol by workers, a recent study reported in the May, 2009, issue of the *Journal of Occupational and Environmental Medicine* has come up with some interesting findings. Dr. Marjo Sinokki and her colleagues at the Finnish Institute of Occupational Health followed 3,347 employees aged between 30 and 64 for a period of three years. The goal was to rate the "atmosphere" in the workplace environment according to four primary descriptions: (1) encouraging and supportive of new ideas; (2) prejudiced and conservative; (3) nice and easy; or (4) quarrelsome and disagreeable.

In addition, employees were asked to note their feelings about team spirit, communications, the amount of pressure they were under, and how much control they had over their jobs. They were also asked about their social lives, where they lived, and what kind of health services they had access to. Their levels of depression, anxiety and use of alcohol were then compared to their taking prescription anti-depressant drugs.

The findings include the following: Those workers who felt team spirit in the workplace was poor were 61 percent more likely to have a depressive disorder. This group was also 55 percent more likely to be taking anti-depressant drugs. No direct link was found with alcohol abuse or anxiety. The authors summed up their study by saying, "A poor team climate at work is associated with depressive disorders and subsequent anti-depressant use."

Stress is Everywhere

Stressful elements of various kinds abound in our everyday lives – indeed, they are pervasive – and they include both *internal* and *external* stressors. Internal stressors are a result of negative emotional experiences we went through as a child or young adult, and have left either temporary, semi-permanent or permanent psychological scars. As a result, people may lack self-confidence, suffer from eating disorders, social anxiety, panic attacks or insomnia, or have difficulty developing/maintaining close and loving relationships.

External stressors originate in our environment and most are almost impossible to avoid. The information explosion is a prime example. Today, we are being impacted by as much information in a few weeks as the previous generation was in a full year. Through mass advertising, we are being told what to eat, how to dress, how to be attractive, what gadgets to buy, how to spend our leisure time … in short, how to live almost every aspect of our lives. Another is the common work environment and the ever-increasing demands being placed on employees at all levels, people who are already struggling to juggle a variety of personal and family-related responsibilities. Globalization, and the rapid rate of change and increased competition it represents in every aspect of our life, is only compounding the problem.

In this regard, it is important to understand that all stressors we encounter are in fact benign (e.g. neutral) in their original form. It is only when we assign a certain meaning to them (say on a scale from minus 50 through zero to plus 50) that they result in an emotional response of one kind or another. This is where our personal belief system plays a key role, as has been explained in PART 1. In other words, it is *not* the stressors themselves that cause problems; it is how we *interpret* them (e.g. our "cognitive" response to them), and this necessarily varies a great deal with each individual.

We know the mind and body are closely inter-connected, each affecting the other. The body is designed to detect and deal with stressors of all kinds as a defense mechanism, primarily to ensure our physical survival. When the mind encounters a stressor of some kind (e.g. one that says extreme danger is present), the body experiences an arousal response of a certain magnitude as a warning. For example, you could experience an adrenaline surge, enhanced sensual acuity and a rapidly increased heart-beat However, if such encounters occur too often and/or are of a major proportion (e.g. repeated traumatic experiences in a war zone), and are fully accepted and internalized, your health can be seriously affected in a variety of ways.

For example, your immune system can be impacted, making you more susceptible to other diseases; you can develop debilitating symptoms associated with post-traumatic stress disorder including fatigue, insomnia and depression; and finally, you may develop chronic medical conditions such as cardiovascular disease and muscle-tension headaches. People who suffer from excess stress are also more likely to turn to drugs and/or alcohol in an attempt to alleviate or escape from their predicament.

Suicide Levels

Regarding youth suicides in the U.S., the rate for 10- to 24-year-olds is on the increase after a steady decrease. The decline took place from 1990 to 2003 (from 9.48 to 6.78 per 100,000 people) and the increase took place from 2003 to 2004 (from 6.78 to 7.32), according to a report released on 6 September, 2007, by the Atlanta-based Centers for Disease Control and Prevention's (CDC) Morbidity and Mortality Weekly Report. In other words, after a decline of more than 28 percent over three years, the suicide rate increased 8 percent in a single year. The study then states that there were **4,599** suicides among young people in 2004.

"This is the biggest annual increase that we've seen in 15 years. We don't yet know if this is a short-lived increase or if it's the beginning of a trend," said Dr. Ileana Arias, director of CDC's National Center for Injury Prevention and Control. "Either way, it's a harsh reminder that suicide and suicide attempts are affecting too many youth and young adults. We need to make sure suicide prevention efforts are continuous and reaching children and young adults."

Regarding this same report, a CBS News article says, "The study also documented a change in suicide method. In 1990, guns accounted for more than half of all suicides among young females. By 2004, though, death by hanging and suffocation became the most common suicide method."

Suicide among teenagers is the third leading cause of death for this group in the U.S. – almost **2,000** teens kill themselves each year, says the National Youth Violence Prevention Resource Center (NYVPRC). Of course, many more *attempt* suicide, estimated to be 8 to 25 times the actual suicide rate.

Female teens are much more likely to attempt suicide than males but male teens are four times more likely to actually succeed in killing themselves.

A recent survey of high-school students found that:

- Almost **1** in **5** had seriously considered attempting suicide;

- More than **1** in **6** had made plans to attempt suicide; and

- More than **1** in **12** had made a suicide attempt in the past year.

In other words, if you look around a class of **25** students, at least **5** are likely to have seriously considered suicide, and at least **2** are likely to have tried to kill themselves in the past year.

The NYVPRC also says over 90 percent of teen suicide victims have a mental disorder such as depression and/or a history of substance abuse. Many of the mental illnesses, including depression, that contribute to suicide risk appear to have a genetic component. (Source: www.safeyouth. org/scripts/teens/suicide.asp)

Here are some specific facts and figures concerning the total population in the U.S. for 2001, a year for which a wide range of statistics is available: (Source: www.familyfirstaid.org/suicide)

- Suicide was the 11th leading cause of death overall in the U.S. It was the 8th leading cause of death for males and the 19th leading cause for females.

- The total number of suicide deaths was **30,622** or **84** a day.

- Suicides outnumbered homicides (**20,308**) by 3 to 2.

- There were twice as many deaths due to suicide than death due to HIV/AIDS (**14,175**).

To note, if we use the 2009 global population figure of **6.8** billion and extrapolate using the 2001 U.S. population of **277** million and suicide rate of **84** per day, we can estimate (using broad assumptions) that there very well might be about **752,630** suicides annually – or **2,062** per day – worldwide. In fact, the actual number is closer to **one million** suicides annually (or **2,739** per day), as a WHO study in 1998 actually found. This larger number is understandable when we realize that many countries in the world lack the advanced knowledge and expertise in medical and mental health care that exists in the U.S. Clearly, **one million** suicides per year on a global basis is a very startling number, yet very few in the general population are aware of it.

Statistics are also available from the National Center for Health Statistics (NCHS) and the American Foundation for Suicide Prevention (AFSP). The data from 2006 indicate that someone commits suicide in the U.S. every **16** minutes, and an attempt is made every minute. There are four male suicides for every female suicide, but three times as many females as males attempt suicide. According to the AFSP, more than 60 percent of all people who commit suicide suffer from depression, but it is also common for suicides to occur with no obvious warning signs at all.

Now consider the following from an article titled, *Active-Duty Soldier Suicides Hit New High* (Washington, 29 May, 2008) regarding the war the United States is waging on terror in Iraq and Afghanistan. Included are some direct quotes:

"A (U.S.) Army official said Thursday that **115** troops committed suicide in 2007, a nearly 13 percent increase over the previous year's **102**." This followed **85** deaths in 2005 and **67** in 2004. These numbers involved active duty soldiers and National Guard and Reserve troops that had been activated. About a quarter of the deaths occurred in Iraq.

"Earlier this year, Lt. General Michael Rochelle, the deputy chief of staff for personnel, directed a complete review of the Army's suicide prevention program, according to the Army's website. He called for a campaign that would make use of the best available science, and would raise awareness of the problem."

"Since the beginning of the global war on terror, the Army lost over **580** soldiers to suicide, an equivalent of an entire infantry battalion task force," the Army said in a suicide prevention guide to installations and units that was posted in mid-March on the site. "This ranks as the fourth leading manner of death for soldiers, exceeded only by hostile fire, accidents and illnesses." As startling is the fact that during this same period, 10 to 20 times as many soldiers have thought to harm themselves or attempted suicide.

The document concludes: "The true incidence of suicide among veterans is not known, according to a recent Congressional Research Service report. Based on numbers from the Centers for Disease Control and Prevention, the VA (Veterans Affairs) estimates that **18** veterans a day – **or 6,500 a year** – take their own lives, but that number includes vets from all wars." (Source: www.cbsnews.com)

Providing an update on 16 January, 2010, the (U.S.) Department of Defense reported that **160** active-duty army soldiers committed suicide in 2009, up from **140** in 2008, a new record high. It also noted that suicides among veterans and female soldiers have also been on the rise compared to previous years. The D.O.D. report concluded by noting that these suicide figures are the highest since the closing days of the war in Vietnam in the mid-1970s, more than three decades ago.

Things You Can Do

Thankfully, most of us are not in a war zone (at least not at the present moment!), although at certain times in our life we may think we are. If you have ever been stressed out and depressed, you know that it drains you of your energy, hope and desire, thus making it even more difficult to do the very things you need to do to begin feeling better. At the same time, while there is no simple formula or quick fix for overcoming depression, it is possible to make meaningful progress. *The key is to realize that you do have an element of control.* In other words, it is important to establish a base of activity e.g. begin doing several small things on a regular, daily basis and going from there.

Here are some options available to you:

1. *Eliminate us many stressors as possible.* Organize your finances carefully to avoid going into debt; this involves setting up and following a detailed budget comparing income and expenses. Don't go on a shopping spree as a way to feel better. Always take a day or two to think twice before committing to any major purchase. Organize the routine you follow at home and at work a little differently. Watch less (local, national and world) news and grisly crime programs on TV. Consider a change in career. Learn to

say "No!" (when and as necessary) to those who make frequent demands on your time and energy including your significant other, children and close relatives. Develop better interpersonal skills (e.g. active listening, empathizing and communicating) in order to avoid needless arguments and unnecessary confrontations.

2. *Find better ways to deal with the stress you cannot avoid.* Take time to relax and get sufficient sleep. Get organized by always having a definitive "to-do" list for important things to finish in the next 5, 10, 30 and 60 days. Set aside more time for yourself including indulging in an occasional sauna/ hot bath or arranging for a weekly massage. Spend more time with family and friends whose company you enjoy and appreciate. Begin an exercise program, even something as simple as "fast walking" for 30 to 45 minutes every day. Spend more time outdoors at some activity that gives you pleasure and changes your mind such as a visit to a beach, a bicycle ride or a weekend trip to the country-side. Become an expert concerning the many ideas and approaches described in this book, especially critical thinking, and practice them on a regular basis.

3. *Seek out community assistance.* Don't fall into the trap of thinking you have to do everything yourself. There is a myriad of offerings from community organizations, colleges, universities, and volunteer and mental health groups in your area to help you deal with stress and depression. Many have toll-free numbers and helpful websites with advice on this subject. (See Annex 9, *The Wellness Workbook.*) Consult your doctor and ask for a list of organizations to contact. Visit your local library or bookstore for books, research studies and articles on this subject. Sometimes a few simple ideas will get you started ... but it is up to you to take the initiative.

4. *Finally, practice regular, daily mindfulness meditation* which is the focus of this part of the text. There is more and more evidence each year that supports the many benefits of this activity. Mindfulness uses your inner resources for healing and is relatively easy to learn (to note, it does require a certain amount of patience and self-discipline). As a natural way to deal with troublesome thoughts and emotions, it is unique: It is available to you at any time, any place and for whatever period of time you want to make available. And you don't have to pay to do it by the hour. It's free!

A Definition

*"Mindfulness means paying attention in a particular way –
on purpose, in the present moment, and non-judgmentally."*

Jon Kabat-Zinn
Author, *Wherever You Go, There You Are*

Mindfulness meditation (also known as insight meditation) is a mental activity wherein we remember to pay *attention* in the present moment. This means a combination of three things: (a) being <u>present-centered</u>, namely directing our full attention in the present moment; (b) being <u>sensation-focused</u>, such as on our regular breathing; and (c) being <u>process-absorbed</u>, which involves sustained attention on the process that is chosen rather than on individual occurrences within that process.

Mindfulness meditation is not a ritual, a dogma or even a methodology. It is the "practice" (not meant in the usual sense of the word) that leads to an enhanced *sense of awareness*. In this practice, we learn to attend to the mind rather than follow it; we engage the mind instead of being engaged by it. The ultimate purpose of the initiatory life is to become one with our essence, to deeply reside in Being, and allow that depth of existence to impact and inspire our whole life.

The Initiatory Life and Transcendence

When we embark on the path of mindfulness meditation, we are living the "initiatory" life, one that involves taking proactive steps towards better understanding and solving life's many mysteries. Life's biggest mystery, some would say, is who we are, our "essence," our innate or inborn nature that is unimaginable, indescribable and ungraspable. Therefore, in a real sense, through mindfulness meditation we are moving towards a better understanding of our true identity at the deepest level.

Exercises in mindfulness meditation are exercises in *transcendence*, of moving beyond the chaos and (some would say) insanity of our everyday world to a new and different level of awareness. Note that transcendence is <u>not</u> something that is in another place or another time, and we have to go out and find it. *It is where we are right now!* It recognizes the existence of an energy, power, intelligence or force that is beyond our ability to fully contemplate and understand, yet it is readily accessible at any time in the present moment.

Transcendence is not an abstract concept. It is a very direct and real *experience,* a liberating force that is accessible through various structured mental and (sometimes) physical exercises (e.g. yoga). This experience is characterized both by its effects (e.g. how certain parts of the brain are activated) as well as by its revelatory nature, meaning what we learn or come to understand from it.

People seek out transcendence for any number of reasons, often for a calmer, more meaningful life and a more focused, perceptive mind. Although there is nothing more natural than our true nature, we tend to function as humans in a way that focuses most of our energies on physiological, security, social, and self-esteem needs and wants. By doing this, we are always getting in the way of being able to experience transcendence as a liberating force and discovering our true nature. Thankfully, this tendency is beginning to change as the current surge in interest in spirituality clearly shows.

When we are able to function at this, the deepest level, we are no longer preoccupied with ego-centered concerns that include physical survival, personal competence or social acceptance (e.g. "Gee, I hope everybody likes me!"). We will know peace, love and joy unconditionally and naturally. Transcendence leads to enlightenment, and with enlightenment comes understanding and uncommon happiness in all aspects of our life.

"Transcendentalism" has evolved as a respected philosophy that places an emphasis on the importance of the spiritual inner self over the materialistic outer world. The teachings of Immanuel Kant, Georg Wilhelm Friedrich Hegel and Johann Gottlieb Fichte are prime examples of transcendentalism. In its most simple terms, it could be said this involves a search for reality and truth through "wakeful awareness," an approach popularized in the late 19th century by New England-based authors Ralph Waldo Emerson, Henry David Thoreau and Walt Whitman in their numerous musings, writings and lectures.

Of course, "mindfulness" is something we can participate in at any time and at any moment in our wakeful state, not just during formal practice once or twice a day. We could also incorporate it into simple, everyday activities including eating, walking, bathing, listening, observing, tasting, touching, smelling or even brushing our teeth … any number of informal undertakings such as these. This way, we experience life and its everyday happenings at a deeper level, and are able to relate and respond to them at a higher level.

Regarding eating, a study in the *Journal of the American Dietetic Association* (July, 2008) shows that "mindful eating" can help you eat less and enjoy your meals more. The process involves eating slowly, chewing the food well, and putting your knife and fork (or food item like a sandwich, sub or pizza slice) down between each bite. You may want to consider this approach, along with keeping a daily food journal, as part of your own weight management program.

Breathing

Breathing as a natural activity is often at the very center of mindfulness meditation. Of course, breathing is a necessary bodily function to exchange carbon dioxide for oxygen to ensure our physical survival but it can also serve a much broader purpose. Through it, we can experience ourselves as living, fully-functioning human beings, opening then closing, presenting then surrendering ourselves to the universe. In mindfulness meditation, breathing is a way to measure how close we are to our true nature, our universal Oneness.

There are good reasons why breathing can play this role. Breath is life. It is what connects all the events in our life from birth to death. Breathing is something we always do and it always takes place in the present; hence identifying with it allows separation between the present moment and past-future preoccupations. It is constant, predictable and life-giving; as well, it is easily observable as an object of our attention. Breathing is not an active "seeking out" activity that requires effort and concentration; rather it is passive and involuntary, a sort of surrendering. In this sense, focusing on our breathing involves a disengagement from the active "doing" mode of mind to engagement with the more passive "Being" mode of existence.

The Kabir Book

The following is from *One Hundred Poems of Kabir* (1961), translated by Rabindranath Tagore. The author, Kabir (1440 – 1518), was an influential Indian poet, mystic and spiritual philosopher.

"He is the real Sadhu, who can reveal the form of the Formless to the vision of these eyes:

Who teaches the simple way of attaining Him, that is other than rites or ceremonies:

Who does not make you close the doors, and hold the breath, and renounce the world:

Who makes you perceive the Supreme Spirit wherever the mind attaches itself:

Who teaches you to be still in the midst of all your activities.

Ever immersed in bliss, having no fear in his mind, he keeps the spirit of union in the midst of all enjoyments.

The infinite dwelling of the Infinite Being is everywhere: in earth, water, sky, and air:

Firm as the thunderbolt, the seat of the seeker is established above the void.

He who is within is without: I see Him and none else."

How to Meditate: Seven Simple Steps

You can teach yourself how to meditate in a matter of minutes using the following seven simple steps:

- Find a quiet place where you will not be disturbed.

- Sit upright in a comfortable chair with both feet on the floor.

- Set your time-clock to 15, 20 or 30 minutes, depending on the time you want to make available.

- Close your eyes (to avoid any visual stimulation) and become an innocent observer to what is going on in your mind.

- Begin taking deep, controlled in-breaths and deep, controlled out-breaths.

- Pick a simple word or phrase such as "only love" (or an image or symbol such as a cross) that is particularly comforting/soothing to you.

- Repeat the word or phase (or visualize the image) you have chosen over and over again with every out-breath. The monotony will help calm you down and assist you in entering a state of no-mind.

Practice only *deep, controlled breathing* for this exercise. In other words, observe your in-breath from start to finish. Be aware of the air entering your nostrils, traveling along your airway, filling your lungs and finally inflating your abdomen. Now the out-breath. Be aware of the air leaving your lungs, moving back up the airway, traveling out your nostrils, all the while deflating your abdomen. In time, breathing this way while meditating will become automatic.

Mindfulness meditation creates a <u>relaxation response</u> throughout your body, the exact opposite of an <u>arousal response</u>. During mindfulness, observe your thoughts without either suppressing them or judging them. Act like an innocent, detached observer of what is impacting/engaging your mind. For each thought, simply observe its contents and how it makes you feel, that's all.

The result? Over time, you will become more aware of how you react to any given stressor; you will have greater insight regarding the range of stressors your mind is dealing with; and you will have developed a new and better way of responding to such stressors in general and accepting them as a normal part of your life. Stressors by themselves need not be debilitating.

Suggested Exercises

1. Here is a meditation exercise I find relaxing and invigorating.

Again, choose a quiet setting where you won't be disturbed. Then, while sitting in a comfortable chair or lying down, close your eyes and begin to focus on your breathing. As you do this, take a few deep breaths and be aware of the sensation that this creates in your nostrils, your abdominal and chest muscles, your shoulders, your neck, your arms and legs, your wrists and ankles, your hands and feet, your fingers and toes, as well as your mind.

Now focus only on your breathing ... no thoughts, no thoughts. Just breathe in slowly ... hold that breath ... then breathe out slowly. As you continue to do this, inhale very slowly ... imagine this as God (or Divine energy, "consciousness" or whatever term you are most comfortable with) sending his love and his joy into your very essence ... now hold it, hold it ... imagine this phase as God hugging, caressing and comforting you ... now begin to

---

exhale very slowly … and imagine this as you sending God's love and his blessings back out to every thing and every one in the universe. Repeat this activity (bring in his love, hold it, hold it … feel its warmth and comfort, then send it back out to the universe) for 20 or 30 minutes, or for as long as you like.

2. Consider the following as a way to come into contact with your inner consciousness, and the power and wonder of universal mind:

Find a quiet place. Close your eyes. Slowly count from one to 10 (*one* … pause … *two* … pause … *three* … pause …) while taking deep breaths, and enter a state of deeper and deeper relaxation. Be aware you are concentrating only on what is going on in your mind. Sense the complete solitude as the physical world begins to retreat from around you and you enter the silent recesses of your inner world.

At last, you are alone. To begin, just let your mind go wherever it wants. Do not try to direct it in any way. If a certain thought enters your consciousness and lets its presence be known to you, simply let it go.

This initial phase can be quite discomforting, even turbulent at times as certain thoughts may try to attach themselves to you, cling to you, fearing to move on to a place they don't know or understand. The experience is not unlike moving through dark, heavy clouds while taking off in an airplane: You hit some rough spots, the plane bounces around a bit, then you finally break out into clear, blue sky. Wow! Clear sailing at last.

I liken meditation (a simple, yet powerful mind-management tool) to your home computer deciding to reboot to reconfigure itself (e.g. reformat its hard-drive). It wants to reorganize and reposition certain memories that are permanently etched in its retrieval system so it can function more efficiently and effectively.

As things continue to unfold, you will see that you are looking out over a vast universe of infinite proportions, a sort of cosmic wonderland whose tranquility is interrupted periodically by streaking comets, which are simply thoughts coming out of nowhere and heading off in various directions. You notice this and marvel at it all, but you just let them pass by. Let none directly enter your consciousness. By focusing on the splendor of what is happening before your very eyes, you become aware how you are able to rise above the noise, clutter and meaningless drudgery of the thoughts and happenings of your everyday life. You need not be preoccupied or consumed by any particular thought. You can choose to be a neutral observer watching everything quietly unfold from a distance, and picking and choosing at will what thoughts you want to consider and what others to simply let pass by.

Divorced from body, all thought and past remembrances, you exist as pure spirit. Here then is your true Self, free from the effects of all physical sounds and sensations. You know whatever you choose, you can have and whatever you reject, will never touch you. In this place, you need only be still, innocently observe and patiently "allow" what is … to be. You are a detached witness of simple "no-thing-ness" existing in a state of no-form.

Ever so quietly and without any prompting on your part, insights and understandings will begin to reveal themselves to you as eternal knowings and simple truths. They do not appear as either foreign or unfamiliar but as friendly and inviting. They come as angels would come to share wisdom that you once knew but have (for a variety of reasons) forgotten about. Just let this process continue to unfold … unfold … unfold.

The experience is like playing an animated computer game, and you control all the activity and initiate all the action. You say to yourself, "Boy, this is a lot of fun!" And it truly is. But you know for sure there is one thing you cannot do – you cannot turn the machine off completely. This "game," after all, does have a mind of its own!

Group-Based Cognitive Therapy

"Remember that our true Self or true nature is not something that is false or fabricated or phony or fluctuating. It is constant, pure, natural and authentic. It is incorrupt and permanent. It is real.
It is also something we dearly love and want to know more about;
in fact, we want to become intimate with it … to become one with it.
Why? Because we know when we are real, we are home;
and when we are home, we are at peace."

The Author

A new study reported on 1 December, 2008, found that group-based psychological treatment – known as Mindfulness Based Cognitive Therapy (MBCT) – is equally effective (e.g. compared to CBT used alone) as anti-depressant drugs for people suffering from depression. The research team was made up of psychologists from Oxford, Cambridge and Toronto, and was led by Professor Willem Kuyken of the University of Exeter. The team conducted a randomized control trial involving over 123 people from both urban and rural areas who had suffered repeated episodes of depression. Participants were referred to the study by their GPs.

Split randomly into two groups, one group continued with their drug treatment and the other participated in an MBCT course, with the option of coming off anti-depressants if they wanted. Over a 15-month period, the researchers found that only 47 percent of the MBCT group experienced a relapse while 60 percent of the anti-depressant group did the same. Those taking the MBCT program also reported another plus: A higher quality of life in terms of their overall enjoyment of daily living and physical well-being.

The researchers compared the cost of providing MBCT programs with the cost of long-term anti-depressant therapy. They believe the former approach is more cost effective because MBCT can be taught in large groups by a single therapist, and patients then continue to practice the skills they have learned at home by themselves. "But while they (anti-depressants) are very effective in helping reduce the symptoms of depression, when people come off them they are particularly vulnerable to relapse," Professor Kuyken commented. He concluded by saying, "MBCT takes a different approach – it teaches people skills for life. What we have shown is that when people work at it, these skills for life help keep people well." (Source: *Journal of Consulting and Clinical Psychology*)

Meditation Retreats

"Awakening is not a single event in time;
it is a river endlessly flowing in this moment now."

Arjuna Ardagh
Author, Speaker and Founder of the *Living Essence Foundation*

The cover of *Time* magazine dated 4 August, 2003, features Hollywood actress Heather Graham performing transcendental meditation. The accompanying article by writer Joel Stein notes the virtual explosion in the number of people in America and elsewhere – most just normal people with jobs and families – who are taking up meditation as a daily exercise, typically 20 minutes twice a day. It highlights the London Buddhist Center, England; Shambhalla Mountain Center, Red Feather Lakes, Colorado; Maharishi University, Fairfield, Iowa; Seoul International Zen Center, South Korea; Insight Meditation Society, Barre, Massachusetts; Spirit Rock Center, Woodacre, California; Marpa Gompa Meditation Society, Calgary, Alberta; and several Catskills hotels and centers in upper New York state as examples of the increasing popularity of this activity, saying that in the New York instance, the Borscht Belt is now better known as the Buddhist Belt.

Stein points out in his article that many meditators are also famous celebrities, listing regular practitioners such as Goldie Hawn, Shania Twain, Richard Gere, Al Gore, as well as Heather Graham. (Graham starred in the TV series, *Twin Peaks* in the early 1990s as well as several movies including *Austin Powers: The Spy Who Shagged Me* in 1999. In 2001, she was voted by *People* as one of the "50 Most Beautiful People in the World.")

Stein goes on. "Meditation is being recommended by more and more physicians as a way to prevent, slow or at least control the pain of chronic diseases like heart conditions, AIDS, cancer and infertility. It is also being used to restore balance in the face of such psychiatric disturbances as depression, hyperactivity and attention-deficit disorder (ADD)." He then cites Daniel Goleman, author of *Destructive Emotions*, as saying, "For 30 years, medical research has told us that it works beautifully as an antidote to stress. But what's exciting about the new research is how meditation can train the mind and reshape the brain."

This fact has been borne out in studies using brain imaging techniques. For example, the brains of several Tibetan Buddhist monks were studied in 2004 while practicing "compassion" meditation which involved generating a feeling of loving kindness towards all things. The monks who were chosen had spent more than 10,000 hours practicing meditation. The result? During meditation, activity in the *left* prefrontal cortex (the seat of positive emotions such as happiness and joy) was found to have much greater activity than in the *right* prefrontal cortex (site of negative emotions and anxiety), something never before seen from purely mental activity. (Source: *The Wall Street Journal Online,* 5 November, 2004.) This is clearly evident in the brain scan shown below. In other studies as well, the physical size of this part of the brain of seasoned meditators actually grew larger compared to novice meditators or non-practitioners.

Hmmm. Thoughts. Our simple, everyday thoughts can actually alter the size, structure and activity levels in certain parts of our brain.

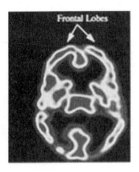

A brain scan of a person in deep meditation. (Source: Wikipedia)

Noble Silence

*"When you live and sense the love that is in all things,
you are never alone. You are in the company of the Sacred."*

The Author

Retreats around the world offer a unique program that involves going into silence for periods of one to 40 days. The kind discussed here (although part of the Buddhist tradition, it has universal application) is called "noble" silence, meaning silence with *full awareness.*

It is almost impossible today to find silence anywhere in the usual places: Our homes, our backyards, the local park, the beach or the community library. They have been invaded by cell-phones, Blackberries, iPods, skate boards, TV, loud conversations, laptops, screaming kids, booming radios, and noisy cars, trucks and motorcycles. All are examples of external stimulation run amuck.

Although many retreats are held in beautiful, often isolated locations, their primary aim is to calm the mind, settle one's thoughts, establish some sort of balance or equilibrium in one's mind, and perhaps offer a different perspective on life.

There are strict rules of conduct at all such retreats, although the list of "do's" and "don'ts" can vary widely. The "don'ts" often include no cell-phones, radios, TV, Internet, newspapers, books, magazines, cigarettes, coffee, alcohol, as well as no eye or physical contact or conversation of any kind. To go and experience noble silence is definitely not a vacation and should not be considered as such. Rather, think of it as an experiential learning exercise in "consciousness-awareness."

Participants have described their experience in different ways. Comments include: "You become more intimate with your mind and your self;" "You get to experience another way to be;" "You come to realize that life is also about being, not only doing;" "You come to see why your normal state of mind is so messed up;" "You lose all sense of immediacy, and come to value and appreciate intimacy and relevancy a lot more."

Some claim that benefits also include positive changes in physical and mental health; others report a greater sense of inner strength and well-being, as well as a better appreciation of the meaning of life. Considerable research over many years indicates that longevity may also be a by-product of meditation and quiet contemplation.

You may want to investigate retreats of this kind if benefits such as these, although primarily anecdotal, are of interest to you. You can find a list of those located in your local area (or indeed, anywhere in the world) by searching for "spiritual retreat" (or some similar term) on your computer.

PART 4

Timeless Quotations that Inform and Inspire

"'Who am I?'
The physical world in which you find yourself
is totally incapable of answering this question.
Oh my goodness, what to do?"

"The key to a joyous and prosperous life is this:
Find out who you are, then live according
to what you have found out."

"You cannot hope to do great things until
you know you have greatness within you."

The Author

Timeless Quotations that Inform and Inspire

"Only the truth of who you are will set you free."

The following quotations represent yet another way of saying many of the same things that have been discussed in this book. They only go to show how confused humankind has been over many, many years – indeed, throughout the course of human history – and how certain people have tried to make some sense out of all this confusion, sometimes in a very serious way and other times in quite a humorous way.

They represent a small yet noble effort in response to that timeless human quest to better understand the seemingly unknowable, namely the Self – "Who am I? Why am I here? Why do I think, feel and act the way I do? Why do I have so much pain and suffering in my life? Why am I often so hostile and intolerant towards others? Why do I do my part to pollute and destroy the very Earth that gives me all my sustenance? Why … why … why? There has got to be a better way, and I need to find that way!"

"When you cease trying
to control and manipulate your experience,
meditation spontaneously happens."

Adyashanti
American Teacher and Practitioner of Zen Buddhism

"You are not a thing. You are not a body-thing
or a mental-thing or an emotional-thing or a thing
with a history in time. You are no-thing.
You are consciousness itself. Let go of your attachment to
thing-ness, and you will awaken to that which is
the Source of all things. Go directly to that Source.
Don't waste your life-time defining yourself as a thing.
Wake up from that dream and you are free."

Adyashanti

*"At the moment of enlightenment, everything falls away –
everything. Suddenly the ground beneath you is gone,
and you are alone. You are alone because
you have realized that there is no other;
there is only THAT, and YOU ARE THAT."*

Adyashanti

"Outside show is a poor substitute for inner worth."

Aesop
(620 – 560 B.C.E.)
Greek Fable Writer

---

*"Thinking means life, since those who do not think do
not live in any high or real sense. Thinking makes the man."*

A.B. Alcott
(1799 – 1888)
American Philosopher and Educational Reformer

---

*"All truth exists within man and never in the world about him.
He who studies the world studies effects.
He who studies his own mind studies
the cause and source of things as they really are."*

U.S. Andersen
(1917 – 1986)
Author, *Three Magic Words*

---

*"A psychological transformation is not possible
without a spiritual awakening, and before a man can change
his kind of thinking, it first is necessary that he alters
his conception of self."*

U.S. Andersen

"I am Light itself, reflected in the heart of everyone;
I am the treasure of the Divine Name, the shining Essence of all things.
I am every light that shines, every ray that illumines the world.
From the highest heavens to the bedrock of the earth,
all is but a shadow of my splendor."

Fakhruddin Araqi
(1213 – 1289)
Sufi Mystic and Poet
From *Two Rising Suns*

"We are here on Earth to do good for others.
What the others are here for, I don't know."

Wysten Hugh Auden
(1907 – 1973)
English Poet

"Some men covet knowledge
out of a natural curiosity and inquisitive temper;
some to entertain the mind with variety and delight;
some for ornament and reputation; some for victory and contention;
many for lucre and livelihood; and but few for employing
the Divine gift of reason to the use and gift of mankind."

Francis Bacon
(1561 – 1626)
English Philosopher, Essayist and Statesman

"To see a world in a grain of sand and heaven in a wild flower,
to hold infinity in the palm of your hand, and eternity in an hour."

William Blake
(1757 – 1827)
English Poet and Engraver

*"... I used to pray that God would give me something –
strength, wisdom, patience, the solution to a problem.
I was forever telling God what was wrong with my life
and what God needed to do to fix it.
Today, I talk things over with God to decide what I can do,
not what God should do. This is the key to spiritual power,
to finding God in so many wonderful places
both ordinary and extraordinary."*

Father Leo Booth
Author and Unity Minister

---

*"When was the last time you embraced a situation that you didn't like?
Did you complain through the entire experience or did you run away
from the situation altogether? If you did either, you missed a wonderful
opportunity to be something that you've never been before.
It just might have been that one thing that you had been wishing for."*

Les Brown
Author, *Live Your Dreams*

---

*"If we could see the miracle of a single
flower clearly, our whole life would change."*

The Buddha
(563 – 483 B.C.E.)
Spiritual Master

---

*"Believe nothing, no matter where you read it
or who said it – even if I have said it – unless it agrees
with your own reason and your own common sense."*

The Buddha

"In separateness lies the world's great misery;
in compassion lies the world's true strength."

The Buddha

"The secret of health for both mind and body
is not to mourn for the past, not to worry about the future,
not to anticipate troubles,
but to live the present moment wisely and earnestly."

The Buddha

"I tried to change my life once.
It didn't work so I gave up."

Archie Bunker
From the TV Sit-Com *All in the Family*

"Too often we underestimate the power of a touch,
a smile, a kind word, a listening ear,
an honest compliment, or the smallest act of caring,
all of which have the potential to turn a life around."

Leo Buscaglia
(1924 – 1998)
Author, *Living, Loving & Learning*

"How far you go in life depends on your being tender
with the young, compassionate with the aged,
sympathetic with the striving, and tolerant of the weak and the strong.
Because someday in life you will have been all of these."

George Washington Carver
(1864 – 1943)
American Botanist and Chemist

"The mind, in proportion as it is cut off from free communication with nature, with revelation, with God, with itself, loses its life, just as the body droops when debarred from the air and the cheering light from heaven."

William Channing
(1780 – 1842)
American Clergyman, Author and Philanthropist

"When we find ourselves looking at the world and saying, 'There's nothing out there for me,' we should probably also look into our hearts and ask, 'If there's nothing out there, is there anything in here?' We need to examine our inner dialogue to discover where we might be blocking the conscious energy flow, then remove the ego, step out of the way, and let the fire of the soul shine through us."

Deepak Chopra
Author, *Unconditional Life*

"Personally, I'm always ready to learn although I do not always like being taught."

Winston Churchill
(1874 – 1965)
Former Prime Minister of England

"The source and center of all man's creative power is his power of making images, or the power of imagination."

Robert Collier
(1885 – 1950)
American Author, *The Secret of the Ages*

"The superior man thinks always of virtue;
the common man thinks only of comfort."

Confucius
(557 – 479 B.C.E.)
Chinese Philosopher and Teacher

"The highest possible stage in moral culture is when
we recognize that we ought to control our thoughts."

Charles Darwin
(1809 – 1882)
English Naturalist

"If you would be a real seeker after truth, it is necessary
at least once in your life to doubt as far as possible all things."

René Descartes
(1596 – 1650)
French Philosopher and Mathematician

"Love all God's creation, both the whole and every grain of sand.
Love every leaf, every ray of light. Love the animals, love the plants,
love each separate thing. If you love each thing, you will perceive
the mystery of God in all; and when once you perceive this,
you will, from that time on, grow every day to a fuller understanding of it
until you come at last to love the whole world with a love
that will then be all-embracing and universal."

Fyodor Dostoyevsky
(1821 – 1881)
Russian Novelist

"It doesn't interest me what you do for a living.
I want to know what you ache for, and if you dare
to dream of meeting your heart's longing.
It doesn't interest me how old you are.
I want to know if you will risk looking like a fool for love,
for your dream, for the adventure of being alive ...."

Oriah Mountain Dreamer
Author, *The Invitation*

"The focus on outward contribution is
the hallmark of the effective human being."

Peter Drucker
(1909 – 2005)
Writer and Father of Modern Management Practices

"There is a divine whisper within you telling you
that this is not your ultimate home and that the things
this life offers are unfulfilling to a part of you.
You sense that the real you does not value appearance,
possessions, achievements, physical strength, talent, or intellect
because all these things eventually atrophy and disappear.
You know that there is an eternal aspect of you beneath the surface
and that for this part of you, only the truth will suffice."

Dr. Wayne W. Dyer
Author, *Your Sacred Self*

Timeless Quotations that Inform and Inspire

*"We can make conscious contact with God,
transcend the limitations of a dichotomous world,
and regain the power that is only available to us when
we're connected to the Source. This is what I call getting in the gap.
It's where we create, manifest, heal, live, and perform
at a miraculous level. The gap is the powerful silence
we can access through meditation."*

Dr. Wayne W. Dyer
Author, *Getting in the Gap*

---

*"Authentic empowerment is the knowing within that you are on purpose,
doing God's work, peacefully and harmoniously. It is knowing that you
can create whatever you need to further that work,
without resorting to manipulating or harming another.
It is a new way of being, and
it can show up in thousands of tiny ways."*

Dr. Wayne W. Dyer

---

*"To find truth, you must experience it in your soul.
You can read hundreds of books or study the religions of all
time, only to find that all of them have one common point,
one common denominator: and this is love – which is another
word for light or soul illumination.
To realize this soul illumination, you have to shut away
the clamor of the lower mind, to become humble, very simple."*

White Eagle
Author, *Beautiful Road Home*

"The Sanskrit word 'ahimsa'
does not contain a negative or passive connotation
as does the English translation 'non-violence.'
The implication of 'ahimsa' is that when all violence
subsides in the human heart, the state which remains is love.
It is not something that we have to acquire;
it is always present, and needs only to be uncovered.
This is our real nature, not merely to love one person here,
another there, but to be love itself ... love in action."

Eknath Easwaran
(1910 – 1999)
Author, *Gandhi, the Man: The Story of His Transformation*

"You need not look for God either here or there.
He is no farther away than the door of your heart:
there He stands waiting till He finds you ready
to open the door and let Him enter ...
There is only one thing you must do: open and enter."

Meister Eckhart
(1260 – 1328)
Author, *Two Suns Rising: A Collection of Sacred Writings*

"The most beautiful thing we can experience is the mysterious.
It is the source of all true art and science. He to whom the emotion
is a stranger, who can no longer pause and stand
wrapped in awe, is as good as dead; his eyes are closed."

Albert Einstein
(1879 – 1955)
German-born Physicist

"A human being is part of the whole,
called by us 'Universe,' a part limited in time and space.
He experiences himself, his thoughts, and feelings as
something separated from the rest – a kind of optical delusion
of his consciousness. This delusion is a kind of prison for us,
restricting us to our personal desires and to affection
for a few persons nearest to us. Our task must be to free ourselves
from this prison by widening our circle of compassion to
embrace all living creatures and the whole [of] nature in its beauty."

Albert Einstein

"I am enough of an artist to draw freely upon my imagination.
Imagination is more important than knowledge.
Knowledge is limited. Imagination encircles the world."

Albert Einstein

"My religion consists of a humble admiration of the
illimitable superior spirit who reveals Himself in the slight details
we are able to perceive with our frail and feeble mind."

Albert Einstein

"We shall not cease from exploration,
and the end of all our exploring will be to arrive
where we started and know the place for the first time."

T.S. Eliot
(1888 – 1965)
American-English Poet, Playwright and Literary Critic

"There's no vocabulary for love within a family,
love that's lived in but not looked at, love within the light
of which all else is seen, the love within which all other love
finds speech. This love is silent."

T.S. Eliot

"It's but little good you'll do a-watering the last year's crops."

Mary Anne Evans
(1819 – 1880)
English Novelist

"The currents of the Universal Being circulate through me;
I am part and parcel of God."

Ralph Waldo Emerson
(1803 – 1882)
American Essayist, Poet and Philosopher

"It is one of the most beautiful compensations
of this life that no man can sincerely try
to help another without helping himself."

Ralph Waldo Emerson

"Here is a mental treatment guaranteed
to cure every ill that flesh is heir to:
sit for half an hour every night and mentally forgive everyone
against whom you have any ill will or antipathy."

Charles Fillmore
(1854 – 1948)
Co-Founder of Unity School of Christianity

Timeless Quotations that Inform and Inspire

"Lord, make me an instrument of your peace.
Where there is hatred, let me sow love;
where there is injury, pardon; where there is doubt, faith;
where there is despair, hope; where there is darkness, light;
and where there is sadness, joy."

Saint Francis of Assisi
(1182 – 1226)

"There is a law of sowing and reaping.
But it lies on the world not like a judgment but a promise.
It is the law of creativity. And it says, sow and
you shall reap. But you shall sow what is yours to sow,
that you may reap what is life's to give. For the seed
is in your hand, but the harvest is in life's hand.
Sow a thought, and reap a revelation.
Sow a hope, and reap a miracle.
Sow a dream, and reap a new life
for yourself and perhaps for all the world."

James Dillet Freeman
(1912 – 2003)
Author, Poet and Unity Minister

"Each of us sends out positive or negative vibrations,
often without being conscious that we are doing so.
What if we made an effort to be consciously positive,
to resonate messages of the highest good for others and ourselves?
What if we made a deliberate attempt
to keep our thoughts aligned with God's spiritual optimism,
to refuse to be stuck in self-centered fear?
Our thoughts speak louder than our words.
In order to change what we create,
we must change our thinking. We must mind our mind."

Albert Clayton Gaulden
Author, *You're Not Who You Think You Are*

*"You have no idea what a poor opinion I have
of myself and how little I deserve it!"*

W.S. Gilbert
(1836 – 1911)
English Poet and Humorist

---

*"The greatest explorer on this Earth never takes voyages as
long as those of the man who descends to the depth of his heart."*

Julien Hartridge Green
(1900 – 1998)
French-American Novelist and Playwright

---

*"The longest journey is the journey inward, for he who has chosen
his destiny has started upon his quest for the source of his being."*

Dag Hammarskjold
(1905 – 1961)
Former Secretary General of the United Nations

---

*"In the infinity of life where I am, all is perfect, whole, and complete.
I believe in a power far greater than I am
that flows through me every moment of every day.
I open myself to the wisdom within,
knowing that there is only One Intelligence in this Universe.
Out of this One Intelligence comes all the answers,
all the solutions, all the healings, all the new creations.
I trust this Power and Intelligence, knowing that whatever
I need to know is revealed to me, and that whatever
I need comes to me in the right time, space, and sequence.
All is well in my world."*

Louise L. Hay
Author, *You Can Heal Your Life*

*"Remember that your real wealth can be measured
not by what you have but by what you are."*

Napoleon Hill
(1879 – 1950)
Author, *Think and Grow Rich*

---

*"What lies behind us and what lies before us
are tiny matters compared to what lies within us."*

Oliver Wendell Holmes
(1809 – 1894)
American Writer and Physician

---

*"Man's mind, stretched to a new idea, never
goes back to its original dimension."*

Oliver Wendell Holmes

---

*"We do our best to disprove the fact, but a fact it remains:
man is as divine as nature, as infinite as the void."*

Aldous Huxley
(1894 – 1963)
English Novelist, Poet and Essayist

---

*"I have often thought that the best way to define
a man's character would be to seek out the particular
mental and moral attitude in which, when it came upon him,
he felt himself most deeply and intensely alive.
At such moments, there is a voice inside which speaks and says,
'This is the real me!'"*

William James
(1842 – 1910)
American Psychologist and Philosopher

---

*"The greatest use of life is to spend it
for something that will outlast it."*

William James

---

*"Your vision will become clear only
when you can look into your own heart.
Who looks outside, dreams; who looks inside, awakes."*

Carl Jung
(1875 – 1961)
Swiss Psychologist

---

*"The dream is the small hidden door
in the deepest and most intimate sanctum of the soul,
which opens to that primeval cosmic light that was soul
long before there was conscious ego and will be soul
far beyond what a conscious ego could ever reach."*

Carl Jung

---

*"Perhaps 'spiritual' means simply experiencing
wholeness and interconnectedness directly, a seeing that
individuality and totality are interwoven,
that nothing is separate or extraneous,
and that everything is spiritual in the deepest sense,
as long as we are there for it."*

Jon Kabat-Zinn
Author, *Wherever You Go, There You Are:
Mindfulness Meditation in Everyday Life*

Timeless Quotations that Inform and Inspire

"Forgiveness is not an occasional act;
it is a permanent attitude."

Martin Luther King, Jr.
(1929 – 1968)
U.S. Civil Rights Leader

"We must work passionately and indefatigably to bridge the gulf
between our scientific progress and our moral progress.
One of the great problems of mankind is that we suffer
from a poverty of the spirit which stands in glaring contrast
to our scientific and technological abundance.
The richer we have become materially,
the poorer we have become morally and spiritually."

Martin Luther King, Jr.

"People are like stained-glass windows.
They sparkle and shine when the sun is out,
but when the darkness sets in, their true beauty
is revealed only if there is a light from within."

Elizabeth Kubler-Ross, M.D.
(1926 – 2004)
Author, *On Death and Dying*

"To be aware of a single shortcoming in oneself
is more useful than to be aware
of a thousand in someone else."

The Dalai Lama
Spiritual Leader of Tibet

---

*"These two things, the spiritual and the material,
though we call them by different names,
in their origin are one and the same."*

Lao-tzu
(604 – 531 B.C.E.)
Chinese Philosopher, Moralist and
Founder of Taoism

---

*"By the accident of fortune a man may rule
the world for a time,
but by virtue of love and kindness
he may rule the world forever."*

Lao-tzu

---

*"When we realize that the strength of the Infinite
is our strength and that the strength of the Infinite is limitless,
we must come to the conclusion that we are capable
of doing anything that the living of a great life may demand."*

Christian D. Larson
Author, *Pathway of Roses*

---

*"To know God is the beginning of wisdom, because God is
the source of wisdom. The nearer we live to the source,
the more we receive of that which comes from the source.
The mind that is not consciously living with God may have intellect
and mental capacity, but the wisdom that knows can come only to that mind
that is walking with God every moment of conscious existence.
The mind that does not know God thinks in the darkness;
the mind that does know God thinks in the light."*

Christian D. Larson

"It may be hard for an egg to turn into a bird;
it would be a jolly sight harder for it to learn
to fly while remaining an egg. We are like eggs at present.
And you cannot go on indefinitely being just
an ordinary, decent egg.
We must be hatched or go bad."

C.S. Lewis
(1898 – 1963)
Author, *Mere Christianity*

"Once, having been asked by the Pharisees
when the kingdom of God would come,
Jesus replied, 'The kingdom of God does not come
with your careful observation, nor will people say,
'Here it is' or 'There it is,'
because the kingdom of God is within you.'"

Luke 17:20-21

"Self is only Being – not being this or that.
It is Simple Being.
BE, and there is the end of ignorance."

Ramana Maharshi
(1879 – 1950)
Advaita Master

"The Self alone exists, and the Self alone is real.
Verily, the Self alone is the world, the 'I' and God.
All that exists is but the manifestation
of the Supreme Being."

Ramana Maharshi

"Distracted as we are by various thoughts,
if we would continually contemplate the Self,
which is Itself God, this single thought
would in due course replace all distraction
and would itself ultimately vanish.
The pure Consciousness that alone finally remains is God.
This is Liberation. To be constantly centered on one's own
all-perfect pure Self is the acme of yoga,
wisdom, and all other forms of spiritual practice.
Even though the mind wanders restlessly,
involved in external matters,
and is so forgetful of its own Self,
one should remain alert and remember:
'The body is not I.'"

Ramana Maharshi

"For the rest of my life, there are two days
that will never again trouble me. The first day is yesterday
with all its blunders and tears, its follies and defects.
Yesterday has passed forever beyond my control.
The other day is tomorrow with its pitfalls and threats,
its dangers and mystery. Until the sun rises again,
I have no stake in tomorrow, for it is still unborn.
With God's help and only one day to concentrate
all my effort and energy on, this day, I can win."

Og Mandino
(1923 – 1996)
Author, *The Richest Man in Babylon*

"Ours is a world where people don't know
what they want, and are willing
to go through hell to get it."

Don Marquis
(1878 – 1937)
American Humorist and Journalist

Timeless Quotations that Inform and Inspire

*"The tendency of man's nature to good is
like the tendency of water to flow downwards."*

Mencius
(371 – 288 B.C.E.)
Chinese Philosopher and Teacher

---

*"But if a man happens to find himself, he has a mansion
which he can inhabit with dignity all the days of his life."*

James A. Michener
(1907 – 1997)
American Novelist

---

*"We are invited to realize the tremendous influence
we wield through the choices we make.
Through the life of Jesus, we are provided a template
for God-like behavior. It is as if He is telling us:
'You want to see God? Then look at me.
There is no separation here. That same Presence and Power is in you.
Follow me. Follow my way of being,
and you will find that Power yourself.
You will do the things that I do and greater things still.'
Our own God-like behavior brings us closer
to our true selves, as children of God."*

Mary Manlin Morrissey
Author, *No Less than Greatness.*

"It is better to be disliked for who you are
than to be liked for who you are not.
How much easier to be authentic than to pretend to be
someone you are not. What a relief just to be.
How clear and simple. How honest. How real.
The only thing you really have to share
with anyone, anyway, is your own state of being."

Judith Ann Parsons
Author, *The Clear and Simple Way*

"Man holds an inward talk with himself alone
which it behooves him to regulate well."

Blaise Pascal
(1623 – 1662)
French Mathematician, Physicist and Religious Philosopher

"We think very little of time present;
we anticipate the future as being too slow,
and with a view to hasten it onward,
we recall the past to stay as it is too swiftly gone.
We are so thoughtless, that we thus wander through the hours
which are not here, regardless only of the moment
that is actually our own."

Blaise Pascal

"What we have to do is to be forever curiously testing
new opinions and courting new impressions."

Walter Pater
(1839 – 1894)
English Essayist, Critic and Novelist

Timeless Quotations that Inform and Inspire

"Finally, brothers, whatever is true,
whatever is noble, whatever is right, whatever is pure,
whatever is lovely, whatever is admirable –
if anything is excellent or praiseworthy –
think about such things."

Philippians 4:8 (NIV)

"The first and best victory is to conquer self; to be conquered
by self is of all things the most shameful and vile."

Plato
(427 – 347 B.C.E.)
Greek Philosopher

"We are all contained within our own mental boundaries,
each according to our own individual awareness.
Many people live bound by the world outside them because they know not
of an inside world. In order to bring a sense of stability into their lives,
people cling to the outside world to control how they feel.
They try to give to themselves a sense of love and well-being,
and yet it is largely beyond their control
because their love is based outside them."

Ron W. Rathbun
Author, *The Way is Within*

"The very nature of the mind is such that
if you only leave it in its unaltered and natural state,
it will find its true nature, which is bliss and clarity."

Sogyal Rinpoche
Author, *The Tibetan Book of Living and Dying*

"I cannot believe that the purpose of life is merely to be happy.
I think the purpose of life is to be useful, to be responsible,
to be honorable, to be compassionate.
It is, above all, to matter:
to count, to stand for something,
to have it made a difference that you lived at all."

Leo Rosten
(1908 – 1997)
Teacher, Academic and Humorist

"There is a force within that gives you life – seek That. In your body there
lies a priceless jewel – seek That. Oh, wandering Sufi, if you are in search
of the greatest treasure, don't look outside, look within, and seek That."

Jalal ad-Din Rumi
(1207 – 1273)
Persian Poet and Mystic

"An amazing thing happens when we slow down.
We start to get flashes of inspiration.
We reach a new level of understanding and even wisdom.
In a quiet moment, we can get an intuitive insight
that can change our entire life and the lives of the people around us
in incredibly positive ways. And those changes can last a life-time.
Living more simply will make it possible to create those quiet moments.
Out of those quiet moments, miracles happen. Be open to them."

Elaine St. James
Author, *Living the Simple Life*

"This one thing I know:
the only ones among you who will be truly happy
are those who will have sought and found how to serve."

Albert Schweitzer
(1875 – 1965)
Alsatian Theologian, Musician and Missionary

*"When you know who you are; when your mission is clear
and you burn with the inner fire of unbreakable will;
no cold can touch your heart;
no deluge can dampen your purpose."*

Chief Seattle
(1786 – 1866)
Leader of the Suquamish and Duwamish Native American Tribes

"We are trampled most often by forces we ourselves create."

William Shakespeare
(1564 – 1616)
English Poet and Dramatist

---

*"Our doubts are traitors, and make us lose the good
we oft might win by fearing to attempt."*

William Shakespeare

---

*"One word frees us of all weight and pain of life:
that word is love."*

Sophocles
(496 – 406 B.C.E.)
Greek Tragic Dramatist

---

*"To be what we are and to become
what we are capable of being is the only end of life."*

Robert Louis Stevenson
(1850 – 1894)
Scottish Novelist, Poet and Essayist

---

*"We need to find God and He cannot be found
in noise and restlessness. God is the friend of silence.
See how nature – trees, flowers, grass – grows in silence;
see the stars, the moon and the sun, how they move in silence ...
We need silence to touch souls."*

Mother Teresa of Calcutta
(1910 – 1997)

---

*"The more we engage in silent prayer,
the more we can give in our active life.
The essential thing is not what we say but
what God says to us and what He says through us."*

Mother Teresa of Calcutta

---

*"Do not lose hold of your dreams or aspirations.
For if you do, you may still exist but you have ceased to live."*

Henry David Thoreau
(1817 – 1862)
American Naturalist, Philosopher and Writer

---

*"As a single footstep will not make a path on the Earth,
so a single thought will not make a pathway in the mind.
To make a deep physical path, we walk again and again.
To make a deep mental path, we must think over and over
the kind of thoughts we wish to dominate our lives."*

Henry David Thoreau

---

*"Man's capacities have never been measured; nor are we to judge
what he can do by any precedents, so little has been tried."*

Henry David Thoreau

*"If one advances confidently in the direction of his dreams,
and endeavors to live the life he has imagined,
he will meet with a success unexpected in common hours."*

Henry David Thoreau

---

*"Language ... has created the word 'loneliness' to express the pain
of being alone. And it has created the word 'solitude'
to express the glory of being alone."*

Paul Johannes Tillich
(1886 – 1965)
German-American Theologian
Author, *The Courage to Be*

---

*"The illiterate of the 21st century will not be those who cannot
read and write, but those who cannot learn, unlearn and relearn."*

Alvin Toffler
Writer and Futurist

---

*"You find peace not by rearranging the circumstances
of your life, but by realizing who you are at the deepest level."*

Eckhart Tolle
Author, *The Power of Now*

---

*"The mind is a superb instrument if used rightly.
Used wrongly, however, it becomes very destructive.
To put it more accurately, it is not so much that you use your mind wrongly,
you usually don't use it at all. It uses you. This is the disease.
You believe that you are your mind. This is the illusion.
The instrument has taken you over."*

Eckhart Tolle

*"The word 'enlightenment' conjures up the idea of
some superhuman accomplishment, and the ego likes to keep it that way,
but it is simply your natural state of felt oneness with Being.
It is a state of connectedness with something immeasurable and indestructible,
something that, almost paradoxically,
is essentially you and yet is much greater than you.
It is finding your true nature beyond name and form."*

Eckhart Tolle

---

*"Life exists only at this very moment,
and in this moment it is infinite and eternal.
For the present moment is infinitely small;
before we can measure it, it is gone, and yet it exists forever ....
You may believe yourself out of harmony with life and its eternal Now;
but you cannot be, for you are life and exist Now."*

Alan Watts
(1915 – 1973)
American Writer, Thinker and Interpreter of Zen Buddhism
Author, *The Way of Zen*

---

*"There are two ways of spreading light:
to be the candle or the mirror that reflects it."*

Edith Wharton
(1862 – 1937)
American Novelist, Short Story Writer, and Designer

---

*"You have to learn to seek first the kingdom of heaven,
the place of stillness and quiet at the highest level of which you are capable,
and then the heavenly influences can pour into you,
recreate you, and use you for the salvation of all human kind."*

White Eagle
Native American Chief

*"Our deepest fear is not that we are inadequate.
Our deepest fear is that we are powerful beyond measure.
It is light, not our darkness, that most frightens us."*

Marianne Williamson
Writer and Social Activist
Author, *A Return to Love*

---

*"Love takes more than crystals and rainbows,
it takes discipline and practice. It is not just a sweet sentiment
from a Hallmark card. It is a radical commitment
to a different way of being, a mental response to life
that is completely at odds with the thinking of the world.
Heaven is a conscious choice to defy the ego's voice.
The more time we spend with the Holy Spirit,
the greater our capacity is to focus on love."*

Marianne Williamson

---

*"There comes a time, not too long into the journey to God,
when the realization that the world could work beautifully
if we would give it the chance, begins to excite us.
It becomes our new motivation. The news isn't how bad things are.
The news is how good they could be.
And our own activity could be part of the unfolding
of Heaven on earth. There is no more powerful motivation
than to feel we're being used in the creation of a world
where love has healed all wounds."*

Marianne Williamson

"Forget the past, for it is gone from your domain.
Forget the future, for it is beyond your reach!
Control the present! Live supremely well now!
It will whitewash the dark past, and compel the future to be bright!
This is the way of the wise."

Paramahansa Yogananda
(1893 – 1952)
Indian Spiritual Master
Author, *Autobiography of a Yogi*

PART 5

Frequently Asked Questions

LOOK; JUDGE; LABEL.
The collective curse of humanity.

SURRENDER; ACCESS; LISTEN.
The collective salvation of humanity.

The student asks …

"Master, can you explain what the
'joy of awakening' is one more time?"

The Master replies …

"No, I cannot. I suggest you go into
the place of no-mind and simply Be,
and find out for yourself."

_____

The student asks …

"Master, how can I find my *true* Self?"
(e.g. enlightenment)

The Master replies …

"Lose your *little* self."
(e.g. stop identifying with your mind
and assuming you are it and it is you)

"You yourself, as much as anybody in the entire universe, deserve your love and affection."

The Buddha
(563 – 483 B.C.E.)
Spiritual Master

"Twenty years from now you will be more disappointed by the things you did not do than the things you did."

Mark Twain
(1835 – 1910)
American Humorist, Satirist, Lecturer and Writer

"Formulate and stamp indelibly on your mind a mental picture of yourself as succeeding. Hold this picture tenaciously. Never permit it to fade. Your mind will (now) seek to develop the picture."

Dr. Norman Vincent Peale
(1898 – 1993)
Protestant Preacher and Author of
The Power of Positive Thinking

Frequently Asked Questions

"Love is simply recognizing the Sacred in another,
in fact, the same Sacred that is in you in another."

The Author

During one-on-one counseling sessions, week-end retreats and various seminars I have conducted on the topic of practical spirituality (by "practical" I mean useful in your everyday life), participants have asked me many questions to supplement the material that was presented. Here is a brief compilation of the most frequently asked questions (FAQs) that I received and the answers I provided:

Question 1. "First, how do you define spirituality? And second, can you explain why interest in spirituality is very much on the increase today at the same time that interest in organized religion, at least in many parts of the West, seems to be decreasing?"

Dr. Staples: "Spirituality can be defined in many ways. I see it as acceptance that there is an element of the Sacred in each of us, that there is a world beyond the world of form (e.g. physical things, objects, thoughts, hopes, fears, events …), beyond what we can perceive with our five senses. It's recognition that we are more than just our physical bodies and the thoughts we think. It's through spirituality that many people find meaning, hope, comfort and peace of mind. Ultimately, spirituality is about understanding our relationship with the Infinite, and taking specific steps to develop and nurture that relationship.

"There are many paths to enlightenment, and each and every religion that exists is potentially one of them. At the same time, some people are finding that their particular religion, likely the one that they were born into, is somewhat archaic, often rigid and perhaps overly ritualistic (e.g. hear this sermon; repeat these words; say this prayer; sing this song). For them, they have decided that it isn't meeting all their needs and aspirations. This group is seeking a more direct, a more meaningful relationship with the Divine.

"And that's their choice. Of course, spirituality doesn't require that you give up your religion or any religious beliefs you may have. It's not a matter of either 'this' (my current religion) or 'that' (the spiritual path). It's just another step – albeit for some, a very important one – to consider as you travel down the road to enlightenment.

"Here is something very important that people are beginning to understand if you remain locked into or obsessed with the everyday world of form. You are limited – there is absolutely no choice in the matter – to bouncing back and forth between pain and pleasure, over and over again. Up one day, down the next; this is the most you can ever hope for. The result? *The experience of pure joy and bliss will always escape you.* Therefore some people decide to move on, going deeper and deeper in search of something that's more meaningful, more impactful, more helpful … indeed, more *liberating* for them."

Question 2. "Walter, as you see it, what are some of the key benefits that people find as a result of spiritual awakening? And why is it that spirituality is able to bring such benefits into our life?"

Dr. Staples: "People who are spiritually 'aware' clearly understand two remarkable things: First, as just discussed, that they cannot find in the world of form – no matter how long or how frantically they search – what exists only in the formless, namely love, joy and bliss; and second, they come to see that they cannot find in the past or in the future what exists only in the Now, namely peace, understanding, meaning, acceptance and fulfillment.

"People who actively practice spirituality are able to evolve naturally, and with minimum effort. They are more at ease with themselves and their world. They are more content, creative, productive, perceptive and empathetic, and are more in harmony with others and with nature. They find it easier to make decisions, both big and small, adjust and change, set priorities and manage their affairs. They feel more inter-connected and grounded, and less controlled by old habits and past conditioning. They manifest great joy and experience bliss, which is our true nature. Personally, I see it as a 'get out of jail' card … you are literally being set free!

"Spiritually-aware people are able to live in such a way that their so-called 'life situation' never takes them over completely, regardless of the extremes of the 'pain-pleasure' spectrum. Because such people are centered at their core, their pain is never so crippling or debilitating (e.g. 'My world is a total disaster!') that they want to do themselves or others harm; and their pleasure is never so euphoric or over-whelming (e.g. 'My world is absolutely perfect!') that they feel they are on top of the world. It's because whichever way it is today, they know that tomorrow it could well be very different ... in fact, even the exact opposite!

"It's been said that some people live by the 'light,' meaning with an inner glow. Imagine this as a candle that is in you. When you are spiritually connected, the flame on this candle is burning and shines brightly. It never brightens, it never dims, and it never goes out completely. It just shines brightly.

"Now, as each day arrives, you lift the 'curtain' of your mind to this new dawning, this new day. Some days, you find that the sun outside is shining brightly; other days, you find that a storm is in full force. Each represents one end of the two extremes that always applies in the world of form (e.g. up-down; over-under; hot-cold; right-wrong; love-hate ...). Neither of these occurrences has any impact on you, however, since your inner candle continues to shine brightly. So you simply proceed to go about your day. Whether the sun is shining outside or not (e.g. whether you life situation is positive or negative), you function as you should, knowing what you know and doing what you need to do.

"A final analogy, if I may, to emphasize this point. When we look at any large body of water such as the ocean, we see that the *surface* is always in a certain state of disarray and disruption e.g. invariably, there are waves of some kind. These may be small ripples, sizable undulations or indeed large white-caps, depending on the wind and other weather conditions at the time. On the other hand, we know that whatever is happening on the surface, if we travel down to the bottom of the ocean, to the very *depths* of the ocean, everything there is calm, everything is peaceful, everything is serene.

"And so it is with your everyday life. On the *surface* (the world of form), everything there is active, busy, in flux and in motion. But while all this is going on, if you travel down to the *depths* of your mind (e.g. to no-mind), into silence, into presence, into the world of no-form, you'll find there that everything is also calm, everything is peaceful, everything is serene.

"It's perhaps why people flock to the oceans of the world in the first place. There, it's much easier to kick back, relax and be yourself (e.g. your Self!). In such a place, close to water, close to Nature, there is much less competition in the way of inner ego and outer stimulation to keep your mind constantly running in overdrive."

Question 3. "Can you explain why you chose the title, *The Hollywood Cure™ for Stress, Anxiety and Depression?*"

Dr. Staples: "Selecting a good and marketable title is always a difficult as well as critical aspect of writing a book. I chose this one because people who are not well just want to feel good again, but lack a detailed understanding and practical way to bring this about. Hence they're not able to help themselves in this process, something I believe is very important. For example, I have come to understand from my studies what lies at the very core of why so many people have serious problems in their life: First and foremost, *they don't love themselves enough* (see Annex 1, *The Wellness Workbook*). They therefore go through life trying valiantly and desperately – yet very often unsuccessfully – to fill this huge and unsightly void. However, if people have the necessary insight, understanding and specific tools – for example, an in-depth understanding the self-concept, self-image and self-esteem – they are in a much better position to bring about a certain amount of self-healing.

"People generally have resigned themselves to the usual ups and downs that they have always experienced in life, from childhood through to adulthood, not realizing they are causing these very feeling themselves. In the text, I liken this situation to Hollywood, which epitomizes for many of us what is wrong with our society today – namely a lot of people focused almost exclusively on the egoic world of form. The result, when things don't turn out as hoped or planned, is as predictable as a ticking time-bomb, namely low self-esteem, stress, anxiety and depression, which on occasion can lead to suicide. Hollywood's reputation for pushing the limits is well known, and the hurt in the lives of many people working there – actors, singers, dancers, musicians, comedians, TV personalities, and so on – is both real and often highly publicized; it's very much part of our reality. So I felt this title was a good choice, knowing I had found ways that people could help themselves with such afflictions, no matter who they were, what careers they had, or where they lived.

"Of course, I considered other titles as I was writing the text. They included *Help Heal Your Life; Feel Good Every Day; One Journey, A Thousand*

Joys – Timeless Insights into the Awakened Mind; Personal Transformation – How to Live a Life of Authentic Power, Passion and Purpose; The Power of the Divine – Perfection is Within You, All Suffering is Without; Life, Love & Much Laughter – Total Wellness through Positive Psychology; and *The Joy of Being – From Depression and Despair to Hope and Happiness.*

"Eckhart Tolle's choice for the title of his first book, *The Power of Now* (1999) is interesting. It's interesting because you could argue that the 'Now' doesn't represent any 'power' at all. More correctly, you could say it represents an opportunity or provides an entry point to *access* the power that in fact lies in the divine or in consciousness. In other words, the power is not the 'Now' per se; it's where being in the Now can take you. Hence a more accurate – but far less catchy – title might be, *The Power of Being in the Now.*

"Then there is the classic book, *The Power of Positive Thinking* (1952) by Dr. Norman Vincent Peale. When the book was first given to Prentice-Hall for its consideration (in fact by Dr. Peale's wife, Ruth, because Norman had thrown it into a waste-paper basket), it had no title. So an enterprising young editor at that publishing house gave it its current title. It went on to become an international best-seller. But again it could be argued that the title misleads people. We know there are special places for people who think only positive, happy thoughts all the time. These places have padded walls, barred windows and securely locked doors! A more accurate title might be, *The Power of Christian Thinking.* But this, too, as a title may be less appealing to a mass market than the one that was actually chosen.

"Finally, Napoleon Hill wrote another classic, *Think and Grow Rich,* published in 1937. It's been said that this book has been read as much as the *Holy Bible.* Evidence of its on-going popularity is that it's still available in bookstores today, more than 70 years after its initial release. That's quite a feat for a so-called 'self-help' book.

"The title infers that you have to first think real, real hard (each Chapter tells you in what specific directions), then you'll become rich in monetary – e.g. "dollar" – terms. OK. Think! … and material wealth will be yours. But how about a book with the title, *Do Not Think – and Become Rich in Every Way.* Based solely on their titles, which book would you buy? Hmmm. OK. Now, which book do you think in fact offers more real value regarding how to live all aspects of your life more fully and more passionately?

"Regarding this book, I would say that *not thinking* is responsible for about 80 percent of it and *thinking* is responsible for the other 20 percent. And the *not thinking* part necessarily took place first! In other words, I believe my book represents about 80 percent inspiration and 20 percent perspiration. I suspect that the book *Tao Te Ching*, purported to be the most widely read book in the world, is 98 percent versus two in this regard.

"So, clearly, book titles are a tricky business. If someone has gotten along to this page, in this text, it would seem my title has done its job. Then, again, if another person isn't reading this book, it has not."

Question 4. "Walter, what would you say is your main reason for writing this book?"

Dr. Staples: "My primary intent is to help people move away from the 'hurt' mode in their life towards the 'heart' mode, from endlessly struggling with themselves to fully validating themselves. People naturally want to make something of their lives and give back, but all too often they have a very hard time getting to their passion. It's extremely frustrating, of course. Many people *sense* their passion but they're not able to reach out and firmly grab onto it."

Question 5. "You say you took almost 10 years to find the 'cure' for low self-esteem, stress, anxiety and depression, at least a cure as successful as any anti-depressant drug. Can you describe what you found?"

Dr. Staples: "I found that there are three components that make up a combined approach to overcoming low self-esteem, stress, anxiety and depression in people. They include (1) Cognitive Behavioral Therapy (CBT); (2) practical spirituality; and (3) mindfulness meditation. All three are drug-free. *Of these, clinical trials conducted over the past 50 years have focused primarily (although not exclusively) on CBT and found it to be just as effective as drug therapy when provided by experienced psychotherapists in treating moderate to severe depression.* Based on my own research, I believe these components when combined together represent the most potent remedy available today for the problems we are talking about.

"People may find one or another of these components easier to understand, internalize and apply. Or they may want to take the best parts from all three and combine them into something that works for them. It's like a menu in a restaurant and from it you can order the appetizer, and feast on that; the entrée, and feast on that; or the dessert, and feast on that. Alternatively, if you are very, very hungry, you can enjoy the 'full course' meal!"

Question 6. "Why do you think as a species we're finding it more and more difficult to live normal, productive and happy lives?"

Dr. Staples: "My research shows that our mind has not evolved, and perhaps is not able to evolve, as quickly as the changes taking place in the everyday world in which we live. Our mind's current development dates back about 50,000 years, yet our society and its level of sophistication is as recent as the last great invention (e.g. the Internet and the information age it has spawned). As a species, then, we're having to play a constant game of catch-up. It's an open debate whether we'll ever succeed.

"This being said, it's no wonder there is friction, indeed conflict, between our 'inner' mind and 'outer' matter, between our mental abilities to adjust and cope, and the technological progress of science and engineering. Marshall McLuhan, the noted Canadian futurist of the 1960s and 70s understood this well when he remarked, 'In the future, everyone will have to learn a living.'

"Yet there is reason for hope. The mind as an organism is still developing, still adapting, still growing, as recent research on the mind's 'plasticity' has discovered. See *The Brain that Changes Itself* (2007) by Norman Doidge, M.D. This is one reason. Another is the fact that the mind is not an isolated instrument, acting all alone and in isolation. It's connected to the great unmanifested, the creative center of the universe.

"We know if the physical brain is dissected into smaller and smaller sections, even very fine slivers that are practically transparent, we still cannot find a single 'thought' in there! Yet in the course of a person's life-time, the brain processes several billion thoughts. (The estimate is about 60,000 a day.) Where did they all come from? Where did they all go?

"Somehow our mind attracts thoughts from some unknown source beyond the physical world. This source forwards them on to us (via space-mail!) and they enter our consciousness. *It could be said that the human mind is designed to receive and decode emanations that represent universal intelligence.* That makes our mind one of unimaginable complexity and infinite proportions. No one should ever discount its true powers."

Question 7. "Walter, if you were to ask yourself the question, 'Who am I?' what would your answer be?"

Dr. Staples: "I believe my answer is similar to what many others would say trying to answer this question. It would be, 'I am love. Love is my very essence, my embodiment, my true Self in the unmanifested state. This is all I am for this is all there is.'"

Question 8. "How would you answer the question, 'Why am I here?'"

Dr. Staples: "Again, my answer is quite simple. I believe we are all here to do our part to further our Creator's divine purpose on Earth. I believe this purpose is *to love and be loved*. This way, we are consciously identifying with God in body, mind and spirit. We are in tune with our soul, 'at one' with our Source."

Question 9. "How would you answer the question, 'What can I possibly hope to accomplish in my life?'"

Dr. Staples: "Each religious faith or spiritual following has its own way of addressing this question. Their teachings and proclamations all talk about the inherent power each individual has to do 'good' in his life, in fact an ability to do good things at a level that most people consider impossible – way beyond their reach, so to speak – because they believe they are limited in some way. But of course they are not … they only *think* they are! Consider, for example, what Christ said in John 14:12: 'Most assuredly, I say unto you, he who believes in me, the works that I do he will also do; and greater works than these will he do ….' So each person has to answer this question in his own way."

Question 10. "When people contemplate their mortality, something we all do from time to time, they are often concerned. They ask themselves, 'When my days here on Earth come to a close, and I look back over my life and wonder what I have accomplished, what relevant question should I ask myself?' What would you say to them?"

Dr. Staples: "I would suggest they ask themselves, 'How well did I love? How often, how deeply, how unselfishly, how universally?' Each of us has the ability to use love to transform the world from one of discord, dysfunction and despair to one of peace, hope and harmony. It's important to realize this sooner rather than later, of course. You don't want to wait until the last week of your life to leave your mark!

"In this regard, I sometimes tell people that I'm looking forward to dying (of natural causes, of course!). And I am. This doesn't mean I'm hoping it will happen sometime sooner rather than later, however. I explain that I just accept that this is the way things have been set up. Everyone is born, lives for a while, then dies. I see arriving, being and departing as a learning experience, really. And if I have learned a lot, shared a lot and loved a lot during my brief time here, there will be a point when it's time to move on and do something else. I'm very okay with all of this.

"Here is an interesting quote from the book, *One Cosmic Instant* (1973) by John A. Livingston:

'Though I do not expect that I shall ever be reborn directly as a crocus, I know that one day my atoms will inhabit a bacterium here, a diatom there, a nematode or a flagellate – even a crayfish or a sea cucumber. I will be here, in myriad forms, for as long as there are forms of life here on Earth. I have always been here, and with a certain effort of will, I can sometimes remember.'"

Question 11. "Walter, you make several references in the text to the 'Now,' to the so-called precious present. Can you elaborate on this point?"

Dr. Staples: "The most important thing you can do to reach a higher level of consciousness is to minimize as much as possible 'past-future' hopes, fears, desires, ruminations and preoccupations. This primarily involves regretting things ... past, and worrying about things ... future. Many people find refraining from this activity extremely difficult, and some virtually impossible! Hence they end up spending a disproportionate amount of their time standing still and going nowhere – at best! *Good grief. The Now is all there is!* If you waste most of your present moments this way, you have no hope of ever moving ahead.

"I'm reminded of this comment by Blaise Pascal: 'All man's miseries derive from not being able to sit quietly in a room alone.'

"You must find a way to spend more time in the present moment, in the Now, *because this is where God is; this is where peace is; this is where acceptance is; this is where all enlightenment takes place.* Hence the choice you have is clear: Either spend time mired in ego-related thoughts about the material world in which you live … or spend time with your Source. The former gets you absolutely nowhere whereas the latter gets you very much somewhere. Only your Source can take you to a place of wonderment and awe, of authentic power, passion and purpose."

Question 12. "Very interesting. So how do people actually do this?"

Dr. Staples: "I described the three primary ways to calm the mind at the very beginning of PART 2, one of which is regular, daily meditation. When we bring the presence of God to bear on our often destructive and self-defeating thoughts, they begin to dissipate and have less effect on us. This allows new thoughts generated by Divine love to enter our consciousness, and we see a new reality being formed and new possibilities being created. This can be a very exciting as well as a very scary experience! But it's one you dearly want to have. Otherwise, your life can be like a boring B-movie that you hope will soon be over."

Question 13. "Walter, can the cure you found for depression be self-administered or self-managed, so to speak, or should a person always seek out professional help?"

Dr. Staples: "This is a very important question. First, anyone suffering from early signs of depression (see Annex 9, *The Wellness Workbook*) should consult with his family physician as soon as possible. Treatment may begin at this stage or, if it's deemed necessary, you may be referred to a psychotherapist, clinical psychologist or psychiatrist who specializes in this field. Unfortunately, in some cases, this may involve being put on a waiting list for treatment or not being able to afford the treatment itself. Even if it is available, the provider may be able to offer only two 45-minute sessions a month (as an example) due to a heavy workload and limited (if any) government financial support. Nevertheless, whatever the circumstances of your case are, you should pursue this avenue as your first priority.

"At the same time, I strongly encourage you to take the initiative early and on your own, and immerse yourself in an intense and all-consuming way in the information contained in this and similar texts (see 'Bibliography'), as well as various websites that offer additional help. There is little or nothing in this book that the average person cannot understand and apply, if sufficient effort and determination are applied. Once it is pointed out to them, for example, most people (1) easily identify with their failings at using critical thinking to address and resolve their current problems; (2) are quick to understand and appreciate various aspects of practical spirituality, and how they can have a positive, healing effect on their everyday lives; and (3) readily see and identify with the many benefits of mindfulness meditation as yet another proactive and productive way to move forward.

"So, in the case of this text, you're free to choose a single approach that particularly appeals to you or any combination of the three that have just been discussed. Even if you're put on an anti-depressant drug (and suffer from certain side effects that may come with it), these self-management approaches may well lead to a quicker recovery and reduce the chance of a serious relapse. I believe the objective should always be to get off any prescription drug you may be taking as soon as possible, of course with appropriate and necessary guidance on when and how to do so from your doctor or primary care-giver. (To note: You should *never* do this on your own.)

"If you're like me, you'll want as much control as possible over your own well-being, and not have to rely exclusively on other people or certain drugs to 'fix' you. So taking the initiative yourself, as just discussed, along with seeking professional help at the earliest sign of a problem, is my first and strongest recommendation."

Question 14. "Can you elaborate on what you mean by the term 'sense of self?'"

Dr. Staples: "Of course. Our everyday lives (e.g. our thinking, our feelings, and in turn our behavior) revolve around one primary aspect of our psychological make-up, namely our *self-identity* (specifically the 'I' in 'Who am I?') or 'sense of self.' If we're confused about who we are, if our sense of self is contrived and only guessed at (and hence is necessarily false), we'll always be looking for ways to complete what we perceive to be our limited self, our inadequate self, our unknown self. Often this is manifested by simply wanting as much pleasure in life as possible and as little pain as possible. At other times, it's manifested by fear, anger, guilt, jealousy, greed or various acts of aggression because of the frustration we feel when we're confused and at our wits' end. This, of course, is the ego at work. Like a leech or parasite, it feeds off our insecurities and fears, our sense of isolation and vulnerability.

"There is much that can be said about this topic. I'll limit my remarks and say that the 'self' can be seen in several different ways. First, it can be seen as the 'little self' or ego, the great pretender, as previously discussed. Second, it can be seen as the broader, larger, more collective 'Self,' the thing of Oneness. And third, it can be seen as the 'non-self' or 'non-entity,' meaning that perhaps we don't want to have any firm belief or notion of who we are at all, knowing that any 'sense of self' we conjure up in our mind is, at least to some extent, false and misleading. In other words, by having a certain 'sense of self' or persona in mind, we're only allowing the ego back into a position of dominance in our life."

Question 15. "Can you explain how practical spirituality can help us with goal-setting in our life? After all, we're always settings goals of one kind or another but very often we don't achieve them."

Dr. Staples: "The first and most important consideration when goal-setting is to ask yourself, 'What is my motivation, my real purpose, for wanting this result (e.g. whatever goal you have decided upon) in my life?' You can answer this question by imagining that you have *already achieved* this goal, that it is already part of your life. This way, as an internalized entity and existing in the Now, you'll be able to sense how it *feels* in your gut, and in turn come to understand if the goal is primarily for personal and selfish reasons or for the common good. It's a significant difference in how you feel. If it's indeed appropriate for you, it will resonate with your energy field and excite you like nothing else can. This invariably is why such goals are ultimately achieved – all this positive energy is directed at them – while others are not.

"When living in the world of form, we tend to organize everything in our life as perfectly as we can, like lining up all the ducks at a shooting gallery. To this end, we set goals, goals and more goals, both major and minor. We then spend an inordinate amount of time each day trying to achieve them: Get this (object/thing) in place, get this (object/thing) in place, get this (object/thing) in place. As a young woman, for example, you may decide to marry your boyfriend, move to California and pursue an acting career. On the few occasions when we are successful at getting everything absolutely perfect – note this only adds to the illusion that we can organize our 'external' affairs exactly the way we want all the time and all by ourselves – we sit back and marvel at how great our life is. 'Wow,' we say, 'I've finally made it. What a smart person I am!'

"But of course in the world of form, the phenomenal nature of events and situations is totally unpredictable and sometimes tragic. So one day everything can indeed be fine while the next day everything can be terrible. It's like always asking (tap, tap on the table) for more and more cards in a poker game, trying to come up with a perfect hand (e.g. a royal flush). We want to get everything just right. We want to win the jackpot. But when even one of these cards is missing (the ace, for example), things necessarily fall back into total disarray. *What a way to live!*

"Imagine that you have just been selected as the first captain of the RMS Titanic, the culmination of a long and illustrious career as a naval officer. You are asked to take this fine ship, the largest and most sophisticated ocean liner in the world at the time, on its maiden voyage. The ship is to leave Southampton (England) on 10 April, 1912, on its way to New York City. Incredible! What an honor!

"The result? On top of the world one moment, at the bottom of the ocean the next! (Captain Edward John Smith chose to go down with his ship.) Win an Academy Award one moment, enter drug rehabilitation the next. Such is the nature of living in the extreme polarized environment of 'object consciousness.'"

Question 16. "Walter, can you comment on 'romantic' love and the important role it plays in our personal life, indeed in our modern society? After all, the family unit traditionally has been the cornerstone of our social order. What is it, really? Why do so many people crave it and feel that life is a total waste without it? Why does it bring so much happiness to some, and so much pain and sorrow to others? With divorce rates in many countries hovering around 50 percent, it seems something is tragically amiss."

Dr. Staples: "Perhaps a little background is in order. In today's world, we see an enormous fixation on the material aspects of life – again, the world of form – from fancy cars, to designer clothes, to over-sized homes, and the belief that these things can make us happy. This is problem # 1. Let's call it the 'toys and trinkets' factor.

"There is also the aspect of instant gratification, especially by the younger generation, the wanting of things that are seen as desirable right now, immediately, if not sooner! This is problem # 2, the 'stress, anxiety and depression' or S-A-D factor. This mind-set places enormous pressure on people which often leads to conflict between couples, major disappointment and often too much debt.

"Then there is the 'status' factor, our compulsive (and often repulsive) need to prove to the world (including ourselves!) over and over again how important, how smart, how capable and how attractive/lovable we are. This is problem # 3, the 'prima donna' factor. With these things just described all happening at the same time, our lives are necessarily in overdrive, with everyone wanting to get somewhere (in fact nowhere) as quickly as possible. To note, a treadmill leads you nowhere, after all. It only causes you to break out in a sweat while standing still!

"And the liberation of sexual mores and practices in many countries continues unabated. As a result, we see higher and higher instances of teenage pregnancies, sexually transmitted diseases, single mothers, single households and common-law marriages, as well as an ever-increasing divorce rate in North America and elsewhere. To note, the U.S. has the highest divorce rate in the Western world. (Source: Wikipedia)

"Indeed, as Bob Dylan told us back in 1964, 'The times they are a-changin.' And we know they are changing faster today than ever before. To deal with these developments, however, we as responsible and caring adults need to better understand the many social and psychological forces that are at play.

"I offer the following observations about romantic love. They are not meant as a criticism or judgment in any way. In other words, I'm not saying romantic love is either good or bad, or somewhere in between; I'm only saying that it needs to be better understood.

"To note, we know romantic love is a euphoric experience of monumental proportions, indeed a magnificent blessing, a unique and enthralling experience quite unlike any other we may hope to have in our life-time. Unfortunately, however, though we readily welcome such feelings, they often 'blind' us concerning what is really going on. So let me now try to explain 'what is really going on.'

"We all experience different kinds of love in our life and they center around the following: (1) **transcendent** or universal love; (2) **familial** or family-centered love; and of course (3) **romantic** love. Regarding the latter, we have seen in the text how the ego is always wanting and needing, always trying to complete and better itself. This is the dynamic, then, that is taking place when two people find each other physically and emotionally attractive, and 'fall' in love.

"The 'attractive' part is the primitive, primordial sex drive we all have that perpetuates our species. The often-called 'chemistry' that causes us to find one person more attractive than another is the luck of the draw, I believe. It's something we're born with … and either blessed or stuck with.

"People who are in love feel that when they're together, they are 'better off,' meaning more happy, playful and joyful … more alive! But we must come back to what is 'real,' what is permanent, to what never changes. And by this criteria, romantic love by itself is neither real nor permanent, although it may be more *convenient* for a time for many personal and societal reasons (e.g. like having a ready sexual partner and the raising of children). But we know people often fall in and out of love (e.g. it comes, it goes, it intensifies, it diminishes). Others may remain in love all of their lives. It doesn't matter. With the death of both parties, it comes to an end (e.g. when a person dies, the ego in that person dies, along with anything and everything that the ego helped create). I suggest, then, it could be argued that every marriage that is based solely on romantic love is simply a marriage of 'convenience.'

"Romantic love usually involves two very different personalities coming together with very different ego-related and trans-egoic drives (see Abraham Maslow's hierarchy in PART 2.). We know these drives often change with age and maturity, hence one person may change in one or more of these areas while the other may change in other areas – or indeed, in none at all. It comes down to how well such aspects of the two people allow them to co-exist as a unit for the mutual benefit of both. In this sense, marriage is very much an on-going exercise in adjusting, in accommodating, in compromising, with the hope that staying married keeps you in a better place.

"A final comment. Can you imagine being a gentleman who is head-over-heels in love with a lady you absolutely adored … but she decides to marry someone else? (Yes, I can.) If you *truly* loved this person (e.g. your ego played *no part*), wouldn't you be the first to step up and cheer her on, knowing she believed she would be happier in this other relationship? (Are you kidding? I can't imagine doing that!)

"Of course, you also might think she was wrong in making the decision she made. (Yes, I sure did!) And you could very well be right. But is this not your ego jumping in, making its presence known, and putting your self-interest first and foremost?

"As an aside, we know there are marriages as well that are devoid of any kind of love at all, including romantic love, that are also marriages of convenience. Here the reasons may be to reduce living expenses and/or to have simple friendship or companionship. It's not unlike having a room-mate in college or university.

"In a typical 'romantic love' marriage, the convenience factors could include any or all of the following: (1) safety and security; (2) acceptance and friendship; and (3) recognition, status and self-respect. In fact, there is no end to what the ego wants for you and no end to its telling you that it can provide it. The constant and persistent message it impresses upon you is, 'Do exactly as I say and I promise to give you everything you want!' Until you find a ready response to this most alluring – but highly misguided – entreaty or learn how to ignore it, I believe you are putting yourself (e.g. your Self) and your well-being (e.g. well Being) at serious risk.

"I offer this final observation, and emphasize that this is very important to understand. There is another possibility in this 'romantic love' scenario and I suggest it is the ideal situation. Consider this: If you are able to bring *transcendent love*, which is not a purely unconscious act as is romantic love, into the relationship as well, then you have something quite remarkable, indeed very, very unique. In this instance, you have nothing less than pure, enthralling, ever-enchanting … *bliss!* And bliss has magical powers attached to it as it allows miracles to show up – not just once or twice – but on a regular basis.

"As you probably suspect, miracles are very interesting things even though you may not have experienced one in your life up to now. So what are they, anyway? Miracles are remarkable, unforeseen occurrences that seemingly defy natural law and hence are thought to result from some supernatural power. (OK, that's simple enough.) And strange as it may seem, miracles have very little (in fact, nothing) to do with you and everything to do with the world at large. They have a sort of 'omni-presence' and 'omni-effect.'

"So here is my challenge to you: Adopt and follow the steps that are described in detail in this book. Do not doubt, do not deviate, and do not procrastinate. Just "be" and "do." As you travel down this path, I know miracles will show up in your life – as they have in mine – and a life sprinkled with miracles here and there is surely one that is worth living."

"For most of us, the inner journey is the journey of last resort;
we go there only after we discover the outer journey doesn't work.
What a shame ... for the inner journey is the only one that has
any meaning, any substance, any real joy."

The Author

Afterword

In PART 1, it was shown how important it is to better understand the process we all use to "think" in the active mode. To assist further in this regard, I present here a detailed explanation about how to avoid what I call the "mind T.R.A.P."

On a regular basis, you need to know how to identify and deal with the possible illogical, irrational, inaccurate, or improbable nature of any particular thought you may have. **The goal is to avoid the "mind T.R.A.P."** This is where you often consider a thought to be 100 percent true when in fact it may very well be partially, mostly or totally false. The exercise described here represents a relatively quick yet effective method that uses _critical thinking_ to weed out thoughts that need to be eliminated from your mind, and thus stopping them from impacting your consciousness and negatively affecting your mood and subsequent behavior.

In the vast majority of cases, you'll find the inquiry in question simply takes your ego out of the situation and replaces it with humility, understanding, acceptance, and love. For if you see things happening to you or around you that you don't particularly like, want or agree with, then in a very real sense **you are pretending to be God and acting as though only you know the "truth" or what is "right" or "wrong" about the situation.** Of course, none of us can know the truth or what is right or wrong about any given situation, and to think we can only leads to unnecessary and unwanted pain and suffering. Invariably, it's arrogance, ignorance, presumption, and pride (namely ego) that lie at the very center of false beliefs.

To the point, the mind T.R.A.P. works something like this. You witness an event or situation that upsets you or makes you angry (at either yourself and/or the "world"). You then formulate a statement of some kind in your mind that portends to accurately describe what you have just witnessed or experienced. Unfortunately, you do a very bad job of it because you do this while in a weakened and unstable cognitive state. But the result represents an unfortunate double-whammy: You end up both upset/angry _and_ stuck with a faulty statement/narrative that you believe justifies your hurt. To correct your predicament, there is only one recourse available to you – **you have to calmly and deliberately deconstruct what you have just built**. In other words, you have to come up with an exit strategy that brings greater logic, accuracy and rationality back into the equation. Only then can you move ahead with clarity, wisdom and understanding, with empowering and uplifting attributes that represent your higher Self.

The inquiry involves the following four questions that you need to ask in order to check the relevancy and accuracy of any given thought you may have:

T. Is the thought 100 percent <u>t</u>rue? Y/N

R. Is the thought 100 percent <u>r</u>elevant? Y/N

A. Is the thought 100 percent <u>a</u>ccurate? Y/N

P. Is the thought 100 percent <u>p</u>roven? Y/N

Let's assume you have a thought that is causing you some hurt, distress, anxiety, pain, dismay, regret, depression or even anger of a certain magnitude. Take a piece of paper and carefully write it down.

e.g. My thought says, " _____ "

Now with this thought in mind, systematically ask these four pertinent questions, carefully consider your answers, then write them all down.

Clearly if you determine that the thought is *not* 100 percent <u>true</u>, *not* 100 percent <u>relevant</u>, *not* 100 percent <u>accurate</u>, or *not* 100 percent <u>proven</u>, **this means that there is no reason to hold on to it**. To do so is only keeping you in an unwanted, unproductive and unhealthy state. So you need to throw the thought away faster than you can say, *"Get out of here!"*

What does this exercise actually accomplish? Specifically, it helps you identify where you might be using prejudgments, total absolutes, over-generalizations, over-simplifications, gross distortions, simplistic rationalizations or false assumptions, all known enemies of critical thinking, to compose a certain statement that describes from your perspective the situation as you see it. "Probabilities" are very important here. For if there is any possibility, even a very small one, that the statement you have in mind is not true, not relevant, not accurate, or not provable, then there is a very real chance that you have over-stated your premise and mistakenly assumed it to be *fact*. Thankfully, by questioning its accuracy and validity, you have determined that it is *fiction*, and hence no longer need to give the matter your focused attention.

Once the thought has been discarded and is no longer a factor in your thinking, something quite remarkable takes place and it is *immediate*. Instead of the hurtful, stressful or sometimes angry feelings you had before when you assumed your thought was 100 percent true, a whole new set of feelings descends and impacts your consciousness ... they include hope, compassion, understanding, joy, wonderment, humility, serenity, beauty and love. Each of these feelings has been described in detail throughout the book.

EXAMPLES TO ILLUSTRATE THE POINT

1. **A distraught daughter might be saying ...**

   "My parents don't listen to me ... they don't understand me ... they don't care about me. This can only mean they don't love me."

   N.B. Inquiry here may prevent a depression or an attempted suicide.

2. **A disgruntled employee might be saying ...**

   "My boss doesn't like me ... he doesn't respect me ... he doesn't appreciate the good work that I do. He probably thinks I shouldn't even be working here."

   N.B. Inquiry here may prevent a verbal outburst or an act of physical violence.

3. **An angry father (perhaps born in Asia) might be saying ...**

   "My daughter (perhaps born in America) is no good ... she is ignoring her culture and heritage ... she dances, she smokes, she has a boyfriend I haven't met, and dresses like all her other friends. She is an embarrassment to her family."

   N.B. Inquiry here may prevent a physical beating or an "honor" killing in a fit of rage.

C O M M E N T S ... from participants at seminars and retreats based on the book, *The Hollywood Cure™ for Stress, Anxiety and Depression* by Walter Doyle Staples.

1. "You cannot help but be impressed by a book that, step-by-step, insight-by-insight, reveals to you who you really are. In the process, you experience an awakening of profound proportions and a realization of your true potential. It's truly life-changing."

2. "A comprehensive and practical approach to personal well-being and authentic happiness. It undoubtedly will positively impact all those who choose to heed its important message."

3. "A remarkable book written with clarity and compassion. It provides a perfect balance between theory and practical application. You need only read, understand and apply the concepts to get optimum results."

4. "I like Dr. Staples' comment, 'You cannot hope to do great things until you know you have greatness within you.' OK, my friends, now that we all know this, we'd better get to work!"

5. "This 'destined-to-be-classic' shows you how to master your moods and take purposeful action. It will bring excitement, energy and fun back into your life!"

6. "Very insightful! This book shows that our species is at risk unless we find a way to transcend our ego. It then goes on to show how, both individually and collectively, we can actually do this. An excellent piece of work."

7. "A masterful guide to peaceful, positive and purposeful living, one that is centered in the stillness and joy of our authentic selves. It's a must-read!"

8. "This is the ultimate 'take-charge-of-your-life' book. Equally important, it offers a prescription for successful living that has proven to actually work!"

9. "Seldom does a book come along that has the potential to change your life in so many important ways. This is such a book. It truly is a recipe for positive mental health."

10. "A masterpiece! This book is a wonderful gift to all of us who want more peace, hope, happiness, success and love in our everyday life."

11. "A fascinating book about the awakening of the human spirit, about how to be fully aware and intensely alive, and fully appreciate all that we are and all that we can be."

12. "'Always up for good reason, never down for any reason.' I really like this awesome message from Dr. Staples' latest book. It's empowering beyond words."

13. "The fact is, a lot of people are tired of feeling down and depressed, and their first priority is to start feeling good again. This book helps you do that … and much, much more."

14. "This book opens up your mind to a whole new concept of happiness called 'authentic happiness' – the incredible feeling of confidence, courage and compassion, and the burning desire to make a difference."

15. "I wish I had written this book … but on second thought, maybe not. Now I can read in one weekend what it took Dr. Staples almost 10 years to research and write!"

16. "Using a vocabulary that is both hopeful and helpful, Dr. Staples treats us to a new and exciting way to understand and apply practical spirituality. It takes us well beyond where many of us have been stuck for most of our lives."

17. "Most people in their heart want to be loving, caring and forgiving, yet struggle to know how to be this way. Now no one has any excuse. You need only understand the message in this text, then apply the principles that are offered."

18. "I found the text of this book easy to read, the advice easy to follow, and the exercises interesting and helpful. The occasional touch of humor also made the reading a lot of fun."

19. "Because of this book, I discovered that I could begin my recovery myself, at my own pace, and not have to rely on other people or prescription drugs to 'fix' me. This feeling – that I am in control – is very important as I gain new insight into the healing process I need to follow."

20. "This book is guaranteed to inform, inspire, delight and create wonder in your world. It is an uncommon book for uncommon times ... so many people are hurting today, and need the help that this book so eloquently and beautifully provides. Thank you, Dr. Staples."

Your Feedback is Welcome

Your comments and feedback are most welcome to help make this book and the information in it as relevant, accurate and helpful as possible for its readers. For example:

1. You could make general comments regarding your overall impression of the book.

2. You could point out (a) topics/areas you found particularly helpful and insightful. e.g. What worked best for you? Was it PART 1, the appetizer; PART 2, the entrée; PART 3, the dessert; or all three, representing the "full course" meal? (b) topics/areas you found that were not that helpful or even somewhat confusing; or (c) topics/areas you think should be expanded upon in either theory or practical application (such as additional questions/answers in the FAQ section in PART 5).

3. Lastly, please advise if information in this text in fact was instrumental in helping you deal successfully with a specific mental challenge, concern, or indeed a moderate or acute depressive episode in your own life. Or did you find that this book was just helpful in a general way, and provided some useful insights and concepts about how to live a more meaningful and satisfying life?

Thank you.

Contact:

e-mail: info@thehollywoodcure.com

See **www.thehollywoodcure.com**

Santa Barbara, CA   Oakville, ON

Begin today to heal your life!

THE
"TOTAL WELLNESS"
KIT

includes

1. The book, *The Hollywood Cure™ for Stress, Anxiety and Depression* (272 pages);

2. The Wellness Workbook: Putting THE HOLLYWOOD CURE™ into Practice (80 pages); and

3. 2 DVDs – 4 hours of teaching modules by the author based on the book.

Order online today

The "Total Wellness" Kit

for

only $197.00

by going to

www.thehollywoodcure.com

Santa Barbara, CA   Oakville, ON

Life Coach & Mentoring

Dr. Staples offers one-on-one coaching and mentoring sessions to a wide range of individuals in all walks of life including accountants, architects, writers, doctors, lawyers, nurses, teachers, military personnel, law enforcement officers, high school, college and university students, actors, singers, dancers, musicians, politicians, amateur and professional athletes, as well as business executives. All arrangements are necessarily personal and strictly confidential.

Sessions may continue anywhere from six weeks to six months, with three months being the average. This offering, called the *total wellness* coaching program, has proven to be highly successful over several years, and is based on the many insights, concepts and themes contained in his latest book, *The Hollywood Cure™ for Stress, Anxiety and Depression* as well as other important life-changing research findings by Dr. Staples.

Contact:

e-mail: info@thehollywoodcure.com

See **www.thehollywoodcure.com**

Santa Barbara, CA   Oakville, ON

If you are interested in having Dr. Staples give a Keynote address or conduct a live Seminar with your group ...

Topics may include:

"The Hollywood Cure™ for Stress, Anxiety and Depression"

"Putting 'The Hollywood Cure™' into Practice"

"Total Wellness in your Personal and Professional Life"

"Integrating Spirituality and Leadership: A New Approach"

"How to Feel Good Every Day"

"From Un-Sad to Up-Beat:
8 Strategies to Elevate your Mood and Stir your Passion"

"How to Kiss Depression Good-Bye and Move On with Confidence"

Contact:

e-mail: info@thehollywoodcure.com

See **www.thehollywoodcure.com**

Santa Barbara, CA   Oakville, ON

Bibliography

Ben-Shahar, Tal (2007). *Happier: Learn the Secrets to Daily Joy and Lasting Fulfillment.* New York, NY: McGraw-Hill.

Bodian, Stephan (2000). *The Impact of Awakening: Excerpts from the Teachings of Adyashanti.* Los Gatos, CA: Open Gate Publishing.

Boswell, Nelson (1985). *Inner Peace, Inner Power.* New York, NY: Random House.

Burns, David D., M.D. (1980). *Feeling Good: The New Mood Therapy.* New York, NY: Avon Books.

Buscaglia, Leo (1982). *Living, Loving & Learning.* New York, NY: Random House.

Chopra, Deepak (1994). *The Seven Spiritual Laws: A Practical Guide to the Fulfillment of Your Dreams.* San Rafael, CA: Amber-Allen Publishing.

—— (1997). *The Path to Love: Renewing the Power of Spirit in Your Life.* New York, NY: Random House.

—— (2000). *How to Know God.* New York, NY: Random House.

The Dalai Lama (2003). *The Art of Happiness at Work.* New York, NY: Penguin Group.

Davich, Victor N. (1998). *The Best Guide to Meditation.* Los Angeles, CA: Renaissance Books.

Doidge, Norman, M.D. (2007). *The Brain that Changes Itself.* New York, NY: Penguin Group.

Dyer, Wayne W. (1995). *Your Sacred Self.* New York, NY: HarperCollins.

Fadiman, James and Robert Frager (1997). *Essential Sufism.* New York, NY: HarperCollins.

Gawain, Shakti (1978). *Creative Visualization.* San Rafael, CA: New World Library.

Guillory, William A. (1997). *The Living Organization: Spirituality in the Workplace.* Salt Lake City, UT: Innovations International.

Hahn, Thich Nhat (1996). *Be Still and Know: Reflections from Living Buddha, Living Christ.* New York, NY: The Berkley Publishing Group.

Harpur, Tom (2004). *The Pagan Christ: Recovering the Lost Light.* Toronto, Canada: Thomas Allen Publishers.

Hay, Louise L. (1999). *You Can Heal Your Life.* Carlsbad, CA: Hay House.

Kabat-Zinn, Jon (1990). *Full Catastrophe Living: Using the Wisdom of Your Body and Mind to Face Stress, Pain, and Illness.* New York, NY: Random House.

Kabir (1961). *One Hundred Poems of Kabir.* A translation by Rabindranath Tagore. Macmillan (London) – UNESCO (Paris).

Kapleau, Philip (1980). *The Three Pillars of Zen.* Revised and Expanded Edition. Garden City, NY: Anchor Books.

Katie, Byron (2007). *A Thousand Names for Joy: Living in Harmony with the Way Things Are.* New York, NY: Random House.

Kersten, Holger (1994). *Jesus Lived in India.* Rockport, MA: Element Books.

Lao-tzu (2005). *Tao Te Ching: A New Translation.* Boston, MA: Shambhala Publications.

Lewis, C.S. (2004). *Mere Christianity.* New York, NY: HarperCollins.

Maharaj, Nisargadatta (1973). *I Am That.* Acom.

McDowell, Josh (1984). *Building Your Self-Image.* Wheaton, IL: Tyndale House Publishers.

Mountain Dreamer, Oriah (1999). *The Invitation.* New York, NY: HarperCollins.

Raymo, Chet (2003). *The Path: A One-Mile Walk through the Universe.* New York, NY: Walker & Company.

Renard, Gary (2004). *The Disappearance of the Universe.* Los Angeles, CA: Hay House.

Selby, John (2003). *Seven Masters, One Path.* New York, NY: HarperCollins.

Simpkins, Alexander C. and Annellen M. Simpkins (1992). *Principles of Meditation: Eastern Wisdom for the Western Mind*. Boston, MA: Tuttle Publishing.

Smith, Douglas V. and Kazi F. Jalal (2000). *Sustainable Development in Asia*. Manila: Asian Development Bank.

Staples, Walter Doyle (1991). *Think Like A Winner*™. Gretna, LA: Pelican Publishing.

—— (1996). *In Search of Your True Self*. Gretna, LA: Pelican Publishing.

Thoreau, Henry D. (1973) *Walden*. Princeton, NJ: Princeton University Press.

Tolle, Eckhart (1997). *The Power of Now*. Vancouver, Canada: Namaste Publishing.

—— (2003). *Stillness Speaks*. Novato, CA: New World Library; Vancouver, Canada: Namaste Publishing.

—— (2005). *A New Earth: Awakening to Your Life's Purpose*. New York, NY: Penguin Group.

Warren, Rick (2002). *The Purpose-Driven Life*. Grand Rapids, MI: Zondervan.

Watts, Alan (1957). *The Way of Zen*. New York, NY: Random House.

—— (1995). *Become What You Are*. Boston, MA: Shambhala Publications.

Williamson, Marianne (1992). *A Return to Love: Reflections on the Principles of A Course in Miracles*. New York, NY: HarperCollins.

—— (1994). *Illuminata: A Return to Prayer*. New York, NY: Penguin Group.

Yogananda, Paramahansa (1999). *Inner Peace: How to Be Calmly Active and Actively Calm*. Los Angeles, CA: Self-Realization Press.

Zukav, Gary (1989). *The Seat of the Soul*. New York, NY: Simon and Schuster.

The Holy Bible (1984). Nashville, TN: Thomas Nelson.

A Course in Miracles® (1975). New York, NY: Penguin Books.*

* *A Course in Miracles*® and ACIM® are registered service marks and trademarks of the Foundation for A Course in Miracles, 41397 Buecking Drive, Temecula, CA 92590-5668.

About the Author

Walter Doyle Staples has been an air force officer, a career diplomat, a corporate executive, a college and university professor, as well as a highly successful professional speaker and internationally acclaimed author. He has lived several years in the U.S., several years in Canada and several years in Europe. As such, he brings with him a global perspective and a myriad of fascinating life experiences.

Walter has written five books over the past 25 years. They include *The Greatest Motivational Concept in the World* (1985); *Think Like A Winner™* (1991) now available in 14 foreign languages in over 45 countries; *Power to Win* (1994); *In Search of Your True Self* (1996); and *Everyone A CEO, Everyone A Leader* (2005).

Those who have provided testimonials for his books read like a "Who's Who" in the field of personal and professional growth and leadership development, and include the following 10 world-renowned authorities: Dr. Kenneth Blanchard (*The One Minute Manager*); Jack Canfield (*Chicken Soup for the Soul*); Art Linkletter (*Yes! You Can*); Dr. Norman Vincent Peale (*The Power of Positive Thinking*); Dr. Laurence Peter (*The Peter Principle*); Paul Zane Pilzer (*Unlimited Wealth*); Anthony Robbins (*Unlimited Power*); Dr. Robert Schuller (*Power Thoughts*); Brian Tracy (*Maximum Achievement*); and Dr. Denis Waitley (*The Psychology of Winning*).

He is currently president and CEO of his own executive training and personal coaching company with offices in Santa Barbara, California and Oakville, Ontario. His typical clients are caring, hopeful and energetic individuals, people who want to discover who they really are and what they are capable of accomplishing, knowing they have discovered and accepted their deepest calling. These individuals are committed to achieving only the highest level of success and fulfillment in both their personal life and professional career.

See **www.thehollywoodcure.com**

Acknowledgments

I wish to acknowledge the friendship and kind support of the following: Jack Canfield, co-creator of the *Chicken Soup for the Soul* series of books, who reviewed an earlier draft of this text; Brian Tracy, whose encouragement and gentle urgings have been forthcoming since 1985 when I first arrived in Los Angeles and spent some time with him; Dr. Wayne W. Dyer, whose many books and audio programs have opened my mind to a new way of Being and seeing; Marianne Williamson, whose insights and knowledge of matters spiritual and transformational have been instrumental in helping me on my own journey; Jon Kabat-Zinn, Ph.D., and his important and on-going research into the many mind/body benefits of mindfulness meditation; and Eckhart Tolle, whose wisdom and deep understandings have had a profound and lasting impact on me. To each of you, a sincere and heart-felt "thank you."

Peer Review

Several people have read this book in part or in its entirety over many months, in fact years, offering their valuable time and professional expertise as part of a "peer review" process prior to its actual publication. I received loving encouragement, wise editing advice, helpful criticism and many practical suggestions that together have necessarily helped make the material more understandable, relevant, detailed and accurate for its readers.

With gratitude, I wish to recognize these individuals as follows:

Lois Gilbert; Robert Gardner, Ph.D.; Agostino Menna, Ph.D.; Debbie Halsted; Tim Elliott, D.Div; Leonard J. Staples, P.Eng; Murielle Gagné; Carmen Dima, Ph.D.; Honey Blaine, RN, BScN; Anterpreet Singh; Tangea Tansley, Ph.D.; and John J. Staples, P.Eng.

Index

A

A-B-Cs of thought process.
    See Systematic thought
    evaluation process (S-T-E-P)
Abraham, 31
Action versus inaction, 11,
    38–40
Activating event, 5–6, 65
Advaita Vedanta, 31
Adyashanti, 164–65
Aesop, 165
Alcohol use, 15–16
Alcott, A. B., 165
Ali, Mohammed, 121
Andersen, U. S., 69–70, 112, 165
Angelou, Maya, 22
Anxiety, xxiii, xxiv, 143–44
Araqi, Fakhruddin, 166
Ardagh, Arjuna, 158
Armstrong, Neil, 101
Auden, Wysten Hugh, 166
Authentic living, 27, 93–94, 110
Authentic power, 96

B

Bach, Richard, 108
Bacon, Francis, 166
Bannister, Roger, 101
Beck, Aaron T., xxiii, 3
Being, 42–43
    defined, 23, 27–28
    knowing Source through, 40
Beliefs, core, 102–6

Belief system, 26, 65, 99–102,
    124
    ego as, 71
Bell, Alexander Graham, 98
Bible
    John 14:12, 206
    Luke 17:20–21, 182
    Philippians 4:8, 186
Blake, William, 166
Booth, Leo, 167
Boswell, Nelson, 62
Brain, effects of meditation on,
    159–60
Branden, Nathanial, 128
Branson, Richard, 119
Breathing, in mindfulness
    meditation, 153, 154, 155
Briggs, Dorothy Corkill, 128
Brown, Les, 167
Buddha, 31, 49, 98, 167–68, 197
Buddhism, 31
    on excessive consumption, 74
    nirvana in, 83
Bunker, Archie, 168
Buscaglia, Leo, 168

C

Carrington, Richard Christopher,
    59
Carver, George Washington, 168
Channing, William, 169
Chardin, Pierre Teillard de, 76
Chopra, Deepak, 169

Christianity, 31
  on excessive consumption, 74
Churchill, Winston, 9, 169
Cognitions, 61, 62
Cognitive Behavioral Therapy
     (CBT), 131–33, 204
  action versus inaction, 11–12
  collective consciousness,
     17–19
  described, xxiii, 3–5
  Great Wheel of Life, 14–17
  group-based, 157–58
  scale of human spirit, 19–20
  self-image, 12–13
  taking responsibility for
     thoughts, 10
  thinking process, 5–9
Cognitive response, 5–6
Cole, Ronald, xxi
Collective consciousness, 17–19
Collier, Robert, 169
Comfort zone, 129–30
Confucianism, on excessive
     consumption, 74
Confucius, 170
Conscious incompetence, 6
Consciousness, 35, 139
  object, 29, 48, 52, 123
  self-, 85
  space, 29–30, 52, 123
  unconditioned, 136
  unity, 83, 85
Core beliefs, 102–6
Cousins, Norman, 49
Creative imaging, 97
Critical thinking, 63, 66–69,
     131
Cure
  defined, xi

Hollywood connection to,
     xxi–xxiv, 202–3
  three components of, xxiii–xxiv

D
Dalai Lama, 135, 180
Darwin, Charles, 170
Das, Surya, 72
Dell, Michael, 119
Depression
  celebrities with, xxii
  defined, 44
  effectiveness of cognitive
     therapy for, 131–33
  effectiveness of mindfulness
     based cognitive therapy for,
     158
  effects of, xxi
  overcoming, 149–50, 204
  suicide risk and, 147, 148
  treating, 208–9
  See also S-A-D factor
Descartes, René, 170
Disease
  meditation and, 159
  mental health and, 16
  stress and, 145–46
Disney, Walt, 98
Doidge, Norman, 205
Dostoyevsky, Fyodor, 170
Drucker, Peter, 171
Drugs, use of illegal, 15–16
Dyer, Wayne W., 171–72

E
Easwaran, Eknath, 173
Eckhart, Meister, 173

Edison, Thomas, 98
Ego, 42–43, 46, 53–54, 63, 108,
    110
  defined, 26, 71
  depression and, 44
  described, 32–36
  effects of, 70–72
  human nature and, 90–92
  letting go of, xxv–xxvi
  object consciousness and, 48
Ego-speak, 49
Einstein, Albert, 75, 173–74
Eliot, T. S., 70, 174–75
Ellis, Albert, 3
Emerson, Ralph Waldo,
    152, 175
Emotional reaction, 5–6, 65
Emotions, 24
Enlightened life, 32–36
Enlightenment, 86
  Buddha's definition of, 49
  transcendence and, 152
Environment, importance of, 27
Evans, Mary Anne, 175
Evolution, 58–60

F

Familial love, 213
Feelings
  thoughts generate, 10–11
  See also Emotional reaction
Fichte, Johann Gottlieb, 152
Fillmore, Charles, 175
Five Great Wonders of the Mind,
    110–19
France, Anatole, 113
Francis of Assisi, 82, 176
Freeman, James Dillet, 176

G

Galileo Galilei, 1
Gandhi, Mahatma, 135
Gates, Bill, 119
Gaulden, Albert Clayton, 176
Gere, Richard, 159
Gilbert, W. S., 177
Goal-setting, 121, 210–11
God. *See* Source
Goleman, Daniel, 159
Gore, Al, 159
Graham, Heather, 159
Great Wheel of Life, 14–17
Great Wonders of the Mind, 110–19
Green, Julien Hartridge, 177
Group-based cognitive therapy,
    157–58
Guilt, 55

H

Hammarskjold, Dag, 177
Happiness, 94–95
Hawn, Goldie, 159
Hay, Louise L., 177
Hegel, Georg Wilhelm Friedrich,
    152
Hierarchy of human wants and
    needs (Maslow), 91
Hill, Napoleon, 178, 203
Hinduism, on excessive
    consumption, 74
Hollywood connection to cure,
    xxi–xxiv, 202–3
Holmes, Oliver Wendell, 178
Hubbard, Elbert, 102
Human nature, 88–90
Human spirit, scale of, 19–20
Huxley, Aldous, 178

I

Imagination, 113
Inaction versus action, 11, 38–40
Initiatory life, 151–53
Inner fitness factors, 14
Inner knowing, xxviii, 80
Insight, 23
Insight meditation. *See*
    Mindfulness meditation
Islam, 31
    on excessive consumption, 74

J

Jackson, Michael, xxix
Jalal, Kazi F., 74
James, William, 14, 95, 178–79
Jesus Christ, 31
Jonathan Livingston Seagull,
    108–9
Judaism, 31
Jung, Carl, xiii, 21, 81, 139, 179

K

Kabat-Zinn, Jon, 151, 179
Kabir, 153–54
Kant, Immanuel, 152
King, Martin Luther, Jr., 135, 180
Knowing, xxviii, 80
    See also Being; Self
Kubler-Ross, Elizabeth, 180
Kuyken, Willem, 158

L

Lao-tzu, 31, 181
Larson, Christian D., 181
Lewis, C. S., 182

Life

enlightened, 32–36
initiatory, 151–53
key areas of, 14–17
Little self. *See* Ego
Living authentically, 27, 93–94,
    110
Livingston, John A., 207
Love, 51, 135, 140, 206
    defined, 84–85
    familial, 213
    romantic, 211–14
    transcendent, 213, 214
    unconditional, 24, 55–56

M

Maharaj, Nisargadatta, xxv
Maharishi Mahesh Yogi, 83
Maharshi, Ramana, 182–83
Maltz, Maxwell, 127
Mandino, Og, 183
Marquis, Don, 183
Maslow, Abraham, 91
Materialism, 73–74
Maturity, levels of (Jung), 81–83
McLuhan, Marshall, 205
Meditation, 28–29
    See also Mindfulness
        meditation
Meditation retreats, 158–61
Mencius, 184
Mental cleansing, 49
Mental illness
    statistics, 131–32
    suicide risk and, 147
Michener, James A., 184
Mind, Great Wonders of, 110–19
Mindfulness, 27–28, 152–53

Mindfulness Based Cognitive
Therapy (MBCT), 158
Mindfulness meditation, 143
breathing in, 153, 154, 155
dealing with stress and
depression through, 150, 204
defined, xxiii, 151
effects on brain of, 159–60
exercises in, 155–57
noble silence in, 160–61
retreats, 158–61
seven steps in, 154–55
transcendence and, 151–53
Miracles, 215
Miracles, A Course in, 106–8,
137–38
Modeling, 97
Mohammed, 31
Morrissey, Mary Manlin, 184
Mother Teresa, 82, 189

N

Nature, 27, 56
Neurosis, 60–62
Newton, Isaac, 75
Nightingale, Earl, 114
Nirvana, 83
Noble silence, 160–61
Noise, 34, 45
Now, 40–42, 53, 110, 207–8
meaning of, 28, 40

O

Object consciousness, 29, 48,
52, 123
One Hundred Poems of Kabir,
153–54

Oriah Mountain Dreamer, 171
Otiosity, 11
Outer acknowledgment factors, 15

P

Pain, 47
cycle of, 4
meditation as relief for, 159
Parsons, Judith Ann, 185
Pascal, Blaise, 185, 207
Pater, Walter, 185
Peace, 47
Peale, Norman Vincent, 197, 203
Perfection, 50–51
Personal belief system, 65,
99–106, 124, 127–28
Plato, 186
Practical spirituality
defined, xxiii
enlightened life, 32–36
frequently asked questions
about, 199–215
goal setting and, 210–11
key concepts in, 23–24
key terms in, 26–31
See also individual entries
Problem-pain cycle, 4

Q

Quotations, inspirational, 163–93

R

Rathbun, Ron W., 186
Rational Emotive Behavioral
Therapy (REBT), 3
Raymo, Chet, 75

Reality
  actual vs. preferred, 44
  true, 44
  what is, 26–27, 77–81
Reframing, 8, 115–16
Rimpoche, Gehlek, 70
Rinpoche, Sogyal, 86, 186
Risk, 122
Rochelle, Michael, 148
Romantic love, 211–14
Rosten, Leo, 187
Rowling, J. K., 4–5
Rumi, Jalal ad-Din, 187

S

S-A-D factor
  dealing with, xxiii, 143–44
  defined, xxiii
  See also Depression
Saint Francis of Assisi, 82, 176
Schuller, Robert H., 19
Schweitzer, Albert, 187
Scientific method, 75
Seattle, Chief, 188
Self
  defining, 73
  little (see Ego)
  meditation and, 157
  search for, 30–31, 37–38
  sense of, 19–20, 24, 123,
    209–10
  Source as, 32
  three pillars of, 125–28
Self-concept, 45, 126–28
Self-consciousness, 85
Self-esteem, 45, 125, 126–28, 133
Self-fulfilling prophecy, 4

Self-image, 12–13, 45, 126–28
Self-image psychology, 12, 45,
    112
  enlightened life, 32–36
  key concepts in, 23–24, 123–31
  key terms in, 26–31
Self-talk, 17–20
Service, 97
Shakespeare, William, 70, 114,
    188
Shankaracharya, Adi, 31
Siddharta Gautama, 31
Silence, 34, 40, 46, 47, 55–56, 98
  noble, 160–61
Sinokki, Marjo, 144
Smith, Douglas V., 74
Sophocles, 188
Soul, 80
Source (God)
  defined, 26
  knowing, 27, 40–41, 46, 50, 54,
    57, 206
  love from, 48
  nature of, in world religions, 87
  noise and, 45
  as Self, 32
  shows us the way, 47, 137
  within us, 51, 58
Space, 79
Space consciousness, 29–30, 52,
    123
Spirituality
  defined, 199
  practical (see Practical
    spirituality)
  universal, 87
Spiritually aware, 200–201
Stein, Joel, 159

Stevenson, Robert Louis, 188
St. James, Elaine, 187
Stress
　　body's response to, 145–46
　　dealing with, 150
　　See also S-A-D factor
Stressors
　　eliminating, 149–50
　　internal and external, 144–45
　　meditation and, 155
Suicide, 131, 145–49
　　among armed forces, 148–49
Supreme virtue, traits of, 92–93
Systematic thought evaluation
　　　　process (S-T-E-P), 5–9,
　　　　63–64
　　A-B-Cs of, 5–6, 64–66
　　defined, 4
　　equation, 65

T
Tagore, Rabindranath, 153
Taoism, 31
　　on excessive consumption, 74
Teillard de Chardin, Pierre, 76
Thoreau, Henry David, 152,
　　　　189–90
Thought process, 5–9, 65–69
　　equation for, 65
　　pictures as part of, 111–19
Thoughts
　　analysis of, 50, 63–64
　　feelings generated from, 10–11,
　　　　63
　　taking responsibility for, 10
　　See also Systematic thought
　　　　evaluation process (S-T-E-P)

Tillich, Paul Johannes, 190
Time, as illusion, 40–41, 52
Toffler, Alvin, 190
Tolle, Eckhart, 32, 190–91, 203
Total wellness, xi, xx
Total wellness coaching, 217
Total Wellness Kit, 216
Transcendence, 151–53
Transcendentalism, 152
Transcendent love, 213, 214
Twain, Mark, 197
Twain, Shania, 159
Two Wolves, 52–53

U
Unconditional love, 24, 55–56
Unconditioned consciousness,
　　136
Unconscious, 45
Unconscious competence, 6
Unconscious incompetence, 6
Unity consciousness, 83, 85

V
Virtue, supreme, 92–93
Visualization, 113–15, 120–21

W
Watts, Alan, 143, 191
Wellness, total, xi, xx, 216, 217
Wharton, Edith, 191
White Eagle, 172, 191
Whitman, Walt, 152
Williamson, Marianne, 106–8,
　　136, 192

World of form, 15, 199
Wright brothers, 98

Y
Yeager, Chuck, 101
Yeats, William Butler, 95

Yogananda, Paramahansa, 193
Yogi, Maharishi Mahesh, 83–84
Young, Margaret, 95

Z
Zukav, Gary, 96